Criminal Justice and the Catholic Church

Criminal Justice and the Catholic Church

Andrew Skotnicki

A SHEED & WARD BOOK

ROWMAN & LITTLEFIELD PUBLISHERS, INC.
Lanham • Boulder • New York • Toronto • Plymouth, UK

A SHEED & WARD BOOK

ROWMAN & LITTLEFIELD PUBLISHERS, INC.

Published in the United States of America
by Rowman & Littlefield Publishers, Inc.
A wholly owned subsidiary of The Rowman & Littlefield Publishing Group, Inc.
4501 Forbes Boulevard, Suite 200, Lanham, Maryland 20706
www.rowmanlittlefield.com

Estover Road, Plymouth PL6 7PY, United Kingdom

British Library Cataloguing in Publication Information Available

Library of Congress Cataloging-in-Publication Data
Skotnicki, Andrew.
  Criminal justice and the Catholic Church / Andrew Skotnicki.
    p. cm.
  "A Sheed & Ward book."
  Includes bibliographical references and index.
  ISBN-13: 978-0-7425-5202-9 (cloth : alk. paper)
  ISBN-10: 0-7425-5202-0 (cloth : alk. paper)
  ISBN-13: 978-0-7425-5203-6 (pbk. : alk. paper)
  ISBN-10: 0-7425-5203-9 (pbk. : alk. paper)
  1. Christianity and justice—Catholic Church. 2. Criminology—Religious
aspects—Christianity. I. Title.
  BX1795.J87S56 2008
  261.8'33088282—dc22

                                                                2007011880

Printed in the United States of America

♾™ The paper used in this publication meets the minimum requirements of
American National Standard for Information Sciences—Permanence of Paper
for Printed Library Materials, ANSI/NISO Z39.48-1992.

Contents

Acknowledgments

This book could not have been written without the help of others. Time and again I enlisted the support of colleagues and friends to check my still questionable Latin skills. Among those who kindly lent their expertise, I would like to mention Archbishop John Quinn and the following faculty members at Manhattan College: Joseph Castora, John Kieber, and Brother Luke Salm.

Portions of the text were read and commented on by Jeanne Flavin, Stephen Kaplan, and Michele Saracino, as well as by my many colleagues in the interdepartmental research seminar at Manhattan before whom I was honored to present drafts of some of the manuscript.

I would like to thank my students in the "Religion and Criminal Justice" seminar, many of whom complemented their research with the kind of compassionate analysis that so often provides valuable insights in an area where compassion is frequently the last value sought after.

My family and my wife, Vivian, mean more than I can say. Their support of this project and countless others, big and small, has given me much of the confidence and determination needed to see them through to completion.

Finally, I must say something about the countless men and women I have known in the jails, detention centers, and prisons of the United States. I beheld the face of God for over thirty-five years either as a volunteer, or as a part- or full-time chaplain. Caregivers have said so often that they receive far more than they give that it has become a well-worn cliché, but it is a cliché precisely because over and over again, experience proves it to be true, and I feel deeply the joy and burden of gratitude to them all. My "conversion," for some reason, took place in the late 1970s on a late afternoon in a cellblock of the Cook County Jail in Chicago. The men were locked up for count and one inmate was quietly pushing a broom down the tier. In that moment of stillness, I heard my heart asking, "Why do we do this?" Much of my life has been spent in a desire to answer that question.

Introduction: Prisons, Punishment, and the Catholic Church

When shall I go and behold the face of God?

—Psalm 42:2

I once saw a Western, the details of which have long since faded away. I do remember one scene, however: the hero and his friend were pinned down behind some rocks. Money was involved, lots of it as I recall, and, of course, desperate people with eyes on its ungainly possession. During a lull in the fighting the hero remarked wearily, "If the world were made of gold, people would kill each other for a handful of dirt."

Our philosophical gunslinger may have employed a unique set of metaphors but hardly a unique point of view. Murder and mayhem have found their way into every human community in every age and noted thinkers as disparate as St. Augustine and Sigmund Freud have argued that political life itself came into being in response to homicide.[1]

Such reasoning, in fact all speculative reasoning, according to Emile Durkheim, can trace its origin to our religious ancestors as they pondered the connection between the familiar and the incomprehensible or, more plainly, between events and their meaning.[2] The opening chapters of the Book of Genesis reveal a primal harmony quickly turned discordant as family members and confidants maltreat one another, solemn oaths are wantonly breached, and the guilty dissemble and shun responsibility. The amazement and confusion of the biblical authors are given voice in the words God asks of Eve, "Why did you do such a thing?" (Gn 3:13); and in those addressed to Cain, "What have you done!" (Gn 4:10). David Garland suggests that these and other

1

"intractable" dilemmas of our human existence are the very soil from which myths, rituals, and symbols develop.[3] There is, in other words, a primal connection between religion and criminal justice.

We all think a lot about crime. It is at various times a cause of terror, entertainment, curiosity, and raw frustration that the human propensity to do harm consistently outwits all of its moral pursuers. And, in a historical period marked by the sustained absence of religion from active involvement in shaping correctional policy, the methods of forcible intervention and social control employed by the state have not proven any more effective in combating the adversary. As this book is being written there are seven million people in the United States alone under some form of penal supervision, the majority being the poor members of racial minorities.[4] Furthermore, the "penal harm" movement has all but replaced "penal welfare" as one of the dominant synonyms for current correctional policy—lending credence to the claim, made all too painfully clear throughout history, that the default value in settling social conundrums is usually some form of violence.[5]

At the outset, one might well ask what relevance a study of specifically Catholic attitudes would have in these pressing but terrestrial matters. Briefly stated, the initial foundations of virtually every system of legal redress and criminal detention in the West can be traced to the Catholic tradition, whether one looks at the impact of canon law upon secular legal systems, of Catholic liturgical practice upon the stylized ritual and geographical organization of the courtroom, or of the monastic penitentiary upon the structure and general ethos of contemporary correctional institutions.[6] A more appropriate question might ask whether a coherent, historically verifiable, and theologically defensible theory can be constructed from mining the long history of ecclesiastical involvement in crime and punishment; a theory that would be harmonious with the biblical, and especially New Testament affinity, even tenderness, for the captive as well as with the normative emphases in Catholic social teaching; a theory that might bring an alternative perspective, so old perhaps that it might appear new, to the fractured and seemingly interminable debate over the present and future shape of the penal system.

What follows, then, is not so much a history of the Catholic Church and criminal justice, although many historical elements will be presented, but an attempt to survey and draw some basic conclusions about the way the Catholic tradition has responded to the great problems each society faces in addressing those who honor the demands of justice badly, or not at all. There are many, given the highly charged debate over the role of religion in public life, who become nervous when people within the church begin to tackle social issues. I do not feel it necessary to address that topic in this volume. There has been too much written already on the warrant for religious voices to speak self-consciously in the public square in matters of concern to us all.[7] That being said, there are two legitimate issues that do require some attention, namely, the audience to whom the text is written and, for lack of better words, the translation problem.

As a Roman Catholic scholar actively engaged in questions of religion and criminal justice, I begin this study with a sense that neither the criminological literature nor many of the documents written on the justice system by religious activists have taken sufficient interest in the theological and historical foundations of the "modern" penal system. An underlying contention of this study is that in whatever future direction criminal justice policy proceeds, it should be undertaken in conversation with its past; a past that is, in large part, religious. The present volume seeks to address those scholars, strategic planners, and concerned men and women, religious and secular, who take an active interest in this future direction, although it may also prove useful to those whose concern is primarily historical.

The translation problem can be summarized in stating that much of what will be discussed in these pages occurred in a world where religious meanings were taken for granted and in which the Roman Catholic Church wielded great political and cultural influence. Clearly that is not the case today, nor is it my intention to suggest that it should be. There are, however, lessons and insights that can be drawn into the conversation over social policy that need not carry the freight of theological orthodoxy to legitimate them. It is my hope that this volume will serve the interests of the church as it continues to refine its own understanding of the relation between present ethical challenges and the glory and shame of its own past; but also that it might, theology aside, enable others to consider the long shadow cast by the ecclesiastical prison, and the ways in which the broad spectrum of ideas that created and sustained it for over a millennium might possibly inform visions of a just and effective penal system.

The organizational template for this study will be provided by my contention that any theory of criminal justice must contain four elements and, as such, address four fundamental questions: Who are the offenders? What is the justification for detaining/punishing them? What is the end at which forcible intervention aims? By what means will the end be accomplished? Other questions undoubtedly have already entered, or might soon enter the mind of the reader. One might ponder, for instance, the dynamics of power, total power at that, and its effects on both the mechanics of justice and its institutional format; or one may focus on the factors used to determine moral or spiritual progress and their relation to hegemonic economic and cultural values. It is my hope that these and other derivative queries will be addressed in the discussion that follows.

Addressing briefly the four institutional aspects just previewed, I will contend concerning the identity question that from a Catholic perspective the one held captive can be no other than Christ himself. The central place that I accord to that statement will be borne out in the pages that follow; but it can also be expressed negatively: history reveals that when Christ is not the prisoner, when degrading or inhumane portraits of the criminal offender inhabit and direct the cultural discourse, then, quite literally, all hell breaks loose.

The response to the second question, concerning the justification for a forcible intervention into the life of the wrongdoer, hinges on the delicate balance between coercion and self-punishment. Ideally, in the theory I am presenting, the prisoner punishes him- or herself. Still, there is a strong warrant in the tradition for imposing detention on those guilty of crime. This warrant receives much of its substance from the concepts of order, justice, and atonement and the particular way they have developed within Catholic thought. Perhaps Anselm expressed best this justification in his argument that the sinner must make amends for offenses against others as well as against the harmony God has established in creation.[8]

The ideal end at which punishment aims is the liberation of the offender from all forms of personal and social alienation, and a return to full participation within the community without stigma or further repercussion for the culpable offense. The fourth question, regarding the means best suited to accomplish the end, derives from the practice of penance and reveals that temporary exclusion from the community, with an accompanying emphasis on contrition and amendment, is the normal method employed to create the conditions for inner renewal and fruitful reintegration into social life.

Of the four elements, the first, the one dealing with social imagination, is the most important, conditioning in a dramatic and possibly determinative way the answers to the other three, particularly the third and fourth. "Guns don't kill, people do," states an epigram of the National Rifle Association. Another might be suggested: "Crime is created by cultures, not criminals." The specific ethos of each society determines what is offensive and projects the images that shape the "dangerous classes," as they were termed in nineteenth-century America.[9] Those cultural images, in turn, anticipate in detail how the "dangerous" will be treated. Punishment is "a cultural artifact," David Garland suggests, echoing Richard Quinney's work on the social origin of crime, and, still earlier, that of Norbert Elias on the relation between social mores and the concept of civilization.[10] In a similar vein, the criminologist Nils Christie states that crime "is like a sponge. The term can absorb a lot of acts—and people—when external circumstances make that useful."[11]

Since images are primary sources of criminal justice policy, they will be referred to often in the text. It will be argued that a set of core and complementary images can be drawn from the Catholic tradition that provide a guide for the construction of a theory that is defensible not only in terms of the historical record, but consistent with the sacred texts of Christianity and the normative principles of Catholic social teaching.[12]

We can, of course, derive a host of negative images and, echoing Elias, "corresponding forms of behavior." The reader will discover or, probably better to say, be reintroduced to sobering displays of cruelty in the way Catholic officials treated their captives. While such "real" episodes will by no means be ignored, the task will be to investigate whether images and practices that correspond to the biblical and the current ideal of criminal justice can be sustained intellectually and historically within the Catholic tradition. I say this aware that abundant evidence exists to raise a hermeneutic of suspicion as to the metaphors and events being selected and the conclusions being reached about them. For example, were the maiming of prisoners and the papal galleys lamentable reminders of the colonization of certain church officials by a violent culture, one in which the "pleasure in killing and torturing others was great," or a sufficient reason to undermine the claim that the prisoner in every age merited dignified treatment precisely because his or her being was perceived as sacred?[13] Readers will make their own conclusions after weighing conflicting practices in the ideological balance. In either case, given the vast amount of material upon which one can draw, any theory on this topic will find it necessary at times to separate fact from value; or, to put it another way, however noble and articulate the vision, it is still people who run the system.

What the "real" is presents a further problem. Researchers must rely on written accounts of the goals, policies, and effectiveness of specific institutions provided by eyewitnesses, contemporary chroniclers of those events, government and ecclesiastical documents, and present-day social theorists and historians. What emerges may not resemble the realities of the institutions under study.[14] A nineteenth-century judge once told a convicted felon: "You are to be literally buried from the world."[15] In our own time, Foucault has noted that punishment is "the most hidden part of the penal process."[16] Prisoners are, and in many ways have always been, the most invisible of the poor. The method employed in this volume aims to offset this problem by relying on a broad sample of textual evidence and secondary sources from numerous disciplinary perspectives. While it is well known that a wide range of scholarly interpretation exists on the meaning and merits of Catholic legal and criminal practice, one also finds substantial critical opinion within the tradition itself. The fact that much of the primary source material is provided by documents and accounts written by monks and clerics is thus not necessarily a barrier to the investigator. A lively and contentious debate surfaces not only by taking a comparative approach in textual analysis but also in the conflicting methodological approaches within specific texts themselves. Furthermore, in cultures where the church was not only hegemonic but also identified consciously with its supernatural warrant and justification, there may have been less motivation to conceal what took place in its prisons and dungeons; and, where there was an attempt to hide or to deceive, there existed voices of protest the cries of whom can be heard at least now if not then.

The fourth element of the theory of criminal justice that I am presenting, concerning the means of accomplishing the goal of full social restoration, raises the question of the origin of the prison and its continuing viability. That issue will be discussed in detail as, arguably, the prison is the one artifact of the Catholic system that remains intact to this day. A pulse that runs through the presentation is whether the cellular prison can function as a humane and effective expression of the desire to successfully address the problem of crime. There are many within the church who contend that a case for the prison can no longer be sustained morally, specifically within a morality that calls itself Christian.[17]

My own conclusion is that the prison as we know it in the West originated in the penitential practice of the early church and in primitive monastic communities. With some reservations, I argue that it thus bears a meaning as valid and necessary as penance and monasticism themselves. Perhaps a more restrained way of phrasing it would be that since the contemporary prison is in many ways a Catholic innovation, whatever hope it may have as a locus and vehicle of criminal justice lies within the history we are about to survey.

Chapter 1 traces the origin of the concepts of the prison and the prisoner in the West and the importance of cultural images in shaping penal policy. In many respects, it presents a somber portrait of how brutally the least among us have been treated throughout history. Invariably, prior to its transformation by the church, the prison served three functions: as a means of custody prior to trial, as a punishment in itself, and as a coercive mechanism to obtain ransom or some parallel favor to the captors.[18] Some notable exceptions to this schema that prefigure later developments in the Catholic tradition were introduced in the Hebrew Scriptures among the people of ancient Israel. Here, God, while by no means eschewing punishment of the guilty, is found to take an active interest in the prisoner and in the return of the exile. The chapter then turns to a fuller exposition of the social reality of crime. It argues that two complementary images developed early in Christian history to create the foundations for a Catholic theory of criminal justice: they are Christ as prisoner and the church as parent. They are accompanied by a consistent theme of liberation that provides a teleological dimension to the images.

In chapter 2 the justification for punishment in the Catholic tradition is discussed. In summary, the argument is that the apprehension and detention of the offender is both fitting and necessary in attaining the goals of recognition of wrongful conduct, contrition, and expiation. The meaning of punishment in both its external and internal dimensions is explored, utilizing the concepts of order, justice, and atonement. Numerous sources are cited, but the argument seeks primarily to harmonize the external/internal dialectic by reconciling the insights of some of the tradition's most seminal figures, notably, Augustine, Aquinas, Anselm, and Abelard.

Chapter 3 discusses the meaning or the end that punishment is meant to achieve. The end is full reconciliation and reinstatement of the offender to the community. Frequently, Catholic writers relied on medical analogies to orient their thinking in relation to the goal of the punitive experience: incarceration, like medical intervention, hurts, but its end is restoration, not pain. Psychological factors such as guilt and shame enter into this dynamic and are explored along with the role of mercy both in sentencing and in regard to the uncooperative or unrepentant captive.

By far the largest chapter is the fourth. It takes us beyond philosophy and theological ethics and into the prison cell. The theory that I present carries no weight if it cannot be redeemed in human experience. The prison developed as a structural expression of the exclusionary and temporal dimensions of the early practice of penance. Thus the chapter covers the origin and shape of penitential discipline in the primitive church and the birth of the monastic prison in which those guilty of serious infractions were forcibly detained as a means of both retribution and rehabilitation. The means of determining guilt are discussed, as well as the prison environment and its variations within monasteries, religious communities, ecclesiastical jurisdictions, and within the penitentiaries established by the Inquisition.

Chapter 5 discusses the social impact of the prison as conceived by the church, particularly its effects on the development of secular prisons and secular understandings of criminal justice down to our own day.

The final chapter presents a theory of criminal justice derived from the Catholic tradition. It essentially restates the four principal theoretical elements discussed in the volume while attempting to locate that theory within contemporary correctional developments.

Amidst the confusion and cynicism in the current discussion of crime and punishment, some things do appear to be undeniably true: people are still killing each other, often for what appears to be no more than a handful of dirt; there are more and more inmates, looking more and more alike; and any sentence, given its social, not to mention punitive, ramifications, increasingly resembles a life-sentence. I am an ethicist, not a historian, and I write this study as an ethicist. Its purpose is not to engage an antiquarian interest, or worse, a prurient one, in dark dungeons and cruel forms of torture, but a concern for the millions being detained and punished in a system that originated with the Catholic Church in the hope that perhaps the ideas that formed the system may prove beneficial in its reform.

NOTES

1. St. Augustine, *The City of God*, trans. Henry Bettenson (Harmondsworth, UK: Penguin, 1984), bk. XV, ch. 5; Sigmund Freud, *The Future of an Illusion*, trans. W. D. Robson-Scott (Garden City, NY: Anchor Books, 1964), ch. 8.

2. Emile Durkheim, *The Elementary Forms of the Religious Life*, trans. Karen E. Fields (New York: The Free Press, 1995), 236–41.

3. David Garland, *Punishment and Modern Society* (Chicago: University of Chicago Press, 1990), 274.

4. According to the U.S. Department of Justice, "Almost 7 million adults were under correctional supervision behind bars or on probation or parole in the community" by year-end 2005, www.ojp.usdoj.gov/bjs (accessed Nov. 2, 2005). Also, "Based on current rates of first incarceration, an estimated 32% of black males will enter State or Federal prison during their lifetime, compared to 17% of Hispanic males and 5.9% of white males." U.S. Department of Justice, Bureau of Justice Statistics, Criminal Offenders Statistics, available at www.ojp.usdoj .gov/bjs (accessed Sept. 6, 2006).

5. See Todd Clear, *Harm in American Penology* (Albany: State University of New York Press, 1994).

6. On legal influence, see Harold Berman, *Law and Revolution* (Cambridge, MA: Harvard University Press, 1983), 49–50, 165–98. On the influence of the Catholic Church on Western penal systems, see Norman Johnston, *Forms of Constraint* (Urbana: University of Illinois Press, 2000), 17; Pieter Spierenburg, *The Prison Experience* (New Brunswick, NJ: Rutgers University Press, 1991), 14.

7. See, e.g., Stephen L. Carter, *The Culture of Disbelief* (New York: Anchor Books, 1993); Michael J. Himes and Kenneth R. Himes, *Fullness of Faith* (New

York: Paulist Press, 1993); Robin Lovin, ed., *Religion and American Public Life* (New York: Paulist Press, 1986); Richard John Neuhaus, *The Naked Public Square* (Grand Rapids, MI: Eerdmans, 1986); David Tracy, *The Analogical Imagination* (New York: Crossroad, 1981).

8. Anselm of Canterbury, *Why God Became Man*, trans. Joseph M. Colleran (Albany, NY: Magi Books, 1969), bk I, ch. 11.

9. In spite of his liberal social views, Theodore Parker was representative of his time in affirming that there is a class composed of "foes of society . . . criminals in soul, born criminals, who have a bad nature." See "A Sermon on the Dangerous Classes in Society" in *Speeches, Addresses, and Occasional Sermons* (Boston: Horace B. Fuller, 1876), 305 [originally published 1847].

10. Garland, *Punishment and Modern Society*, 193; Richard Quinney, *The Social Reality of Crime* (Boston: Little Brown, 1970). Elias writes: "The 'civilization' which we are accustomed to regard as a possession that comes to us apparently ready-made . . . is a process or part of a process in which we are ourselves involved. Every particular characteristic that we attribute to it—machinery, scientific discovery, forms of state, or whatever else—bears witness to a particular structure of human relations, to a particular social structure, or to the corresponding forms of behavior." See Norbert Elias, *The Civilizing Process*, vol. I, trans. Edmund Jephcott (New York: Urizen Books, 1978), 59 [originally published 1939].

11. Nils Christie, *A Suitable Amount of Crime* (London and New York: Routledge, 2004), ix.

12. The social encyclicals of popes since Leo XIII and statements by episcopal conferences on social themes have produced a core list of ethical directives. Although there is not unanimity as to their number or their ontological weight vis à vis one another, there is a broad consensus that would confirm the following themes: human dignity, human sociality, human rights, the common good, solidarity, and the preferential option for the poor. See Kenneth R. Himes, *Responses to 101 Questions on Catholic Social Teaching* (New York: Paulist Press, 2001).

13. "Outbursts of cruelty did not exclude one from social life. They were not outlawed. The pleasure in killing and torturing others was great, and it was a socially permitted pleasure. To a certain extent, the social structure even pushed its members in this direction, making it seem necessary." Elias, *Civilizing Process*, vol. I, 194.

14. Trevor Dean, for example, cautions against the writing of social history solely from legislative texts. See *Crime in Medieval Europe 1200–1500* (Harlow, UK: Longman, 2001), 133. See also Johnston, *Forms of Constraint*, 3.

15. W. D. Lewis, *From Newgate to Dannemora* (Ithaca, NY: Cornell University Press, 1965), 114–15.

16. Michel Foucault, *Discipline and Punish*, trans. Alan Sheridan (New York: Vintage Books, 1979), 9.

17. See, e.g., Timothy Gorringe, *God's Just Vengeance* (Cambridge: Cambridge University Press, 1996), esp. ch. 10; Lee Griffith: *The Fall of the Prison: Biblical Perspectives on Prison Abolition* (Grand Rapids, MI: Eerdmans, 1993); Mark Lewis Taylor, *The Executed God* (Minneapolis, MN: Fortress, 2001). Several outright calls to limit or eliminate the prison have been made by the bishops of the United States.

See Catholic Bishops of the United States, "Rebuilding Human Lives," *Origins* 3 (1973): 345; United States Catholic Conference, "A Community Response to Crime," *Origins* 7 (1978): 598; New York State Bishops, "Reforming the Criminal Justice System," *Origins* 12 (1983): 572.

18. See Jean Dunbabin, *Captivity and Imprisonment in Medieval Europe, 1000–1300* (Houndmills, UK: Palgrave Macmillan, 2002), 2–3.

1

What Is the Prison and Who Is the Prisoner?

> Let us fear, my sisters, let us fear; for if God withholds his hand from us, what wicked things are there that we shall not do?
>
> —St. Teresa of Avila (Letter 274)

Anyone attempting to study the Catholic Church and criminal justice must spend considerable time investigating and reflecting upon jails and prisons and upon those forced to inhabit them.[1] While the meaning of penal confinement changed dramatically in early Christian communities, it would be foolish to suggest that the inspiration for these new ideas suddenly fell from the sky after the death of Jesus of Nazareth. Indeed, the method of punishment introduced was in many ways a variation on themes whose roots extend to some of the earliest historical records.

In this chapter, I give an overview of the prison and the functions it fulfilled at the beginning of the Christian era and continued to fulfill in the secular arena well into the second millennium. It is necessary to examine the evolution of criminal justice in the Hebrew Scriptures, as themes that emerged there were highly influential in the formation of Catholic practice. Less explicit attention is paid to the prison systems of other important political centers, for example, Assyria, Egypt, Greece, and Rome, although certain lines of continuity can be drawn between these systems and post-exilic Hebrew practice, and thus, by extension, the Catholic perspective. I next turn to the question of the cultural representation of crime and criminals. These symbolic portrayals have a decided impact on the determination of those classified as delinquent and on the treatment they receive. Some of the conflicting images that have surfaced in the history of the church are examined in support of this contention. I argue that a Catholic interpretation of criminal justice should draw upon those strands within the tradition in which Christ is portrayed as the prisoner and the church as a caring and attentive parent committed to the liberation of her captive children. Finally, the meaning of the prisoner as person is discussed. Important anthropological and ethical emphases in the tradition are introduced in support of this designation, especially the sacredness of each human being, the freedom of the will, the centrality of virtue in the moral life, the duty of forgiveness, and the need for reconciliation.

THE PRISON

The church, through its unique fusion of time, isolation, and repentance had a powerful influence on the shape of penal systems in the West; but this impact was not fully realized until the latter part of the second millennium. Before then, incarceration of any kind was not frequently utilized in civil society. History provides few instances of buildings erected for the sole purpose of confinement. Most frequently, suspects, enemies, or the condemned were detained in makeshift cells created in a castle, chateau, gatehouse, or town wall.[2] This lends credence to the etymology of the word "jail," stemming as it does from the Latin word *caveola*, signifying a hollow cavity or cage.[3]

The following summary of medieval English penal experience could be employed, with perhaps only minor variation, to depict premodern secular practice throughout the lands inhabited by the church: "From a punitive standpoint mutilation, death, outlawry, and above all, compensation in cash were, in a general way, the proper punishments for what are now called crimes."[4] Pecuniary compensation is found, in fact is dominant, in the most ancient legal samples and collections of which we have record, those of the Sumerians.[5] Harold Berman, commenting on the earliest of the Anglo-Saxon legal codes and their complex system of monetary reparation, notes that these penalties enjoyed such widespread favor because they provided benefits more socially advantageous than death or disfigurement.[6] Still, pragmatic outcomes in criminal justice need not be viewed solely in economic terms. Elias attests to the prevalence of violence and penury in medieval society, and the high place, even esteem, attributed to the former. The detention of criminals or those captured in battle was costly, and to return them unharmed merely recreated the threat they had formerly posed; it was frequently determined to be far better to kill them or send them back mutilated and consequently unfit for war or criminal activity.[7]

It is perhaps more accurate to state that the fine and sanguinary vengeance, the latter normally in the form of the vendetta, accompanied and often anticipated one another as the most common ways to address criminal wrongdoing.[8] Like pecuniary sanctions, the roots of the vendetta are very ancient. In the Bible, it first appears in the story of Cain's descendant, Lamech. He bears the "sign" of Cain that distinguishes him not as a member of a condemned group but one "in which blood vengeance is ruthlessly exacted": "I have killed a man for wounding me, a boy for bruising me. If Cain is avenged sevenfold, then Lamech seventy-seven fold" (Gn 4:23–24).[9] Because Israelite legislation did not favor monetary compensation, the shadow of blood vengeance lingers even in the divine command to establish cities of refuge (Nm. 35: 9–34; Dt 19: 1–13).[10] The practice resurfaces after the establishment of the Hebrew tribes in Canaan. A poignant example is found in the murder of Abner by Joab to avenge the death of his brother (2 Sm 3: 22–27, 30).[11] The vendetta was a prominent part of Germanic law and came into widespread use in the West with the successful incursion of the Visigoths and Franks into Roman lands.[12]

Confinement, although infrequently found in the historical record, was still occasionally utilized, usually with one of three ends in mind: custody, punishment, or coercion.[13]

The custodial function of imprisonment refers to detention while awaiting some form of trial or inquiry. This purpose in contemporary experience is fulfilled by the jail; it is perhaps the oldest and most consistently employed use of forcible detention. Moses, on hearing that an Israelite had committed blasphemy during an argument had him placed under guard until the will of God for him might be revealed (Lv 24:10–12). A similar approach was adopted in the case of someone gathering sticks on the Sabbath: "they kept him in custody, for there was no clear decision as to what should be done with him" (Nm 15:32–36). Norman Johnston states, "Before the early modern period, imprisonment was almost always an interlude between court appearance and ultimate punishment, usually torture or death."[14] Ulpian, the great Roman jurist, on seeing confinement deployed by his contemporaries as a means of exacting retribution, issued a strong objection and made clear his contention that incarceration was only to be adopted as a means of pretrial restraint: "Prison is properly regarded as a means of detaining men, not punishing them."[15]

What was so reprehensible to Ulpian was the use of imprisonment for punitive ends, making detention a punishment in itself. The book of

Ezra contains a judicial decree of punitive incarceration by the Persian king Artaxerxes II, revealing the influence of foreign legislation on the postexilic Hebrew community: "Whoever will not obey the law of your God and the law of the king, let judgment be strictly executed upon him, whether for death or for banishment or for confiscation of his goods or for imprisonment" (Ez 7:26). King Jehoiachin spent thirty-seven years imprisoned in Babylon (2 Kgs 25:27; Jer 52:31). Jeremiah was beaten and placed under punitive restraint on several occasions (Jer 20:12; 32:2–5; 37:13–16) and John the Baptist was held captive as punishment for reviling King Herod for marrying his brother's wife (Mk 6:17–18). Among the correspondence of Cyprian is a letter written by a confessor, Lucianus, imprisoned during the Decian persecution of the mid-third century. He writes of fellow Christians "Victorinus, Victor, Herennius, Credula, Hereda, Donatus, Firmus, Venustus, Fructus, Iulia, Martialis, and Aristan—all by God's will starved to death in prison."[16] Eusebius writes of some early Christian martyrs who had survived the torture meant to kill them: "The devil resorted to other devices—confinement in the darkness of a filthy prison . . . and other agonies which wardens when angry and full of the devil are apt to inflict on helpless prisoners. Thus the majority were suffocated in prison."[17] Julius Caesar, in his sentence against Lentulus and his compatriots, reveals the Roman practice of *libera custodia* in which detainees, invariably members of the upper class, were impounded for long periods under what is now termed "house arrest."[18] In other words, despite the objections of Ulpian, Roman law frequently reproduced the practice of punitive incarceration, not only in sentences of exile and enforced labor, but also confinement while enchained.[19]

One of the common justifications for the third function of imprisonment, coercion, was the collection of debt. The Gospels reveal this ancient Hellenistic practice in the warning that disputes settled in court will lead to a detention that will not end until the last penny is paid (Mt 5:25–26; Lk 12:58–59), and in the parable of the unjust servant who was "delivered to the jailers, till he should pay all his debt" (Mt 18:34). A corollary to this form of arrest was incarceration for the purpose of obtaining ransom. Examples are found in the miracle stories, a genre common in Christian hagiography in which saints deliver those held in bondage. Here, important details of social and institutional life are revealed.[20] In one of the miracles attributed to Ste. Foy, a certain Rainhold, held for ransom in a dungeon, is delivered from his captors by the saint's intervention.[21] Dunbabin corroborates this evidence, noting that imprisonment in the early Middle Ages was "almost exclusively of captives of high status who were kept for financial or political motives."[22]

However its use was justified, confinement was invariably brutal unless the captive was rich, and even that was no sure means of avoiding cruel treatment. The Roman historian Diodus Siculus describes a prison in the Republic in the early second century before Christ: "[T]he poor wretches were reduced to the appearance of brutes, and since their food and everything pertaining to their needs was all so foully commingled, a stench so terrible assailed anyone who drew near it that it could scarcely be endured."[23] In the early third century of the Christina era, St. Perpetua speaks of her terror for herself and new baby, confined with her in a "dark hole" with a crowd of other unfortunates in the stifling heat.[24] The story of a captive freed by the intervention of Ste. Foy presents a startling variation on the common practice of chaining the incarcerated. In this instance, the "upper arms were crossed in front of the chest and bound with tightly fastened coils of rope. After this each hand was brought around his neck and tied down very forcefully between his shoulders. And the ropes were pulled under his armpits and tied tightly with crude knots across his belly."[25] The miracles associated with Our Lady of Rocamadour reveal an incident in which a victim of slander was thrown by his lord into a tomb dug into the floor of the jail. His feet and hands were bound and a chain placed around his neck. The tomb was then sealed save for a small hole through which he could fight for breath.[26] Guibert, an abbot of the early middle ages, describes how a French bishop dealt with those protesting his politically charged appointment: "Some of the prisoners traveled too slowly and he ordered the bones under their necks . . . to be pierced, and had cords inserted through the holes in five or six of them, and so made them travel in terrible torture, and after a little while they died in captivity."[27] There is thus ample evidence to suggest that the graphic mutilation described in this medieval war ballad was hardly an exaggeration: "I laugh at what you say, I care not a fig for your threats. I shall shame every knight I have taken, cut off his nose or his ears. If he is a sergeant or a merchant he will lose a foot or an arm."[28]

Social class was given some recognition in the fact that in Greece and Rome, for instance, there were what are now called graded prisons and a parallel system of classification based either on the gravity of the crime or, perhaps, on one's rank in the social hierarchy. The house arrest ordered for Lentulus by Caesar has already been mentioned (even though he was murdered in prison before it could be realized).[29] In the *Laws*, Plato gives witness to three types of facilities arranged according to the degree of wrongdoing.[30] There is legitimate doubt as to whether such a systematic division actually existed in Athenian society, but the case of Socrates as well as that of Seneca in Rome reveal that elevated social standing provided options certainly lacking to the lowly.[31]

Sometimes the three grades were contained in a single edifice, as in the Mamartine prison in Rome. The lower part was composed of a vast system of dungeons, constructed over the main sewer, perhaps meant as a punishment in lieu of the death penalty; the intermediate level held those in chains awaiting punishment; while the upper level was used to house minor offenders.[32] There is evidence to suggest, however, that regardless of offense, towers and upper levels of buildings were the normal places where the wealthy were confined, while the dungeons were reserved for the poor and those of low esteem.[33] Dunbabin speaks of "honorable captivity" in this regard as opposed to what Ives calls "the ghastly mutilations" reserved for the common criminals.[34] In Rome, this may have been an expression of the fact that honor was a deeply embedded social value, respected even when the mighty had fallen.[35]

CRIMINAL JUSTICE IN THE OLD TESTAMENT

The understanding of justice in the Old Testament had a deep influence on Catholic thinking. A God of justice is consistently paralleled with a God who seeks the return of the exiled captive. Crime, law, and expiation are intertwined in a way that prefigures much of what will appear in the early Christian communities, especially in the acclamation that once the debt of justice has been paid, full restoration to the community is mandated (Lv 5:20–26).[36] Yahweh instructs Moses in one passage that justice is to be achieved by means of law and not the vendetta: the Israelites are to establish cities of refuge on their entry into Canaan that will "serve as places of asylum from the avenger of blood, so that a homicide shall not be put to death unless he is first tried before the community" (Nm 35:9–15).

Undoubtedly, violence was commanded and exhibited against those guilty of violations of the covenant established with God. Those whose disobedience threatened the holiness of the chosen people were often dealt the most severe punishments. The death penalty is prescribed for numerous offenses, usually exacted by lapidation (stoning), although there are also instances of strangulation, decapitation, and burning to death (Lv 21:9).[37] Most commentators agree, however, that the tendency in the postexilic community was to seek to moderate such punishments.[38]

There were instances of confinement in ancient Israel, but prisons in a formal sense were unknown until after the Exile.[39] Frequently, that most ancient of receptacles, the empty cistern, was employed for such confinement (Lam 3:53; Is 24:22; Zec 9:11), with prisoners often bound with chains and irons (Pss 105:18; 107:10).

The Hebrew word *bor* is frequently used to describe the place of confinement. It is a term that variously refers to a well, a pit, a prison, or the entrance to Sheol.[40] The choice of this term and its connection to a gloomy isolation seems to suggest the custodial and, in some respects, the punitive function of prisons. The book of Job, however, introduces a more permanent transformation of the meaning of imprisonment with the acknowledgment of the concept of "moral death" as a reaction to the Deuteronomic legal code. The latter conceives of justice as a phenomenon only experienced or withheld in this life, with a concurrent disbelief in an afterlife, at least in a moral sense.[41] The author of Job, however, challenges this belief. For when his friends argue in Deuteronomic fashion that Job surely must have committed some terrible wrong in order to be visited with such suffering, he cries out in protest against this perception of justice and the moral indifference of the grave (Job 16:18); insisting, instead, that the innocent often suffer without recompense in this life and that justice must not perish with our bodies in death.[42] Psalm 49 surely echoes this theme as it announces the passing of the nefarious rich with the warning that "death shall be their shepherd, and the upright rule over them" (49:15), and yet, for the just, the author proclaims "that God will redeem me from the power of the nether world by receiving me" (49:16). This theme of deliverance from the dark cistern, the pit, or prison is often mentioned in the psalms (Pss 30:4; 40:3; 107:10–16). The psalms contain, then, not only a justification for a punitive confinement, but a moral and redemptive justification conceived in a notion of justice that allows deliverance. For the psalmist laments, "You plunged me into the bottom of the pit, into the dark abyss" (Ps 88.7), but also rejoices to say that God "shattered the gates of brass and burst the bars of iron" (Ps 107:16).

Overall, what is most important in the experience of imprisonment in the ancient Hebrew world is not the novelty of the form, but the theme of redemption by a just God who punishes transgressions of the Covenant but who, after penitential expiation, delivers prisoners from the shadows of incarceration (Is 42:6–7).

THE IMAGE OF THE PRISONER AND ITS IMPORTANCE

The legacy of the Athenians to the shape and practice of criminal justice in the West is found principally in the images of the prison and the prisoner, the literary metaphors that they have bequeathed to us. The Platonic dialogues, whether focusing on the death of Socrates or discussing the prison as a metaphor of the body, have long been a part of the canon of Western education and have contributed significantly to the ideational reservoir of the Western imagination.[43] What these sources enable us to do is reflect upon the cultural processes that govern the discourse and create the social vision in regard to crime and criminals. They give evidence, in other words, of the social reality of crime.[44] While this theme is frequently invoked in modern penology, the latter has tended to be governed by theories that interpret the punishment response in light of those elements of the social structure holding sway over the exercise of power, for example, Foucault's dominated and docile bodies, or an economic perspective that asserts: "Every system of production tends to discover punishments which correspond to its productive relationships."[45]

Several authors have investigated how the literary metaphors and cultural codes prevalent in specific locales have impacted the formation and transformation of social policy with regard to the offender. Louis Masur, for example, writes that the realm of the sacred, with its beliefs and rituals, constitutes "a text" enabling one to view ideological development and social relations.[46] Randall McGowen points to the reinterpretation of the body by eighteenth-century social reformers in England as instrumental in channeling public sentiment toward the curtailing of capital punishment.[47] Others have traced the impact of the rise of middle-class sensibilities, tutored on the literary images of romanticism, on the quelling of blood lust and the softening of the image of the criminal.[48] This does not so much discount the thesis of Foucault and neo-Marxist thinkers concerning the impact of political or economic ideology on correctional policy, as much as it widens the field of influence to include other cultural forms and practices, including the literary and the religious, that contribute significantly to how criminals are understood and punished.[49] David Garland writes that penal laws "are framed in language, discourses, and sign systems which embody specific cultural meanings, distinctions, and sentiments, and which must be interpreted and understood if the social meaning and motivation of punishment are to become intelligible."[50]

This influence of cultural forms on penal customs is, of course, reciprocal and open-ended. As with any text, the meaning of these symbolic representations cannot be controlled but continues to refine perception and provoke the members of society, sometimes in ways unintended by the architects of social policy. Aside from the examples just mentioned, one might look to the influence of Florentine art during the Middle Ages on the re-imaging of the offender and the awakening of public empathy and care for the incarcerated. In Florence, artists were frequently enlisted to craft paintings and sculptures for public spaces that depicted biblical stories and motifs. One such work pictures Jesus in the garb of a medieval magistrate with a suppliant humankind as the defendant. In this and similar scenes, not only was it intended that respect for the transcendent foundation of law be imparted to the populace, but also that trials and sentences resemble morality plays drawing their legitimation from these same religious images.[51] What occurred in practice, however, was often quite the opposite of the intent of those interested in using art for the purpose of social control. For these artistic creations, often showing Christ and the saints in penal settings, were influential in igniting a novel sense of compassion in many areas of medieval Europe for the poor and for criminals, regardless of what they had done.[52]

A small tabernacle is still extant that was once a part of the exterior of the (in)famous *Carceri delle Stinche* in Florence. The name can be appreciated phonetically, as the stench emanating from the prison came to provide its lasting appellation.[53] A painting remains visible on the fragment in which a Florentine merchant shares alms with the destitute and emaciated inmates as they gather at the bars of the windows. Christ and two saints are standing on either side of the merchant as angels hover over him.[54] An example of the transformation of social policy by the tutoring of the public imagination came with regard to the portrayal of decapitation. In this form of capital punishment, the victim would assume the position of one kneeling in prayer. Samuel Edgerton notes that such a representation summoned a spiritual metaphor with the condemned "actually appearing to be imploring for divine mercy at the moment of the fatal blow." The poignancy of the ritual inspired hundreds of paintings in medieval and renaissance Europe that depicted Christian saints being martyred in this manner: "Indeed, the image of the martyr, preferably a young female, kneeling in fervent prayer while a cruel male executioner prepares to let loose his terrible sword, was one of the most moving in all of Christian art."[55]

This makes all the more relevant the claim by Elias that civilization is a relative term.[56] Institutions do not evolve from a time that was uncivilized; rather, stories, symbols, and rituals in every age create the images, motivations, and dispositions that give life and direction to cultural practices. What scale could be employed to judge adequately the degree of civilization between the bloody torments of medieval imprisonment and Foucault's antiseptic account of the contemporary prison where the condemned are given aspirin to combat headache right up to the moment they are executed?[57]

The church, above all else, is chartered as preserver of the memory and interpreter of the meaning of the life, death, and resurrection of Jesus Christ. Needless to say, images of a nonviolent Savior, confined, tortured, and murdered by state justice will inspire a different understanding of penal procedure than will a depiction of Christ in one late-fourteenth-century Florentine "miniature." In that work Christ as judge examines the moral record of humanity; directly beneath him sits the pope in a duplicate pose, to whose left burns a heretical bishop while his two accomplices are being herded into a jail cell.[58] A similar clash of meanings arises as one seeks to compare the heavenly deliverance of St. Peter from the dungeon (Acts 12:6-10) with the chaining and imprisonment of the recalcitrant and rebellious angels in the book of Jude (1:6) and in second Peter (2:4). Wayne Meeks sheds light on the origin of this tension in his moral analysis of early Christian communities. His work reveals that questions of group cohesion and moral identity could not be extricated from the reality of violent persecution and the inevitable process of cultural assimilation into a non-Christian world.[59] John Noonan remarks that such pressure is felt by the church in every age: "Yet it would be preposterous to imagine that all these profound changes [in moral doctrine] occurred simply by the acquiring of deeper insights into Christ. Human beings do not reach moral conclusions in a vacuum apart from the whole web of language, custom, and social structure surrounding them."[60]

The reader is familiar enough with the warrior popes of the Renaissance and the images of bishops riding with their armed bands of conscripts to know that the church, like any institution, is the captive of the symbolic universe into which it accommodates itself. Despite a recent record of stern ecclesial opposition to the death penalty and torture, both were sanctioned, albeit in restricted circumstances, for well over a millennium.[61] Gratian writes in the *Decretum* that in cases falling outside the purview of church law, secular mandates in no way threaten ecclesiastical prerogatives and require the obedience of the faithful and, by extension, the clergy.[62] Elias notes that only "a small elite" stood apart from the trend to identify leadership with the frequent and deadly use of violence.[63]

When the prisoner is imaged as a political or social threat, as morally repugnant, or, simply put, as a means to an end, virtually any punishment is possible. A medieval abbot showed approval when the fervent laity ignited heretics despite the squeamishness of their pastors: "[T]he faithful people, fearing weakness on the part of the clergy, ran to the prison, seized them and having lighted a fire under them outside the city, burned them both to ashes. To prevent the spreading of their cancer, God's people showed a righteous zeal against them."[64] The rules for religious orders gave regular witness to the need for shackles, chains, and other devices for the discipline and "more effective custody" of delinquents.[65] The Benedictine historian, Jean Mabillon, spoke of excesses by his fellow monks that were "difficult to believe": "[T]hey mutilated the limbs and sometimes stuck out the eyes" of their brothers who had fallen into serious error.[66] The work of Rene Girard is helpful in this regard. He has pointed to the fact that the execution of the innocent one (Christ) was meant to relieve the debt of punishment owed by the guilty and end the process of scapegoating once and for all. It has not, however, always had that effect on succeeding generations of Christians, who have continued to express the need to crush the criminal beneath the weight of their own guilt.[67]

Despite this, a "small elite" has existed, and probably many more, who have beheld a different kind of God. Their chronicles, stories, and essays abjured the violence of the age in which they lived, refashioned penal imagery and, in the process, altered the meaning of incarceration. For them, it was not possible to see the prisoner without somehow seeing the battered body of Jesus, who had been arrested and cruelly treated while in confinement. The New Testament contains numerous texts provoking an identification between the imprisoned and God's own self. Pilate asks the crowd, "which [prisoner] do you want me to release to you?" (Mt 27:17), and Jesus reveals to the surprised persons gathered at his left on the day of judgment, "what you did not do for one of these [prisoners], you did not do for me" (Mt 25:44–45). Jesus was, in fact, a prisoner even in death as Pilate ordered a guard to be placed at his tomb lest his disciples try to recover the body (Mt 27:62–66).[68]

The same theme of Christ as prisoner and as friend of the imprisoned is repeated often in the historical accounts and devotional literature of the Christian community. In "The Martyrdom of Pionius," probably written in the time of Marcus Aurelius, the author concedes to detractors that Christ "died a criminal." He then continues: "[W]hat other criminal has filled the world with his disciples? What other criminal had his disciples and others with them to die for the name of their master? By what other criminal's name for so many years were devils expelled, are still expelled now, and will be in the future?"[69] In the "Acts of Cyprian," the author states that, despite "the grim terrors of a murky cave," captives are cared for by Christ, who shares their imprisonment: "no place is loathsome . . . their brothers care for them by day, Christ by night as well."[70] St. John Chrysostom chides his parishioners in a homily: "[Y]ou decorate floor and walls and the capitals of the pillars. You provide silver chains for the lamps, but you cannot bear even to look at [Christ] as he lies chained in prison."[71] Cyprian writes that Christ will say to the righteous: "I was in the prison of captivity . . . I was prostrate and from that prison of servitude you freed me."[72]

The image of a captive Savior leads to a theological association with a captive church. Thus Augustine can write that the heavenly city on pilgrimage in the earthly realm "leads what we may call a life of captivity."[73] It is a small step, then, to the creation of an understanding that the very conditions of imprisonment confer a certain degree of holiness on the prisoner. St. John Climacus (579–649?), having lived among those held in the prison near his monastery in Egypt, writes: "For I shall certainly not hide this most moving lowliness in these blessed men."[74] He also writes: "I saw them, Father, and I was amazed; and I consider these fallen mourners more blessed than those who have not fallen."[75] The medieval lay society known as San Giovanni Decollato (St. John the Beheaded) assisted the condemned in Rome on the way to execution, reverently dressed and buried their bodies, and cared for their dependents. Their influence was such that one day a year, on the feast of the martyrdom of St. John the Baptist (August 29), one condemned prisoner would be chosen by lot from the city's jails and granted freedom by the civil authorities. The confraternity sponsored a public pageant in honor of the suddenly liberated prisoner. The one who moments before awaited only the day of execution would be warmly embraced, crowned with a gilded olive wreath, placed on the shoulders of the members of the society, and carried triumphantly through the streets of the city.[76]

One need not dig far to uncover a rich association between confinement and some of the most hallowed stories and sentiments nourishing the Christian imagination. One could even rightly wonder whether the unambiguous presentations in the New Testament and early Christian history of noble saints undergoing torture and execution creates, among some, a strain of sympathy with the incarcerated that obliterates the demands of justice. As the corpse of St. Germanus was being carried through a prison in Paris, several prisoners invoked the departed bishop in prayer. Gregory of Tours relates that at that point the casket became very heavy with the weight of the freed convicts but then became light again as the grateful recipients of mercy joined the procession and afterwards the funeral liturgy at the church where the saint was buried (Ste. Germain-des-Pres).[77] Two saints, who accompany Ste. Foy and Our Lady of Rocamadour in the tradition of heavenly agents who shatter chains and crumble prison walls, add weight to the contention that imprisonment in itself merits divine concern, often miraculous. One early friend and liberator of the incarcerated was St. Quentin, himself a prisoner of the Roman prefect Riciovarus. He was freed from his cell by an angel and, like Sts. Peter and Paul before him, then began to preach and baptize in the town square, including among his converts his fearful and amazed captors.[78] Another heavenly liberator was St. Leonard, to whom a rich collection of miracles are attributed. As one confident testimony reveals, concerning a British captive shackled by the neck and feet and soon to be freed by the saint's intervention: "to those who call upon him, St. Leonard is never late."[79]

The ransoming orders and the charitable movements of the Middle Ages, with their emphasis on the imprisoned and other unfortunates as the "poor of Christ," add another dimension to the long narrative of compassionate care given to those sequestered in dungeons and jails. The Trinitarians and Mercedarians were formed in Spain in the twelfth and thirteenth centuries to foster the release of captives taken by the Muslims, continuing a practice of redemption whose roots can be traced to Catalonia in the tenth century.[80] Part of the mystique attached to the orders was the "fourth vow" of substitution of oneself for the sake of a captive: "I will remain, held as pledge, in the power of the Saracens if this be necessary for the redemption of Christ's faithful."[81] The historical evidence is not strong to suggest that this sacrifice was actually carried out, but the orders did enter into negotiations with Muslim officials, effect the liberation of numerous captives with monies they had raised, and in some instances they personally received the prisoners and escorted them home.[82] Moreover, the movement had the effect of awakening the populace to the plight of the imprisoned by appealing to religious sensibilities in which the captive is understood to be none other than Christ himself.

If the image of the prisoner as *alter Christus* can inspire such compassionate sentiment and such uncritical affirmation, one must surely question the legitimacy of imprisoning anyone. That question is taken up in the following chapter; however, suffice to say, at least at this juncture, that confinement is not the problem, per se, but rather it is the insinuation or assumption, fed by cultural stereotypes, that prisoners are worthless, or at least worth less than members of the noncaptive population. One recent study remarked that a synonym for criminal justice among many advocates of the "new penology" is "waste management."[83] In light of such shameful appellations, a more immediate question might be: If images ultimately control the correctional machinery, and if Christ is portrayed as the prisoner, then what image befits those who design, operate, or at least underwrite the penal complex with their political and moral support? It is this question that provokes my contention that the Catholic Church has been most faithful to its tradition regarding criminal justice when it images itself as the father/mother who loves the child who is punished.

Parental analogies lend themselves easily to theological approaches to punishment in the Judeo-Christian tradition. Yahweh may not be imaged in the ancient Hebrew texts, but the parental parallels are un-mistakable: "So you must realize that the Lord, your God, disciplines you even as parents discipline their children" (Dt 8:5). Christian understandings of punishment have relied consistently upon this metaphor. Origen writes that "fathers," like teachers and doctors, in-flict pain on their children in order to educate and to cure what troubles them: "so also if Scripture says that God inflicts pain on this nature in order to convert and heal those who are in need of such punishment, there can be no ground for objection."[84] Augustine states that corrective punishment is most appropriately administered by one "who by the greatness of his love has overcome this hatred with which those are wont to be inflamed who desire to be avenged." Such love can be seen in "the benevolence of a father towards his young child" who desires not that the child go unpunished but be "happy through the correction he receives."[85] Pope Gregory the Great writes to Augustine of Canterbury: "For we ought to exercise discipline over the faithful, as good fathers do over their carnal children, whom they whip for their faults, and yet desire that they whom they afflict should be their heirs."[86] St. Theresa advises one of her communities on the treatment of a rebellious nun: "Your love for God, my sisters, must show itself in your pity for her, which must be as great as though she were as much the daughter of your own father as she is of this our true Father . . . Whom the poor creature has wanted to serve all her life."[87] Dom Jean Mabillon writes that justice in the monastery "should be paternal since it is the justice meted out by a father to his son."[88] Pope Pius XII insists that, despite the necessity of penal expiation, the foundation of a Catholic approach to criminal justice cannot be based on "a set of ideas that she proposes, no matter how right they may be," but rather the warmth and affection of a mother who "never grows tired of giving herself."[89]

What this parental image has tended to invoke in the theory of punishment is that the end of the disciplinary process is not absolute justice, or vindictive punishment, or even deterrence, but liberation.[90] God, through the words of Isaiah, ordains "liberty to the captives and release to the prisoners" (Is 61:1). When Jesus, in the synagogue at Nazareth, inaugurates his public mission, he announces its meaning with the same emphasis on the liberation of the incarcerated (Lk 4:18). Ambrose writes that God, in driving Cain into exile, "preferred the correction rather than the death of the sinner." Therefore, those who are guilty should not be destroyed by a premature punishment for they "could well procure forgiveness," redeeming themselves "by an act of repentance, however belated."[91] Pius XII frequently pointed to liberation as a principal element in crime and punishment. He surmised that serious crimes signify an "enslavement" and "bondage" that lead to a caricature of human freedom. The process of punishment must aim at "a psychological, juridical, moral and religious liberation."[92]

These images of Christ as prisoner and the church as parent seeking the freedom of her children are critical foundations for a Catholic theory of criminal justice. They remain in firm tension with cultural images that dehumanize and demonize the perpetrators of crime. The contemporary context has seen an unprecedented expansion of those detained in the correctional system; a refashioning of sentencing guidelines to expand exponentially the time penalty for, at times, the most minor felonies; and a deep public desire for, and resultant institutional practice of, violence and harm inflicted on the convict population.[93] The roots of all of this, if the forgoing discussion is correct, need not be uncovered in the criminology section of the nearest library; they are portrayed daily on local newscasts, in reality television, prime-time dramas, and popular literature and cinema. The average citizen, in this or any other time, may not have delved into the history and theory of punishment but can likely reveal in vivid detail which groups or individuals constitute the "dangerous classes" and how they should be punished. This verifies the assertion that any theory of justice proclaims an anthropology; it tells something about what it is to be human, about what people are and are not capable of doing and becoming These are moral and ontological questions that a Catholic theory of criminal justice must address.

THE PRISONER AS PERSON

The images that inform a Catholic theory of criminal justice reveal, among other things, a view of the human person. The interpretation of the tradition being offered here will proclaim the personhood of prisoners and the consequent moral obligations that this designation entails. The term "person" has been used extensively in Catholic theology and social ethics to portray an image of the human that honors the participation of each in God, more specifically, in the eternal triune nature of God, an identity that is at once unique and communal. Furthermore, scripture proclaims the creation of each in Jesus, who is both human and divine.[94] Augustine expresses well the ontological value of all created beings from a Catholic perspective: "There cannot exist a nature in which there is no good."[95] Within Catholic anthropology, one finds the affirmation that the one who has fallen is capable of rising again, that there is no single action that defines the transcendental worth of the agent, but that one's being and actions exist in a creative and formative tension that is never final until one's death, and, perhaps, not even then.[96]

Such a commitment to the human elicits a belief in the inviolable sacredness and dignity of every individual, regardless of what they have done.[97] This, however, does not mean that deliberate violations of human law should be met with unfettered sympathy. Many years ago, an ethics professor of mine summed up a principal canon of Catholic ethics when he stated, "you always do what you want to do." Our backs may be against the wall and the choices before us unappealing, or even appalling, but, in the end, we will choose the course of action that we think best. The limitations on perspective set into motion by environmental and psychological factors not withstanding, criminals freely choose to commit crime. Ambrose writes: "You have dominion, therefore, over your own acts; you are master of your own transgressions. You cannot enter a plea of ignorance or compulsion . . . . It was not by accident or by guile that you put yourself in the category of one accused of inflicting injury on God."[98] Anselm has a similar view: "Man, created in paradise without sin . . . . freely permitted himself to be overcome, by urging alone, in accordance with the will of the devil and against the will and honor of God."[99] Aquinas echoes Augustine in affirming that sin "is principally in the will," and that the one who "believes that something is a command and decides to violate it wills to break the law."[100]

The fact that people voluntarily create evil in the world means that they must accept responsibility for the world they have created. This belief that punishment has retributive value is hardly unique. What distinguishes the Catholic approach is its contention (to be discussed in the next chapter) that, although coercion is involved, punishment ideally takes place in the hearts of offenders, not as an end in itself, but as a path to discovering the inestimable worth of all in God's creation, including the offenders themselves.

Determinism or theories of absolute punishment are thus rejected in favor of an emphasis within the tradition on questions of virtue and character. Human choices lend force to the dispositions and motivations that initiated them. Central to the ethics of Aristotle was the initiation of citizens into a political environment that fostered virtue and restrained vice.[101] Aquinas, following Aristotle, made virtues central to his theory of the moral life and, particularly important, insisted that all were capable of learning them, including those undergoing punishment.[102] A Catholic theory of criminal justice, proceeding from such an anthropology, will not ask whether inmates are fully human, or whether they can be reintroduced to the virtues necessary to personal and communal well-being, but what kind of environment best creates the conditions for the affirmation and inculcation of the virtues. It is my contention that the tradition consistently proclaims that there is something in the environment of separation, solitude, and silence that is congenial to these commitments.

With such an understanding of the human person in which one can clearly detect an attempt to overcome the distinction of the inmate as the separated or despised "other,"[103] there is ideally a thin line that separates the confined from those outside the walls of the prison. The goal of reintegration of the offender is paramount in a Catholic theory, for it recalls the fundamental commitment, indeed the fervently held one, that by the merits of the death of Christ, any action, no matter how venal, can be forgiven.

CONCLUSION

The prison and the prisoner have had a sad and violent history; yet each developed a unique place in the Christian tradition in those instances in which they were portrayed in a set of transcendent and benevolent images, a process that reaches back to the legacy established by the ancient Hebrews and their understanding of criminal justice. Images are critical in all times and places to cultural understandings of the confined and the meaning of their confinement; it is from them that criminal justice policy tends to develop. I have argued that despite the images often employed in penal history by church and state that sanction a disdain for the offender and a punitive imprisonment, there arose at the dawn of the Christian era a contrasting identification of Christ with the prisoner, as well as penitential images in which the church was depicted as a parent with a paternal/maternal love for all of the imprisoned. I have suggested that a tension has thus developed within the tradition: there often appears an uncritical regard for the incarcerated regardless of their crime; at the same time, however, there exist the demands of justice stating that although they should be treated with the care owed to every human being, those guilty of legal infractions must undergo punishment. These contentions have been supported with some brief remarks on Christian anthropology as it has been interpreted by some in the Catholic tradition.

The overall logic of the chapter leaves us, then, with an intriguing if not unsettling conclusion: if Christ is the prisoner, and if those who err seriously must be imprisoned, then, a fortiori, Christ must be imprisoned. I believe such a conclusion is consonant with a clear line of argument within the tradition as well as with the normative emphasis in contemporary Catholic social ethics on the preeminent place of the poor; the poor, I might add, as they exist now, "in darkness and the shadow of death" (Lk 1:79), not in some reified conceptual framework. Since, in Catholic theology, people freely choose to do what is evil and must be placed in a penal environment, I believe it is essential that Christians find Christ in the prisoner, or that Christ *be* the prisoner. This is true not only because Jesus was (is) poor and rejected, but, in social-political terms, lest the deplorable things that have been done, and are being done, to prisoners be given the warrant of theological support or, perhaps worse, indifference. Christ as the one enduring confinement is a provocative statement; I am arguing the necessary one upon which to construct a Catholic theory of criminal justice; one that can ensure at least a humane vision of prisons and punishment for the untold millions currently confined, if not always the practices such a vision recommends. Such a position will require a strong justification for punishment. It is to that justification that we now turn.

NOTES

1. While there is a clear distinction in contemporary parlance between jails and prisons: the former to detain those awaiting trial/sentencing and those serving time for misdemeanors, the latter to confine those convicted of felonies, in this study I will use the term prison to refer to any type of publicly imposed involuntary confinement.

2. Dunbabin, *Captivity and Imprisonment in Medieval Europe*, 23; Johnston, *Forms of Constraint*, 16.

3. Dunbabin, *Captivity and Imprisonment in Medieval Europe*, 36.

4. Ralph Pugh, *Imprisonment in Medieval England* (Cambridge: Cambridge University Press, 1970), 2. See also George Ives, *A History of Penal Methods* (Montclair, NJ: Patterson Smith, 1970), 7 [originally published 1914].

5. See Israel Drapkin, *Crime and Punishment in the Ancient World* (Lexington, MA: Lexington Books, 1989), 26.

6. Berman, *Law and Revolution*, 54–65.

7. Elias, *Civilizing Process*, vol. 1, 193–94. See also Pieter Spierenburg, *The Spectacle of Suffering* (Cambridge: Cambridge University Press, 1984), 55–57.

8. George Ives notes that if fines were not paid, and they were often heavy in cases such as murder, the families of victims were permitted to execute vengeance against their assailants. See *A History of Penal Methods*, 4. F. W. Maitland, in somewhat different fashion, states that due to the strength of the family bond, the legislator often found it difficult to restrain "a blood feud, a private war" by simply ordering the kin of the slain person to accept compensation in money. See *The*

Constitutional History of England (Cambridge: Cambridge University Press, 1968), 4 [originally published 1908]. See also Julius Goebel Jr., *Felony and Misdemeanor* (Philadelphia: University of Pennsylvania Press, 1976), 21–25 [originally published 1937].

9. Roland de Vaux, O. P. *Ancient Israel: Its Life and Institutions*, trans. John McHugh (New York: McGraw-Hill, 1961), 11.

10. Ibid., 11–12.

11. Ibid.

12. Goebel, *Felony and Misdemeanor*, 89; John T. McNeill and Helena M. Gamer, *Medieval Handbooks of Penance* (New York: Columbia University Press, 1938), 22.

13. Dunbabin, *Captivity and Imprisonment in Medieval Europe*, 2–3.

14. Johnston, *Forms of Constraint*, 1.

15. Quoted in Peter Garnsey, *Social Status and Legal Privilege in the Roman Empire* (Oxford: Clarendon Press, 1970), 149.

16. St. Cyprian, *The Letters of Saint Cyprian of Carthage*, trans. G. W. Clarke (New York: Newman Press, 1984), vol. 1, no. 22, 2.2.

17. Eusebius, *The History of the Church*, trans. G. A. Williamson (Harmondsworth, U.K.: Penguin, 1965), bk. V, 1.

18. Garnsey, *Social Status and Legal Privilege in the Roman Empire*, 148.

19. Ibid., 149. Even attempts at humane imprisonment reveal the chaining of inmates. The Theodosian Code (438 AD) contains a Constantinian regulation stating that "the man who has been produced in court shall not be put in manacles of iron that cleave to the bones, but in looser chains, so that there may be no torture and yet the custody may remain secure." See *Letters of Saint Cyprian of Carthage*, vol. 1, no. 22, n. 16.

20. Marcus Bell notes that it was essential to the power of the stories that the miraculous be superimposed on details of ordinary life with which the hearers of the stories would be familiar: "The 'residue' of the story, sifting out the miracle, reveals important material about social, economic, cultural, and religious conditions of the world at that time." See *The Miracles of Our Lady of Rocamadour*, ed. and trans. Marcus Bell (Woodbridge, UK: Boydell Press, 1999), 11.

21. Pamela Sheingorn, ed. and trans., *The Book of Sainte Foy* (Philadelphia: University of Pennsylvania Press, 1995), 185.

22. Dunbabin, *Captivity and Imprisonment in Medieval Europe*, 31.

23. Edward Peters, "Prison Before the Prison," in Norval Morris and David Rothman, eds. *The Oxford History of the Prison* (New York: Oxford University Press, 1995), 19.

24. Herbert Musurillo, ed. and trans., *The Acts of the Christian Martyrs* (Oxford: Clarendon, 1972), 109.

25. Sheingorn, *Book of Sainte Foy*, 128.

26. Bell, *Miracles of Our Lady of Rocamadour*, 109–10.

27. Guibert, *The Autobiography of Guibert: Abbot of Nugent-Sous-Coucy*, trans. C. C. Swinton Bland (London: Routledge & Sons, 1925), 193.

28. Quoted in Elias, *Civilizing Process*, vol. 1, 193.

29. Peters, "Prison Before the Prison," 19.

30. Plato, *Laws*, trans. R. G. Bury (Cambridge, MA: Harvard University Press, 1926), vol. 2, bk. XI.

31. Socrates, on hearing Meletus call for his execution, proposes possible sentences in lieu of death. See Plato, "The Apology," in *Plato: Complete Works*, ed. John M. Cooper, trans. G. M. A. Grube (Indianapolis, IN: Hackett, 1997), 37C. Similarly, beginning with Claudius, Roman law allowed for *liberum mortis arbitrium* (free choice in the manner of death); renowned figures (e.g., Seneca) could choose the manner in which they would die. See Richard Bauman, *Crime and Punishment in Ancient Rome* (London and NY: Routledge, 1996), 7, 87–88.

32. Johnston, *Forms of Constraint*, 6–7.

33. Dunbabin, *Captivity and Imprisonment in Medieval Europe*, 38, 104.

34. Ibid., 114–15; Ives, *History of Penal Methods*, 12.

35. Garnsey, *Social Status and Legal Privilege in the Roman Empire*, 1–5.

36. See Timothy Gorringe, *God's Just Vengeance* (Cambridge: Cambridge University Press, 1996), 40–41.

37. For a discussion of these issues, see Drapkin, *Crime and Punishment in the Ancient World*, 54–83.

38. See, e.g., E. Christian Brugger, *Capital Punishment and Roman Catholic Tradition* (Notre Dame, IN: University of Notre Dame Press, 2003), 62; Vaux, *Ancient Israel: Its Life and Institutions*, 149–50; Lee Griffith, *The Fall of the Prison: Biblical Perspectives on Prison Abolition* (Grand Rapids, MI: Eerdmans, 1993), 91–92; James J. Megivern, *The Death Penalty: An Historical and Theological Survey* (New York: Paulist Press, 1997), 10–12.

39. Vaux, *Ancient Israel*, 160; Peters, "Prison Before the Prison," 12.

40. See Alan E. Bernstein, *The Formation of Hell* (Ithaca, NY: Cornell University Press, 1993), 141; Griffith, *Fall of the Prison*, 106–07.

41. Bernstein, *Formation of Hell*, 3, 146–53.

42. Ibid., 157–61. Griffith seems to miss this point in his singular contention that prisons in the Bible "are identical in spirit to the violence and murder that they pretend to combat." See *Fall of the Prison*, 106.

43. Peters, "Prison Before the Prison," 8.

44. "Wherever the concept of crime exists, images are communicated in society about the meaning of crime, the nature of the criminal, and the relationship of crime to the social order." Quinney, *Social Reality of Crime*, 277.

45. Foucault, *Discipline and Punish*, 136-38; Georg Rusche and Otto Kirchheimer, *Punishment and Social Structure* (New York: Russell & Russell, 1968), 5.

46. Louis P. Masur, *Rites of Execution* (New York: Oxford University Press, 1989), 5.

47. Randall McGowen, "The Body and Punishment in Eighteenth-Century England," *The Journal of Modern History* 59 (1987), 675–76.

48. Just as Elias traced the influence of a culture obsessed with death and judgment on the violent punishments of the Middle Ages, Pieter Spierenburg writes of the cultured members of the early nineteenth century who eschewed the carnage of public floggings and executions: "the elites had reached a new stage and identified to a certain degree with convicts on the scaffold. These delicate

persons disliked the sight of physical suffering: even that of the guilty." See *Spectacle of Suffering*, 204; see also Svend Ranulf, *Moral Indignation and Middle Class Psychology* (New York: Schocken Books, 1964).

49. Garland writes of the "overdetermination of the cultural realm as it relates to practice. In every case, a specific cultural form comes to influence or acts upon penal practice only through a process of struggle, compromise, and alliance with a range of competing forms." See *Punishment and Modern Society*, 209.

50. Ibid., 198.

51. See Samuel Y. Edgerton, *Pictures and Punishment* (Ithaca, NY: Cornell University Press, 1985), 22–23.

52. Edgerton writes: "By comparing the plight of the poor criminal on the scaffold with vividly realistic portrayals of martyred saints and Jesus' suffering, Christians slowly became aware of their own inhumanity in the practice." See *Pictures and Punishment*, 14.

53. Machiavelli was imprisoned in the *Stinche* temporarily for his alleged role in a local conspiracy. He complained "of the stench and the fact that the walls were crawling with vermin so big and swollen that they seemed like moths." See Marvin E. Wolfgang, "A Florentine Prison: Le Carceri delle Stinche," *Studies in the Renaissance* 7 (1960):150–51.

54. Ibid., 153.

55. Edgerton, *Pictures and Punishment*, 132.

56. Elias, *Civilizing Process*, vol. 1, 59.

57. Foucault, *Discipline and Punish*, 11.

58. Edgerton, *Pictures and Punishment*, 30–31.

59. Wayne A. Meeks, *The Origins of Christian Morality* (New Haven, CT: Yale University Press, 1993), 43–46.

60. John T. Noonan, "Development in Moral Doctrine," *Theological Studies* 54 (1993), 673.

61. Francesco Compagnoni, "Capital Punishment and Torture in the Tradition of the Catholic Church," *Concilium* 120 (1979): 41–44, 47–50.

62. "Constitutiones vero principium Ecclesiasticu constitutionibus non praeminent, sed obsequuntur" [Constitutions in fact are not a priori a threat to ecclesiastical authority but by means of the constitutions they defer to it]. Gratian, "Concordia Discordantium Canonum," in *Corpus Iuris Canonici* (Lyon: 1616), dist. 10, ante c.1.

63. Elias, *Civilizing Process*, vol. 1, 195.

64. Guibert, *Autobiography of Guibert*, 208.

65. "In omnibus nostris Conventibus . . . sit locus securus . . . et sint in eo compedes, vincula, aliaque necessaria ad poenam, et majorem custodiam delinquentium." [In all of our convents, may there be a secure place and let there be in it shackles, chains, and other things necessary for the punishment and more effective custody of delinquents.] "Constitutiones Fratres Trinitariorum," in *Codex Regularum Monasticarum Et Canoniciarum*, ed. Lucas Holstenius (Graz: Akademische Druck–U. Verlagsanstalt, 1957), VI, cap xxi, iv, i [originally published 1759].

66. See Thorsten Sellin, "Dom Jean Mabillon: A Prison Reformer of the Seventeenth Century," *Journal of the American Institute of Criminal Law and Criminology* 17 (1927): 584.

67. Rene Girard, *Things Hidden Since the Foundation of the World*, trans. Stephen Bann (Books II & III) and Michael Metteer (Book I) (Palo Alto, CA: Stanford University Press, 1987), 174–85.

68. Griffith, *Fall of the Prison*, 125.

69. *Acts of the Christian Martyrs*, 153.

70. Ibid., 201.

71. St. John Chrysostom, "Homilies on the Gospel of Saint Matthew," in Philip Schaff, ed., *A Select Library of the Nicene and Post Nicene Fathers*, vol. X (New York: The Christian Literature Company, 1888), no. 50, 4.

72. St. Cyprian, *Letters*, trans. Sister Rose Bernard Donna, C.S.J. (Washington, DC: Catholic University of America Press, 1964), no. 62, 3.

73. St. Augustine, *The City of God*, bk. XIX, ch. 17.

74. St. John Climacus, *The Ladder of Divine Ascent*, trans. Archimandrite Lazarus Moore (London: Faber & Faber, 1959), 13–14, V, 21.

75. Ibid., V, 26.

76. Edgerton, *Pictures and Punishment*, 178–79, 185–88.

77. Gregory of Tours, *The History of the Franks*, trans. Lewis Thorpe (London: Penguin, 1974), V, 8.

78. "S. Quintino Martyre," in *Acta Sanctorum*, 31 Octobris, Tomus XIII (Paris: 1883), 781–82.

79. "Sanctus . . . Leonardus, qui numquam se apellantibus fuit tardus." Sanctus Leonardus, *Acta Sanctorum*, 6 Novembris, Tomus III (Brussels: 1910), 157–58.

80. James William Brodman, *Ransoming Captives in Crusader Spain* (Philadelphia: University of Pennsylvania Press, 1986), 11–14.

81. Ibid., 111.

82. Ibid., 104.

83. Malcolm Feeley and Jonathan Simon, "The New Penology: Notes on the Emerging Strategy of Corrections and Its Implications," *Criminology* 30 (1992): 470.

84. Origen, *Contra Celsum*, trans. Henry Chadwick (Cambridge: Cambridge University Press, 1953), bk. 6, ch. 56.

85. St. Augustine, *The Lord's Sermon on the Mount*, trans. John J. Jepson (Westminster, MD: Newman Press, 1948), bk I, ch. 20, 63.

86. John Johnson, ed., *A Collection of the Laws and Canons of the Church of England* (Oxford: John Henry Parker, 1850), I, 68–69.

87. St. Theresa, *The Letters of St Theresa of Jesus*, trans. E. Allison Peers (London: Burns, Oates, and Washbourne, 1966), vol. 1, 274.

88. Sellin, "Dom Jean Mabillon," 583.

89. Pius XII, "Prisoners, Punishment, and Pardon," *The Pope Speaks* 4 (1957): 172–73.

90. It is worth noting that one of the most respected of contemporary criminologists, John Braithwaite, has argued that, to be effective, crime control strate-

gies must base themselves on the model of the family, where discipline is not es-chewed but carried out by parents who deeply love their errant children and de-sire their full reintegration into the family. See *Crime, Shame, and Reintegration* (Cambridge: Cambridge University Press, 1989), 54–68.

91. St. Ambrose, "Cain and Abel," trans. John J. Savage, in *The Fathers of the Church*, vol. 42 (New York: Fathers of the Church, Inc., 1961), bk. II, ch. 9, para. 38.

92. Pius XII, "Crime and Punishment," *The Catholic Mind* 53 (1955), 374.

93. See David Garland, *The Culture of Control* (Chicago: University of Chicago Press, 2001), 8–15; Michael Tonry, *Sentencing Matters* (New York: Oxford University Press, 1996).

94. The literature on these foundational themes is extensive and consistently affirmed in both ecclesiastical and academic circles within the Catholic Church. See, e.g., Jacques Maritain, *The Person and the Common Good*, trans. John J. Fitzgerald (Notre Dame, IN: University of Notre Dame Press, 1966); Emmanuel Mounier, *Personalism*, trans. Philip Mairet (Notre Dame, IN: University of Notre Dame Press, 1970); Pope John Paul II (Karol Wojtyla), *Person and Community*, trans. Theresa Sandok (New York: Peter Lang, 1993).

95. St. Augustine, *The City of God*, bk. XIX, ch. 13.

96. Karl Rahner is perhaps the best-known figure in support of these positions. On his transcendental anthropology and his view of the moral life see, e.g., *Theological Investigations* vol. II, trans. Karl H. Kruger (London: Darton, Longman & Todd, 1963), 217–34; on his theology of death, see *Theological Investigations*, vol. VII, trans. David Bourke (London: Darton, Longman & Todd, 1971), 287–91.

97. This belief in, and commitment to, a view of the sacredness of each human life forms the basis of the recent trend in the Catholic Church to reject the use of the death penalty. See *Compendium: Catechism of the Catholic Church* (Washington, DC: United States Conference of Catholic Bishops, 2006), #2266, 2267; John Paul II, *The Gospel of Life (Evangelium Vitae)* (Boston: Pauline, 1995) and "Homily in the Trans World Dome," *Origins* 28 (1999): 600–601; The Catholic Bishops of the United States, "Statement on Capital Punishment," *Origins* 10 (1980): 373–77.

98. St. Ambrose, "Cain and Abel," bk. II, ch. 7, para. 25.

99. St. Anselm, "Why God Became Man," bk. I, ch. 22.

100. St. Thomas Aquinas, *Truth*, trans. James V. McGlynn (Chicago: Henry Regency, 1953), vol. II, q.17, a.4.

101. Aristotle, *The Politics*, trans. T. A. Sinclair (Harmondsworth, UK: Penguin, 1981), III, ix, 1280b29.

102. "Alio modo dictae poenae comparantur ad eos quibus infliguntur, ut medicinae: quia poenae sunt quaedam medicinae . . . vel sibi, inquantum scilicet praeservant a culpa, sue ad virtutem promovet; vel aliis, inquantum scilicet est aliis exemplum." [In another sense, mandated punishments, for those upon whom they are imposed, can be compared to medicine; because punishments are a kind of medicine . . . either to the person himself insofar as they keep him

from doing harm and motivate him to virtue, or for others insofar as it gives an example to others]. See St. Thomas Aquinas, *Petri Lombardi Sententiarum libre quatuor* (Excudebat Migne, 1841), III, d. 19, q.1, a.3, sol.2.

103. I use the term "other" deliberately since it occupies so prominent a place in postmodern accounts of ethics, including accounts suggesting changes in the system of criminal justice. See Jacques Derrida, *Of Hospitality*, trans. Rachel Bowlby (Palo Alto, CA: Stanford University Press, 2000); George Pavlich, "Towards an Ethics of Restorative Justice," in Lode Walgrave, ed., *Restorative Justice and the Law* (Cullompton, UK: Willan, 2002), 1–18.

2

The Justification for Punishment

In secular justice the principal purpose is to conserve and repair order and to instill fear into the criminals, but in ecclesiastical justice one considers above all the welfare of the soul.

—Dom Jean Mabillon

A penitent is the inflictor of his own punishments.

—St. John Climacus

The first chapter took as its main theme the question of the identity of the prisoner. It is the task of this chapter to address the first of three questions a theory of criminal justice must confront concerning the prisoner: By what justification is he or she punished? This is a particularly delicate question for a theory based in the Catholic tradition because two seemingly irreconcilable claims emerge consistently over the long history of the church: the first, what might be termed a "top-down" approach, is that punishment by lawful authority is both just and necessary for those who have freely chosen to disrupt the harmony established within and intended by God for creation; the second, however, reverses the direction of the coercive action, stating that punishment does not achieve its true meaning until it arises from within and is willed by the offender, that is, until it becomes self-punishment.

Like the conflict inherent in affirming the prison even though Christ himself is the prisoner, this double-sided retributive posture requires a careful analysis of historical and textual sources, since it seems to take back with one hand what it gives with the other. The method I employ

35

in presenting this argument is largely comparative. I summon a number of theological interlocutors whose insights on the justification for punishment are vital to the development of Catholic thought in this area but whose particular contribution also stands in need of expansion or revision. The largely top-down position of Augustine, for example, is presented in conjunction with the interiority that arises in the thought of Aquinas. It is my contention that the twin principles underlying the justification for punishment can best be reconciled by harmonizing the sometimes divergent claims that have appeared among the most notable contributors to Catholic thought relating to criminal justice.

The structure of this chapter focuses mainly on three interconnecting and ascending concepts necessary to the Catholic argument for punishment of the wayward: order, justice, and atonement. A pivotal relationship surfaces within this schema, one that is as precarious as it is crucial—the association of church and state.

THE RETRIBUTIVE DIMENSION OF PUNISHMENT

The way in which criminal justice has been conceived and practiced within the church cannot be understood apart from its primary source of revelation, sacred scripture, nor from one of its most ancient rituals, the practice of penance.

Given the frequent mention in the Bible that God not only punishes intentional evil, but *must* punish it (Ps 58:11–12, Ex 23:7, Is 13:11, Jb 36:17, Rom 2:5–8), and given the necessary demands of both contrition and expiation within penance, one might also say that retributive justice, or what is often termed "just desserts," has always figured prominently in a Catholic understanding of criminal justice.

Aquinas provides the classic warrant for a theory of just desserts when he writes that it is the very nature of punishment to be "contrary to the will, painful, and inflicted for some fault."[1] Augustine states that a God who is just "both rewards the good and punishes the bad" and "these punishments are evils to those who suffer them."[2] Tertullian's view is similar but he also adds that the Christian should not experience gratification in sanctioning retributive suffering—no matter how much it may be deserved: "It is good, no doubt, to have the guilty punished. Who but the criminal himself will deny that? And yet the innocent can find no pleasure in another's sufferings: he rather mourns that a brother has sinned so heinously as to need a punishment so dreadful."[3]

It is my contention that the Catholic tradition strongly favors the hope that the offender will interiorize the punishment being imposed, leading to his or her conversion or amendment of character. Yet, despite strong evidence to support the internal healing power of penitential discipline, I believe that the external retributive component must stand on its own as an independent variable, regardless of how it is received by the guilty party. Employing Thomist terminology, punishment is not the "final cause" of apprehending lawbreakers but is necessary as an "efficient cause" in the creation of justice.

The claim within Catholic thought that retribution, usually expressed as forcible detention, must be recognized as a principal value in achieving criminal justice contains two significant assumptions: the first is that the state has a moral obligation to punish offenders; the second is that state-imposed punishment must never be viewed in absolute terms but always as a pretext and an invitation to inner renewal and conversion.[4] Each assumption is addressed in turn.

THE STATE AND THE PUNISHMENT OF OFFENDERS

To be faithful to the Catholic tradition, a theory of criminal justice must first testify to the natural sociability of human beings. It was noted at the conclusion of the last chapter that a Catholic anthropology is personalist, emanating from a view of both the Godhead and society as a community of persons.[5] Lodged, however, within the notion of a community, even a divine one, is a set of spatial and orientational metaphors.[6] It is proclaimed in the Nicene Creed that Jesus "descended into hell" and "rose from the dead." Often, in scripture, spatial metaphors are combined with judicial-penal ones. In the parable of the wedding feast and that of the wise virgins, the vigilant and cooperative are "invited into the feast," the dilatory and rebellious are "cast out into the darkness" (Mt 22:13; 25:10–11). Theses images lend credence to the notion that all communities, even the Trinity, have boundaries. Hans Boersma notes that, despite the limitations of metaphors such as these, they are, in the end, "all we have to talk about God."[7]

The same sense of linguistic differentiation is replicated in the earthly realm. There are, for example, specific communities within the church, clerical and lay, that aspire to an inclusive love and profess a radical openness to the stranger and the poor. However, these very commitments subordinate values such as property, wealth, and the use of violent means in their defense to Gospel directives deemed "above" the opposing or "lower" values of the world. Thus, despite the expansiveness of the theological or social perspective, certain ideologies, moral commitments, and social structures lie outside the ethos of any given social order and must be held at bay lest the integrity of such a social order be compromised or destroyed.

Reflection on linguistic practice and political experience readily reveals that military metaphors of conflict and defense define a significant part of reality for nations and kingdoms, but they were similarly employed by primitive Christian communities for whom nothing was more important than the clear sense of separation and difference between themselves and their non-Christian contemporaries. Wayne Meeks reveals that in the earliest of the Pauline epistles this sense of defending the purity of the community against the corruption outside was preeminent: "It is obvious in Paul's letter to the Thessalonian Christians that their 'turning from idols' to the 'living and genuine God' was simultaneously a transfer of loyalty and sense of belonging from one set of social relations to another."[8] This theme of protection from the "enemy" also dominates Paul's letters to the Colossians and Ephesians, where other military metaphors are presented. Christians are repeatedly called upon to take off the "old human" with its evil inclinations and vest themselves in the "armor" of God's righteousness (Eph 6:10–17).[9]

Such rigorous attempts to define boundaries against the "pollution" of the non-Christian world are also legitimated in many scriptural texts wherein the delinquent are reproved and, in varying degrees, isolated from the community at large (Mt 13:25–26; 2 Cor 11:13–15; Gal 5:10–12). Paul shares his profound sadness as he reproves the Christians at Corinth for allowing a man living with his stepmother to remain active within the community. He commands that the man be expelled at once and "handed over to Satan," asserting that the destruction of his body may still invite new life in the spirit at the coming of Christ (1 Cor 5:1–5). St. Ambrose, commenting on this passage, states that "the sinner is delivered to Satan for the destruction of the flesh, that the serpent may lick the dust of his flesh, but not hurt his soul."[10] Thus, both church and state share a resemblance in the attempt to legitimate a given set of internal practices and isolate those who threaten them.

That there are inevitable quandaries inherent in punishment hardly needs mention at this point, the immediate question is how a community so clearly intent on maintaining its distinctiveness from the social and political system surrounding it, and so clearly convinced of the superiority of its notion of justice, could arrive at the conclusion that the state was "morally" charged to punish malefactors. To arrive at this position some intervening value would need to surface that both communities shared, one that harmonized the need of both church and state to defend boundaries while at the same time protecting the integrity of the former and its sense of divine origin and mission. The vital thread that linked the two communities, however tentatively, was order; the one figure most responsible in promoting its significance was Augustine.

Order

It was noted in the first chapter that Christians, however diligent their attempts, could not extricate themselves from the cultures in which they resided. As a new religious movement, the early church was largely composed of adult converts who had initially been socialized into other religious and social frameworks. Furthermore, as a largely urban phenomenon, early Christian communities lived and interacted in close quarters with their non-Christian neighbors. They also were citizens of municipalities and of the Empire to which they owed, and often demonstrated, a degree of allegiance.[11]

Given the strain caused by this inside/outside dynamic and the questions concerning social ethics that it inevitably engendered, Augustine's shrewd insight was to magnify the importance of the one value that both the earthly and heavenly "cities" had in common: the order that proceeds from peace. His reasons may have been more utilitarian than strictly theological: defending the police function of the state in order to then direct its power to suppress the threat he saw in opposing religious ideologies. The result, however, was to link the notions of justice of both cities, ambiguity notwithstanding, once and for all, at least as far as the social thought of the church was concerned. The earthly city, though it is to be "condemned in the final punishment . . . . has its good in this world," Augustine writes, "and rejoices to participate in it."[12] Peace is the good to which he refers. In some of his most famous and trenchant images Augustine reflects that even bands of robbers desire to live in peace with one another and, therefore, Christians must make use of the "peace of Babylon."[13] They "must needs make use of this peace" and obey the laws of the earthly city "since the mortal condition is shared by both cities."[14]

Analysis yields abundant evidence that the Catholic tradition has always held order in the highest esteem, drawing legitimation for it from scripture, the writings of the "fathers," as well as ecclesiastical organization. Its context and interpretation may have been different than in other political units but it was an essential value for a community whose foundation was the gift of the spirit of peace at Pentecost (Acts 2:1–13; Gal 5:22). Meeks relies on Pliny to depict the meetings of early second-century Christians wherein those seeking baptism pledged an oath "to abstain from a series of vices: theft, robbery, adultery, breach of trust, and embezzlement."[15] Violations of these and other ethical directives, seen as sacred and inviolable for those who had received the gift of the Holy Spirit at baptism and who dwelt in a sanctified congregation, were primary threats not only to personal holiness but also to communal viability.

Order is not the same as justice, however, and Augustine was careful to distinguish between the two. He did not believe that it was within the capacity of the state, due to its earthly origin, to exact or even enact justice in any true sense. For him, the justice of God was far too glorious and beyond human understanding to be recognized, let alone practiced (a very important insight to which we will return).[16] In a significant passage, he notes that the secular judge could never know if he was condemning an innocent or guilty person.[17] Augustine was thus reticent to embark on an elaborate theory of justice beyond the fundamentally utilitarian desire to support the state in its mission to keep the peace.[18] That, however, does not mean that the stewardship for order, entrusted to the state, was not a divine concern and mandate, despite the fact that the state could do little more than seek retribution, and do even that in a fashion reflecting its fallen nature.[19] The mission to maintain order, thought Augustine, was still so vital that even though Christians might be innocently victimized by what, it could normally be assumed, would be a city driven by a "lust for domination," they were exhorted to "consider in humility the sins which have moved God's indignation" and "not regard themselves as so far removed from such wrongdoings as not to deserve to suffer temporal ills which are the recompense for sin."[20] Besides, Augustine reasoned, God's providence was ultimately guiding history, and the powerful within history, toward the fulfillment of God's own perfect plan.[21]

Stanley Chodorow notes that Gratian shared a similar understanding of the dichotomy between order and justice. For the legitimacy of an ordinance was not equated with notions of justice or injustice but with the power entrusted to the monarch or political official to secure social stability and thereby preserve ecclesiastical sovereignty. Thus Gratian maintains "that unjust sentences—*ex causa*, *ex ordine*, or *ex animo*—ought to be obeyed."[22] Gratian references a letter of St. Jerome in which it is stated that the power of the sovereign is divinely ordained to control evil and protect the good. He also quotes Isidore of Seville: "What priests are not able to do by teaching, power compels by the terror of discipline."[23]

Order and Justice

We have now seen that the first of three justifications for punishment in a Catholic understanding of criminal justice is the emphasis on order. Augustine advanced it as the one value that, in his mind, the doomed earthly city shared with those whose true allegiance was to the city of

God. However, as to our goal of clarifying the ecclesiastical affirmation of the state as a moral agent of punishment, all we have thus far is a military or penal metaphor that reduces the state to a necessary bulwark against disruption of the peace, whether internal or external. I now turn to St. Thomas Aquinas for an explanation of the relationship between order and justice and the role of the state in fulfilling that reconciliation.

Aquinas placed a similarly high value upon order, as did his theological forebears, stating that its removal from created things would "deprive them of their best possession."[24] He saw order as necessary to the three levels of the cosmos relevant to human life: the divine, the political, and the personal: "Accordingly, man can be punished with a threefold punishment corresponding to the three orders to which the human will is subject . . . . one, inflicted by himself, viz. remorse of conscience; another, inflicted by man; and a third, inflicted by God."[25] He thus affirms Augustine's contention that the state has a moral duty to exact retribution even as he points to the internal sense of contrition so essential to the contention that the final end of punishment can only be fulfilled within the heart of the offender.

But what lies at the heart of the qualitative difference between Aquinas and many of his predecessors in the faith, most notably Augustine, was his insistence that the state is a natural institution ordained by God for human governance and, as such, a positive good from which good can be both expected and summoned. Recalling Aristotle, he claims that the human is "a social and political animal" ordained to "live in a group."[26] The state must seek to ensure that the interchanges between group members are conducted peacefully: "The people of Israel is commended for the beauty of its order . . . . But the beautiful ordering of a people depends on the right establishment of its rulers."[27] It is, however, also the divinely appointed duty of political leadership to secure the common good and promulgate, as well as defend, those human laws that underlie social institutions, such as the family and the church, that are the primary loci for training in the cardinal virtues, one of which is justice.[28]

In providing an independent sanction for the state within God's cosmic plan, Aquinas reflects important distinctions between sin and crime and the internal/external forum that were appearing at the time he wrote. Recall that until the introduction of the first universal system of law (canon law), begun after Pope Gregory VII declared the independence of the Catholic Church from all forms of secular authority in 1057, there was little distinction made between a transgression against the community and one against God. Offenses were assumed to be both against the victim and God rather than an affront to a sovereign political jurisdiction.[29] As Harold Berman notes: "All major 'secular' offenses . . . were

also sins to be atoned for by penance; and all major 'ecclesiastical' offenses . . . were also crimes prohibited by folklaw and subject to secular
sanctioning."[30]

The inauguration of a body of law to govern the entire church solidified the emerging autonomy and legitimacy of the secular realm by underscoring the distinction between the internal and external forums; the
former being the domain of privacy and conscience that exists between
priest and penitent; the latter embracing offenses affecting the common
life. Wrongful acts in the external forum, what were termed "criminal
sins," would have to be accounted for publicly. In effect, the public sinner was also a criminal who must repent both the sin and the violation
of order and justice.

The Thomist theological system sharpens these distinctions even further. God and the state each have their own complementary plane of the
universal order. There is an organic relationship between the divine and
human rather than the strained and inevitably disparate cosmic trajectories of the two cities of Augustine. Certainly God is the origin of law and
all social projects receive their sanction and authenticity from their resonance with the divine plan for creation, but humans and the state are imparted freedom and "an active role in the production of natural effects,"
a theological quality John Mahoney terms "instrumental causality."[31]
The ultimate end of all persons is the *visio Dei*, the beatific vision, the
fullness of happiness in God's presence. However, a secondary aim or *telos* exists necessarily: that citizens be habituated into the virtues that
complement and point toward the final end of human history. The state
is a principal agent in the achievement of those exalted ends. Aquinas
writes that the "governance of every provident ruler is ordered either to
the attainment, or the increase, or the preservation of the perfection of
the things governed.[32] He also states: "[S]ociety must have the same end
as the individual man. Therefore, it is not the ultimate end of the assembled multitude to live virtuously, but through virtuous living to attain the possession of God."[33]

Of the four cardinal virtues—prudence, fortitude, temperance, and justice—the first three are concerned with the interior life, while justice governs all human social interchanges.[34] Aquinas defines justice as "a habit
whereby a man renders to each one his due by a constant and perpetual
will."[35] This is essentially the same as Augustine's definition: "the virtue
by which each man is given his due."[36] But whereas the Augustinian
schema despaired of achieving, or even approximating, justice until the
dawning of the day of the Lord, the tradition takes a bold turn with the
claim of Aquinas that the state is to oversee the social project within
which justice is to be fostered and honored. The basis of the state is thus

not a homicide, as Augustine claimed, but "to procure the unity of peace," a phrase which seems to assume not simply order but an order wherein citizens are consciously united by formation in the virtues in pursuit of social concord.[37] This implies that the demands of virtue not only must apply to the average citizen but that a certain degree of nobility should be expected and, to some degree, demanded from the one who oversees the administration of justice. [A kingdom] "easily degenerates into tyranny unless he to whom this power is given be a virtuous man."[38]

Not everyone will be virtuous, however. Like Aristotle before him, Aquinas was careful to distinguish between virtues and the vices poised to efface them.[39] Where disorder threatened social well-being, he adamantly sanctioned repression of the perpetrator, never forgetting that without order "the benefit of social life is lost."[40] For in criminal behavior, as with all sin, the offender "prefers his own will to the divine will by satisfying it contrary to God's ordering. Now, this inequity is removed when, against his will, man is forced to suffer something in accord with divine ordering."[41] In a similar vein, he writes that "whoever sins, commits an offense against an order: wherefore he is put down, in consequence, by that same order, which repression is punishment."[42]

Punishment of the delinquent, however, does not simply react to the offense in terms of the threat to civic tranquility. To be true to the Thomist system, it must direct itself to the levels of disorder and seek to repair the harm done to each. This carries retribution into the realm of justice and its demand for the restoration of equality and anticipates the goal of internal renewal.[43]

By constructing a more positive and attainable understanding of justice, Aquinas is able to add an important dimension to the Augustinian concept of order: structures do not just restrain evil; they have the capacity to make us better.

There are intriguing theological repercussions to this discussion over the role of the state in seeking to create both order and justice. For certainly political structures can also make us worse. As with lawbreakers, however, there are limits in the thought of Aquinas to what the Christian citizen, or any citizen, due to universal participation in the natural law, can accept in the way of comportment by civil authorities. To be sure, Aquinas argues, in cost-benefit fashion, that if the disorder caused by principled resistance to corrupt authority is greater than the harm borne as a result of the "perversion of law," then one should accept the miscarriage of justice in deference to the greater good.[44] In this he lies closer to the thought of Augustine. However, in a theoretical sense, as opposed to the practical one just outlined, tyranny is seen in his thought as a robbery committed against the entire social body.[45] Therefore, one is not obliged to obey that which is unjust.[46] This proviso has been upheld in Catholic teaching to this very day.[47]

The importance of this qualification gains interest in this study since it attests to the fact that injustice is done not only by those who break the law, but also by those who punish the lawbreakers. It is one thing to claim that the state has a moral obligation to punish legal infractions; it is quite another to suggest that the state is the bearer of justice, human and, in a real but limited sense, divine. Too close an association between the state and the creation of justice, notwithstanding its moral mandate to punish, can lead to the very deformation of justice that has so often characterized criminal justice in every period of human history.

This extension of moral responsibility to the state, based on the organic relationship between all parts of creation with God, and likewise based on a natural law that imparts rational apprehension of the foundations of law and morality to all humans, leads to a more exact understanding of order. But does it yield justice? Ideally, Aquinas would answer in the affirmative. For what emerges from the structure of his thought is the creation of the public person, one who does not obey out of fear of "the terror of discipline," but who has cultivated a sense of social responsibility that imparts a series of obligations that are superior to individual human desires just as the whole is superior to any of its parts. This civic-minded citizen is guided by the internal virtues of prudence, fortitude, and temperance, and the social virtue of justice. He or she "is in harmony with the law which directs the acts of all the virtues to the common good."[48]

The vision of society that ennobles each element of the social hierarchy by its connection to the divine provides a compelling foundation for the justification for punishment in the Catholic tradition. I believe it is a necessary element in that it brings the question of justice into the picture with the same immediacy as the normative significance of order that Augustine and his followers introduced. However, on its own, the state is a necessary but limited player in the pursuit of criminal justice.

The Moral Ambiguity of Punishment

What we have thus far provided is an appreciation for order and justice as fundamental components in the justification of punishment; but each implies coercion and, that element, the coercive, is the Achilles heel in all retributive theories. As John Milbank states, it is "always a tragic risk" for "the trial and punishment of Jesus itself condemns, in some measure, all other trials and punishment."[49] For now we must address the question of power and its relation to justice. Foucault may not have been right about his theoretical history of the prison; nevertheless he saw, perhaps better than anyone, the coldly efficient and hidden quality of contemporary punitive regimes and the extent of their grasp on social organization. In the prison at Mettray he found "the emergence or rather the institutional specification, the baptism as it were, of a new type of supervision—both knowledge and power—over individuals who resisted disciplinary normalization."[50] David Rothman has noted that all attempts to reform the captive stumble over the antinomy between coercion and rehabilitation. Or, as he phrases it, over the fact "that there [is] inherent conflict between guarding men securely and making them better."[51]

As we saw in the first chapter, a focus on retribution without compassion for the imprisoned Christ leads to guiltless violence. John of Salisbury, echoing an exegetical inference of Aquinas concerning the command in Matthew's Gospel to mutilate the sinful eye (Mt 18:9), states: "This precept . . . should be followed by the prince in the case of all the members so that not only should they be plucked out, cut off, cast away if they become an offense to the faith or to public safety, but should be utterly consumed and destroyed to the end that by extermination of one, the soundness of all may be procured."[52] James Given notes that as thirteenth-century rulers came to understand "that imprisonment could be used to punish offenders, they were learning that it could also be an effective form of behavior modification." He relates that a protracted struggle ensued between the inhabitants of the town of Albi and their local bishop, whose prison "came to have an evil reputation," as he "made extensive use of imprisonment in his effort to break the will of his opponents."[53]

Certainly, Aquinas was more sanguine than Augustine that such tendencies can be controlled, or at least mitigated, since power must not simply be used by social necessity to quell human sinfulness, but emerges from within a rational system of law legitimated by divine authority.[54]

Perhaps it is best to seek to harmonize the Augustinian and Thomist contributions to the justification for punishment at this point. To be faithful to the Catholic social tradition, a theory of criminal justice must recognize the state as having not only a legitimate right but also a moral duty to punish, a duty coherent with God's own design for the human project. This satisfies the goal of this first section: to derive a justification within the Catholic tradition for the moral obligation of the state to punish. However, what Augustine emphasized, more strongly than Aquinas, is that we cannot expect the state to assume full responsibility for criminal justice. Despite its critical role and the legitimacy of its desire for order, justice is found, finally, only in Christ and in love.[55] John Milbank argues similarly in reminding us that there is no fitting closure for the victims of crime because no one can surmise the extent of damage done by an act of violence and because "true victims do not survive at all to be able to proffer pardon."[56] He states that forgiveness is not within the province of the state but only comes in the life of the offender through "re-narration" and through appreciating that true forgiveness is divine, "since the prime paradigm for positive forgiveness is the Incarnation and Atonement."[57]

There is thus an ironic element in punishment, a baffling middle ground between the justifiable need for order and the demands of justice on one hand and the release of the responsible and repentant captive on the other. This is the area that was spoken of in the last chapter, where divine intent to liberate stands outside and above the parameters of human justice.[58] This leads to the need for creating a "mystical" space wherein God's designs can be accomplished in a way that is outside the gaze and understanding of human judges and human authorities. And in that observation we confront our second principle in the effort to construct a justification for punishment based in the Catholic tradition: retribution, in its truest expression, cannot be imposed but must be self-inflicted.

CRIMINAL JUSTICE AND SELF-PUNISHMENT

If order represents the practical foundation upon which the interests of church and state first came to coincide, and justice the expression of that mutuality on a speculative moral level, then the belief that "external" punishment can be understood most properly as the means to create the conditions for internal transformation sharply demarcates the church from preexisting models of criminal justice, as well as from the retributive and coercive models so often employed in secular penal justice down to our own day. Augustine states that in the punishment of Adam's sin "the retribution for disobedience is simply disobedience itself. For man's wretchedness is nothing but his disobedience to himself."[59]

Here we confront the subjective component of the Catholic justification for imposing detention on the culpable offender, one who has manifested what Aquinas understood as internal disorder. This component focuses properly not on social theory but on theology. It is revealed in the chapter's introductory quote from Mabillon: "In ecclesiastical justice one considers above all the welfare of the soul."[60] It is also expressed in this statement by Pope Pius XII: "The good will of the prisoner must match any outside influence, but that cannot be gotten by force. May divine grace arouse and direct that good will."[61]

My contention that the Catholic tradition favors the view that external punishment must be linked to, and find its ultimate justification in a personal sense of contrition and reparation is best expressed by a brief analysis of theological speculation concerning the Atonement, and particularly of the figure whose view of the Atonement has been most influential upon criminal justice in the West: St. Anselm.

The Atonement and the Gift of Contrition

Christians, notable scholars among them, have always pondered the question of why Christ had to suffer so tragic an end. At least three theories have arisen over time: the idea of *Christus Victor* maintains that the defeat of the power of evil was the primary meaning of the passion of Christ; the recapitulation model, most often associated with Irenaeus, argues that Christ, the new Adam, fulfilled perfectly in his life and death what our primordial parents distorted by their disobedience; finally, the theory of penal substitution argues that Jesus suffered in compensation to God for human sin.[62] These brief descriptions belie the complexity of the arguments and the fact that the models are more interdependent than might at first appear.

The substitutionary model, especially in its rendering by St. Anselm, has been the most instrumental in shaping Catholic thought concerning criminal justice. Many, owing to the trail of blood left by those who have experienced systems of "justice" in lands where the church is prominent, have seen this influence as largely negative.[63] I will contend that Anselm's focus on penal substitution cannot be separated from a similar commitment to the interiority often associated with figures such as Irenaeus and Abelard, and thus effectively expresses the dual objectives of punishment in a Catholic context. In Anselm's presentation, Christ willingly becomes the prisoner and transforms the meaning of confinement, despite the punitive spirit that initiated it, thereby revealing the subjective pole of punishment as the true bearer of the justification for coercive action against the offender. Moreover, Anselm's particular taxonomy of human sin has been reproduced often in subsequent reflection on the question of punishment and is reflected in the way Aquinas understood the internal demands of contrition.

Critics of Anselm, indeed of Atonement theology generally, rightly ask why God, who, in Christ, demands restitution from humanity, did not simply extend forgiveness without requiring the divine offspring to perish so cruelly in the effort to vindicate human sinfulness. That is somewhat of a rhetorical question at this point, since Catholic anthropology has always affirmed that people are the authors of and must be held accountable for their own actions. On a purely logical level, and this is not where the strength of Anselm's theory lies, the answer is that God can do no other than be just, as God can do no other than be merciful.[64] The two virtues coincide perfectly in God but exist only as an antinomy for us. Were God not just, Anselm argues, human disobedience would be more godlike than divine obedience, since the former is subject to no law while the latter is subservient to it. Secondly, the fracture of God's ordered universe would not only go unaccounted for, it would encourage further scarring of creation.[65]

The preceding rationale reveals that according to Anselm, as we saw with Aquinas, willful legal transgressions create multiple levels of distortion against both God and creation. Recall, however, that Aquinas adds, as did Abelard, a third internal source of dereliction. Anselm states that disobedience to the divine, or as he terms it, "dishonor," is sinful and rightly requires compensation on the two levels mentioned. He expresses it thus: "Neither is it enough merely to return what was taken away . . . he must give back more than he took away. For example, one who harms the health of another does not do enough if he restores his health, unless he makes some compensation for the injury of pain he has inflicted."[66]

However, demanding restitution from guilty humans is one thing, requiring the same of the just and guiltless one is quite another. Anselm's argument here is that human rejection of the divine covenant reverberated to the very depths of creation. For, echoing Augustine, Anselm saw the will poised between the gift of paradise being offered by God and the willful rejection of that gift at the urging of Satan.[67] Men and women chose the latter.[68] The cosmic dimensions of human sin are so great that they surpass the ability of any one person, or of all persons collectively, to repay. Yet, only humans caused the rupture of the divine order and they thus bear the onus of responsibility to redress the fault. Therefore, in loving obedience, the Word of God became incarnate to offer to God what we could never supply: the price of our rejection of the offer of salvation.[69]

What Anselm emphasizes for a Catholic theory of criminal justice, in conjunction with Irenaeus, is the introduction of Christ as *the* integral part of the drama of human failing, contrition, and liberation.[70] Christ fulfills the demands of justice for the rebellion against the divine order. However, free will leaves us still responsible to make some attempt at satisfaction for the specific harm done to one another and to the rest of creation. Or, in terms of the classification of sins, the death of Christ addressed the mortal sin of rebellion, but individuals still must make restitution for actual sins that they commit.[71] This creates the context not only for self-punishment but for the role of Christ as a model for those undergoing punishment and the true exemplar of both justice and internal renewal.

It would be both logically and theologically false to suggest that God needs anything from humanity.[72] Moreover, it has already been established that the moral right and responsibility of the state to punish does not fulfill either the deepest demands of justice (i.e., internal amendment) nor God's own revealed desire for the liberation of captives from all that binds them. Punishment, therefore, must principally be understood to be for the sake of the offender; not strictly to punish but to reacquaint him or her to the public order from which they have fallen away and the internal disorder that prompted the neglectful act.

The ultimate goal of this, according to Aquinas, is that lawbreakers may refrain from crime not simply as a result of "force and fear" but "by being habituated in this way, might be brought to do willingly what hitherto they did from fear, and thus become virtuous." Similarly, he states that punishment is sanctioned by God so that the unruly may be "directed to the good of virtue," and that they may "arise from sin, more humble and more cautious."[73] Finally, the intervention is adequately ordered only if there is love for the one whose correction is being sought. Augustine expressed this well: "Wrongdoing can better be punished in a spirit of love than be left unpunished; that the one who punishes does not wish the one punished to be unhappy by the punishment but happy through the correction he receives."[74]

Christ, who bore his captivity humbly and prayerfully, in silence, obedience, and fidelity, becomes the model for the repentant prisoner. Anselm states that prayer is central to the demands of justice and the remission of sin.[75] Irenaeus states that the Word of God, who addressed human apostasy in his own person, "did righteously redeem from it His own property. . . by means of persuasion, as became a God of counsel, who did not use violent means to obtain what he desires; so that neither should justice be infringed upon, nor the ancient handiwork of God go to destruction."[76] In Christ, God's righteousness and love, God's mercy and forgiveness come together in perfect union. In that same Lord it is possible to experience a captivity in which forgiveness and liberation come to the fore as the true justification for punishment.

Thus, in the end, Anselm's penal substitution embraces Irenaeus and the recapitulation theory of the Atonement. Christ takes human flesh to retell the world's story correctly: how to live and die, how to stand before

God as one who is not "good" (Mk 10:18), how to bear liberty and incarceration in a spirit of freedom and peace so as to attain what God had intended from the beginning—to bring all things in creation into one in Christ (Eph 1:10).[77]

The theology of the Atonement gives the decisive justification for detention of the erring brother or sister: to enable them to restate the story of their lives, including the very act of embracing a false account of the meaning of existence, in terms of the life of Christ who suffered the pain of confinement out of love for the guilty.

In summary then, order first binds church and state in common cause as each seeks peace and cessation of violent conflict. Justice deepens this relation as it is the virtue overseen by the political authority in service, proximately, to the common good and, ultimately, to the human quest for spiritual union in Christ. Finally, atonement involves a process of renarration in which the life of Christ becomes the paradigm of one's existence and, specifically, in which the captivity of Christ—an experience of prayer, forbearance, forgiveness, and new life—becomes the model for one's captivity. The justice model on its own is rightfully suspect because many, in both secular and ecclesiastical authority, have distorted the meaning of incarceration due to a spirit of vengeance, or have failed to appreciate the natural antinomy between confinement for a noble purpose and the violence of confinement itself. This last critique, more than others, begs to be addressed more fully because the brutality of Western correctional regimes must be seen as an aberration from what is described above, not as the inevitable consequence, as many have claimed, of the theory itself.

CONCLUSION

Miroslav Wolf comments that, in a perfect world, the blindfold would be removed from Lady Justice "and she would delight in whatever she saw; she would lay aside the scales because she would not need to weigh and compare anything; she would drop her sword because there would be nothing to police. *Justitia* would then be like the God of justice in a world of justice—the God who is nothing but perfect love."[78] In tracing the justification for punishment in the Catholic tradition we have seen that order, the first component, restrains violence, but is not necessarily just. Justice, the second component, seeks equity, but it falls short of God's inscrutable will and certain knowledge and only addresses, at best, one dimension of human rebellion. Atonement theology addresses the shortcomings of order and justice by confronting the act of rebellion itself, not only its external dimension, but the internal weakness that fostered it, and the role of Christ in providing a model for its amelioration. But, like order, certain readings of the Atonement often have a cold, arithmetic tone, not to mention a violent and abusive one that misses the complexity of the internal life. I have suggested in this chapter that not only is this last dimension the most critical and unique in a Catholic theory, but that Anselm presents a compelling reading of the Passion, one that complements the insistence that the story of Christ narrates the perfect human life, particularly, for our interest, his willful subjection to punishment.

The various figures cited in this chapter have been used to construct an approach to criminal justice that is, in the end, larger than the insights of any one interpreter of the tradition. Despite these variations, I believe an indisputable commitment can be distilled from the range of thought presented here: the social ethic of Catholicism favors state-sponsored retributive intervention but, principally, the true work of criminal justice must be internal to the process itself and contained in the heart of the individual offender.

NOTES

1. St. Thomas Aquinas, *Summa Theologica* [ST], trans. Fathers of the English Dominican Province (New York: Benziger, 1947), I-II, q. 46, a. 6.

2. St. Augustine, *The Problem of Free Choice*, trans. Dom Mark Pontifex (Westminster, MD: The Newman Press, 1955), bk. I, 1.

3. Tertullian, "De Spectaculis," in Rev. Alexander Roberts and John Donaldson, eds., *Anti-Nicene Christian Library*, vol. XI (Edinburgh: T&T Clark, 1869), ch. XIX.

4. Concerning the first assumption, see Chana Kasachkoff Poupko, "The Religious Basis of the Retributive Approach to Punishment," *The Thomist* 39 (1975): 528.

5. *Catechism of the Catholic Church* (New York: Doubleday, 1995), 260, 1910, 1920.

6. See George Lakoff and Mark Johnson, *Metaphors We Live By* (Chicago: University of Chicago Press, 1980), 14–19.

7. Hans Boersma, *Violence, Hospitality, and the Cross* (Grand Rapids, MI: Baker Academic, 2004), 106–07.

8. Meeks, *Origins of Christian Morality*, 31.

9. Ibid., 34.

10. St. Ambrose, "On Repentance," trans. Rev. H. De Romestin, in *St Ambrose: Select Works and Letters*, vol. 10, *A Select Library of the Nicene and Post Nicene Fathers, Second Series*, Philip Schaff and Henry Wace, eds. (New York: The Christian Literature Company, 1890), I, xiii.

11. Tertullian, despite a resolute Christian pacifism, still insisted that Christians support the state in other ways: "[W]e are ever making intercession for all the Emperors. We pray for them a long life, a safe home, brave armies, a faithful senate, a quiet world—and everything for which a man and a Caesar can pray." See *Apology*, trans. T. R. Glover (Cambridge, MA: Harvard University Press, 1960), XXX. A similar view was shared by Origen: "And in fact when war comes you do not enlist the priests. If, then, this is reasonable, how much more reasonable is it that, while others fight, Christians should also be fighting as priests and worshipers of God . . . striving for those who fight in a righteous cause and for the emperor who reigns righteously, in order that everything which is opposed and hostile to those who act rightly may be destroyed?" See *Contra Celsum*, trans. Henry Chadwick (Cambridge: Cambridge University Press, 1953), VIII, 73.

12. St. Augustine, *City of God*, bk. XV, ch. 4.

13. Ibid., bk. XIX, chs. 12, 17, 26.

14. Ibid., bk. XIX, ch. 17.

15. Meeks, *Origins of Christian Morality*, 67.

16. Augustine states that the only true justice is when God rules and humans obey. See *City of God*, bk. XIX, ch. 27.

17. Ibid., bk. XIX, ch. 6.

18. This is not to say that the state should not be "laboring at her task" to procure justice; only that, like heavenly beatitude itself, "we do not enjoy a present happiness, but look forward to happiness in the future." See *City of God*, bk. XIX, ch. 4. See also Poupko, "Religious Basis of the Retributive Approach to Punishment," 532.

19. Augustine did not discount the possibility of a Christian sovereign, e.g., Theodosius. See *City of God*, bk. V, chs. 24, 26.

20. Ibid., bk. I, preface, ch. 9.

21. Augustine writes: "God, whose foreknowledge is infallible, has foreknown the strength of our wills and their achievements, and it is for that reason that their future strength is completely determined and their future achievements utterly assured." See *City of God*, bk. V, ch. 9.

22. Stanely Chodorow, *Christian Political Theory and Church Politics in the Mid-Twelfth Century* (Berkeley: University of California Press, 1972), 122.

23. Ibid., 237.

24. St. Thomas Aquinas, *On the Truth of the Catholic Faith*, trans. Vernon J. Burke (Garden City, NY: Image Books, 1956), III, 69, 17.

25. Aquinas, ST, I–II, q. 87, a. 1.

26. St. Thomas Aquinas, *On the Governance of Rulers*, trans. Gerald B. Phelan (London: Sheed & Ward, 1938), bk I, ch. 1.

27. Aquinas, ST, I–II, q. 105, a. 1.

28. On the common good, see Aquinas, *On the Truth of the Catholic Faith*, III, 69, 16; ST, I–II, q. 96, a. 1; *On the Governance of Rulers*, bk. I, ch. 1. On the family as a natural institution, see ST, I–II, q. 94, a. 2.

29. Berman, *Law and Revolution*, 181.

30. Ibid., 73. Julius Goebel, writing of law in the Carolingian period, adds: "Even the power of corporal punishment that the bishop may exercise in a tem-

poral capacity is applied to spiritual offenses." See *Felony and Misdemeanor*, 170–71.

31. Aquinas, *On the Truth of the Catholic Faith*, III, 69, 1; John Mahoney, *The Making of Moral Theology* (Oxford: Clarendon Press, 1987), 247.

32. Aquinas, *On the Truth of the Catholic Faith*, III, 73, 2.

33. Aquinas, *On the Governance of Rulers*, bk. I, ch. 14.

34. Aquinas, ST, I-II, q. 66, a. 4.

35. Ibid., II-II, q. 58, a. 1.

36. St. Augustine, *The Problem of Free Choice*, bk. I, 13, 27.

37. Aquinas, *On the Governance of Rulers*, bk. I, ch 2.

38. Aquinas, ST, I-II, q. 105, a. 1.

39. Aristotle, *Ethics*, trans. J. A. K. Thompson (Harmondsworth, UK: Penguin, 1955), bk. II, ch. 7.

40. Aquinas, *On the Governance of Rulers*, bk. I, ch. 2.

41. Aquinas, *On the Truth of the Catholic Faith*, bk. III, 140, 5.

42. Aquinas, ST, I-II, q. 87, a.1.

43. "Now it is evident that in all actual sins, when the act of sin has ceased, the guilt remains; because the act of sin makes man deserving of punishment, in so far as he transgresses the order of Divine justice, to which he cannot return except he pay some sort of penal compensation, which restores him to the equality of justice." Aquinas, ST, I-II, q. 87, a. 6. See also *On the Truth of the Catholic Faith*, bk. III, 141, 4.

44. Aquinas, ST, II-II, q. 42, a. 2.

45. Aquinas, *On the Governance of Rulers*, bk. I, ch. 11.

46. Aquinas, ST, II-II, q. 42, a. 2.

47. "The citizen is obliged in conscience not to follow the directives of civil authorities when they are contrary to the demands of the moral order, to the fundamental rights of persons or the teachings of the Gospel." *Compendium: Catechism of the Catholic Church*, No. 2242.

48. Aquinas, ST, II-II, q. 58, a. 5. On the "public person" as opposed to the private individual, see ST, II-II, q. 65, a. 1; II, II q. 67, a. 4.

49. John Milbank, *Theology and Social Theory* (Oxford: Blackwell, 1990), 420–21.

50. Foucault, *Discipline and Punish*, 295–96.

51. David Rothman, *Conscience and Convenience* (Boston: Little Brown, 1980), 385–86.

52. John of Salisbury, *The Statesman's Book of John of Salisbury (Policraticus)*, trans. John Dickinson (New York: Russell & Russell, 1963), VI, 26.

53. James B. Given, *Inquisition and Medieval Society* (Ithaca, NY: Cornell University Press, 1997), 53.

54. Aquinas, ST, II-II, q. 65, a. 1; q. 67, a. 4.

55. In his neo-Platonic schema, Augustine believed that it was possible to contemplate the "form" of justice, but that such a splendid reality could not be experienced in the realm of sense. See "On the Trinity," in *Basic Writings of Saint Augustine*, trans. A. W. Haddan (New York: Random House, 1948), II, bk. VIII, ch. 6.

56. John Milbank, *Being Reconciled: Ontology and Pardon* (London: Routledge, 2003), 50.

57. Ibid., 51, 60.

58. Jean Dunbabin writes of the eleventh-century Christians for whom the miracle stories of saints rescuing prisoners were so appealing: "[They] had been taught to believe that, although . . . necessary to render unto Caesar . . . the only true justice . . . was to be found in God." They also learned : "To be condemned to prison by the powers of this world was not therefore proof, or even a *prima facie* case for wrongdoing; and where wrong action was involved, God would hear the prayer of the repentant sinner." See *Captivity and Imprisonment in Medieval Europe*, 134–35.

59. St. Augustine, *City of God*, bk. XIV, ch. 15.

60. Sellin, "Dom Jean Mabillon," 583.

61. Pius XII, "Crime and Punishment," 372.

62. For an overview of these theories read against the contention that the cross was the perfect expression of divine hospitality, see Boersma, *Violence, Hospitality, and the Cross*.

63. Anselm has many critics, none perhaps more adamant than Timothy Gorringe, who rejects what he terms Anselm's "mysticism of pain" that complements and justifies a sadistic correctional mechanism that "reeks of cruelty." See *God's Just Vengeance* 101, 102. Gustaf Aulen, in his renowned work on the atonement, *Christus Victor*, captures the gist of the above sentiment when he writes that Anselm serves "as the exemplar of everything decadent and legalistic in Medieval Catholic theology." Quoted in D. Bentley Hart, "A Gift Exceeding Every Debt," *Pro Ecclesia* VII (1998): 339.

64. St. Anselm, *Proslogion*, trans. M. J. Charlesworth (Oxford: The Clarendon Press, 1965), chs. 9–10; *Why God Became Man*, bk. I, ch. 12.

65. See R. W. Southern, *Saint Anselm and His Biographer* (Cambridge: Cambridge University Press, 1963), 97–98.

66. St. Anselm, *Why God Became Man*, bk. I, ch. 11. Despite the fact that he is often placed in theological tension with Anselm, Abelard held a similar view: "For when God pardons penitents their sin, he does not forgive them every penalty but only the eternal one." See *Peter Abelard's Ethics*, trans. D. E. Luscombe (Oxford: Clarendon Press, 1971), 89.

67. "Evil is the turning of the will away from the unchangeable good, and towards the changeable good. Since this turning away from one to the other is free and unforced, the pain which follows as a punishment is fitting and just." St. Augustine, *The Problem of Free Choice*, bk. II, ch.19, 53.

68. "Man, created in paradise without sin, was placed, as it were, on God's side, between God and the devil, to overcome the devil by not consenting to his temptation to sin . . . And although man could have done this easily . . . he freely permitted himself to be overcome, by urging alone, in accordance with the will of the devil and against the will and honor of God." St. Anselm, *Why God Became Man,*, bk. I, ch. 22.

69. Ibid., bk. II, ch. 6.

70. Irenaeus states:

Long-suffering therefore was God, when man became a defaulter, as foreseeing that victory which should be granted to him through the Word. For, when strength was made perfect in weakness, it showed the kindness and transcendent power of God. For as He patiently suffered Jonah to be swallowed by the whale . . . so also, from the beginning, did God permit man to be swallowed up by the great whale, who was the author of transgression, not that he should perish altogether when so engulfed; but, arranging and preparing the plan of salvation, which was accomplished by the Word . . . . For he (Satan) thus rendered him (man) more ungrateful towards his Creator, obscured the love which God had towards man, and blinded his mind not to perceive what is worthy of God, comparing himself with, and judging himself equal to, God.

See "Against Heresies," in *Ante-Nicene Fathers,* vol. I (New York: Charles Scribners' Sons, 1900), III, ch. 20, 1.

71. Southern, *St. Anselm and His Biographer,* 101.
72. St. Anselm, *Why God Became Man,* I, 21.
73. Aquinas, ST, I-II, q. 87, a. 2, ad. 1.
74. St. Augustine, *The Lord's Sermon on the Mount,* bk. I, ch. 20, 63.
75. St. Anselm, *Why God Became Man,* bk. I, ch. 19.
76. Quoted in Boersma, *Violence, Hospitality, and the Cross,* 129.
77. Hart, "A Gift Exceeding Every Debt," 348.
78. Quoted in Boersma, *Violence, Hospitality, and the Cross,* 36.

3

The End of Punishment

Coming to himself at last.

—Luke 15:17

Many of the saints have fallen and then become saints again.

—St. Teresa of Avila

From a Catholic perspective, one's life is a pilgrimage, both in an external/historical sense as well as an internal/spiritual one. The events of each human life have an origin and a finale that are far from random. This does not deny free will and the autonomy it grants to the decision maker, but central doctrinal commitments such as the Incarnation and the sacramental quality of life contend that the apprehension of external events and the interpretation of internal impulses condition decision making in a way that supersedes linear and rational thought patterns and after-the-fact explanations. One looks back at events and life-altering decisions and is at times captured by the thought that there was more than transition; there was direction. This same sense pervades the Catholic understanding of the internal life. The rich genre of contemplative and mystical literature attests to a movement downwards into the depths of the self as life proceeds. Critical to this perspective is the sense that each event in one's life story potentially reveals a deeper apprehension of the mystery and beauty of God and of one's radical connection to God in the depths of the self. This, too, is a journey that surprises and enlightens, particularly when viewed over the course of time. Wherever one is, there is still so much farther to go, and every encounter, every moment, is a doorway to fuller union with the source of life and, through God, with all of creation.

It is in that framework that punishment from a Catholic viewpoint, in the double sense discussed in the last chapter, is best understood. When viewed in the light of the imprisoned Christ, punishment is not absolute and closed as advocates of retribution would contend, or simply a means to a desired social state of affairs, as those who favor deterrence or incapacitation would contend, but always part of the ongoing narrative of a life touched by grace and designed for human and spiritual fulfillment. Specifically, the third element of the theory presented here, the goal of criminal justice, builds on the argument of the last chapter and argues that, just as punishment has two justifications, one internal and one external, so also it has two ends. The first is liberation and reconciliation. It coincides with the inner justification for punishment in that there is recognition of fault, a sense of contrition, and at least a desire to make reparation for harm done to others. It also transcends this subjective emphasis. It seeks, as Pope Pius XII stated, to reconcile the offender to the relationships fractured by the errant behavior.[1] The second end of punishment is the full reinstatement of the offender to the life of the community with no accompanying stigma or no further need to pay for one's mistakes.[2]

Since much of the material on the inner dimension of punishment in the previous chapter suggests the goal of personal liberation, I offer only a brief reflection on this matter. However, there is an issue relating to conversion and reconciliation that does require our attention: the role of mercy and forgiveness in the case of those who resist or deny the subjective meaning of the punitive process. Following this, the second aim of full social reintegration is discussed.

INTERNAL REFORM

It has been argued that punishment should be fundamentally understood as an internal phenomenon. Recall that in Catholic anthropology the core of the self is never alien to the presence of the One in whom it was formed. This view of human nature is grounded in scripture. In the book of Genesis, the story of the origin of human life and human sinfulness testifies to the commitment that, as Ricoeur argues, sin is radical, but goodness is primordial.[3] The tempter is not located within the first humans but beguiles from without. Certainly Adam and Eve are responsible for their act of disobedience, but the explanatory power of the narrative sets the tone for a deep reverence for the fundamental goodness of the human person—a contention that is at the core of Catholic social thought.

Similarly, Hebrew accounts of divine chastisement often frame the punishment as parental or familial, summoning the better part of the person by way of the disciplinary action. In Proverbs, the image is that of a father correcting his son (Prv 20:1). In the book of Judith the author states that "not for vengeance" does God puts us in the crucible; rather, it is "by admonition that he chastises those are close to him" (Jdt 8:27). The prophets consistently stress the fact that the return of the sinner is what God desires, not punishment for its own sake. The New Testament is also replete with references to the fact that God, in Christ, uses human alienation caused by sin to spark the desire for repentance and personal transformation. It was the baptism of repentance administered by John the Baptist that enabled its recipients to "behold the Lamb of God" (Jn 1:29). The first public statement of Jesus is one of repentance leading to internal reform (Mk 1:15). The alienation and separation endured by the prodigal son are essential to his "coming to himself at last" (Lk 15:17). True to the tradition in which he was formed, Jesus sought reconciliation with sinners and that reconciliation became the precondition for the desire to accompany him.[4] There was nothing in an ontological sense that separated the fallen from integrity or wholeness, only the willingness to undergo contrition as a condition of renewal. It bears repeating that it was the tax collectors and prostitutes who were the "little ones" to whom the Kingdom of God was given (Mt 21:31–32).

This scriptural anthropology has been reproduced often in the Catholic tradition. Cyprian states that those who betrayed their faith in times of persecution are not to be abandoned. Moreover, he says: "If we know what made us fall, we can learn how to heal our wounds."[5] Ambrose, employing agrarian imagery, writes that, for the sinner, the shame of penance "ploughs his land, removes the . . . brambles, prunes the thorns, and gives life to the fruits he believed were dead."[6] Augustine states that "the punishment of sin has been turned by the great and wonderful grace of our Savior to a good use, to the promotion of righteousness . . . . So by the ineffable mercy of God even the penalty of man's offence is turned into an instrument of virtue."[7]

In particular, the tradition emphasizes that seclusion, whether voluntary, as in the case of the monk or contemplative nun, or involuntary, as with the prisoner, can dynamically transform the internal and, by extension, the social life of the one so involved. St. Basil utilizes the image of writing upon wax to emphasize this belief. He likens the practice of solitude to the friction necessary to disengage "the spirit from sympathy with the body." Only this smoothing down of "the conceptions arising from worldly experiences" can then enable "divine teachings" to be imparted to the soul.[8] St. John Climacus, using the popular medical analogy, wrote that the more recent the transgression, the more easy to heal through penitential discipline. However, he also stated that even the long-neglected and embedded faults are not without remedy, although they require "much treatment, cutting, plastering and cauterization." For "with God all things are possible."[9]

Certainly, there have been many instances where penal conditions and the attitudes and actions of penal authorities failed to honor this liberating goal of punishment. There may be some ironic understatement in the claim of Ralph Pugh that Catholic penitential practice "at least sometimes" had recognized "that forced confinement could furnish opportunities for reflection upon past misdeeds and a change of heart."[10] Less subtle is the statement by Henry Charles Lea that the Catholic penitential system consisted in grouping the confined in "hideous squalor."[11] Aware as we are that cruelty so often accompanies the practice of punishment, even a practice that seeks to be humane and restorative, it is impossible to deny the inhumanity suggested in the above accounts. It is my contention, however, that when the image of the imprisoned Christ has been invoked, the liberation of the prisoner has been the end most consistently sought, rather than social defense, deterrence, or retribution. It is much more difficult to stipulate whether this end was the one most consistently desired.

Perhaps Pius XII sums up best the first end of punishment in the Catholic tradition: "May human penal law, in its judgments and in the execution of those judgments, never forget the [human] in the culprit and never omit to strengthen him and assist him to return to God!"[12]

Mercy and the Limits of Punishment

But what of the imprisoned man or woman who fails to meet the expectations of reform desired by his or her captors? This is a deeply perplexing issue. All are aware that high rates of recidivism cast shadows of doubt upon projects designed to reduce criminogenic tendencies. At the same time, one's imagination may quickly be drawn to the disorderly and violent images of the contemporary correctional experience portrayed in a host of prison dramas in the entertainment and publishing industries. Not many years ago I visited a cell block at San Quentin State Prison in California. It summoned the spirit, if not the exact detail, of John DiIulio's rhetorical snapshot of a correctional facility he had studied:

Inmates roamed about virtually unimpeded, glaring, making threatening gestures, often shouting profanities at the officers. One cellblock was "trashed" by the inmates who lived there to underscore some grievance that nobody, including the inmates themselves, was able or willing to articulate. Officers wearing rubber boots and carrying shovels waded ankle-deep into the mess and were showered with insults and debris and human excrement. The inmates were rarely more charitable to each other. . . . [They] spent their days in idleness punctuated by meals, violence, and weightlifting.[13]

Part of the intent of this book is to address the religious legacy of the correctional enterprise and the restricted options left to penal officials who must craft a meaning to the punishment process without the teleology and accompanying institutional values and practices utilized historically by the church. The dramatic and degrading images just utilized to reflect on the current penal environment are not meant to beat the straw man of secular correctional institutions; they are presented, rather, to suggest that conversion or change of heart are first of all highly subjective categories and that, in the absence of at least verbal, if not behavioral, evidence of change, it is no easy matter to determine in many instances what meaning if any can be ascribed to continued confinement, other than the infliction of pain. Discretion in sentencing, even for its proponents, is a policy shrouded in ambiguity. Indeed, the increasing shift in courtroom dynamics to the use of sentencing grids to determine punishments for the guilty, whatever else may be the motivation, is certainly driven in part by the demonstrable inequality in sentences accorded to, for instance, persons of different races whose criminal profiles are otherwise identical.[14] It also owes some of its impetus to the strained logical attempts by parole boards to determine who has actually reformed or, in the increasingly dated parlance, been rehabilitated.

It is with this in mind that the question of mercy enters the equation in the discussion of the goals of liberation and reconciliation. How has the church addressed this most sensitive issue and what position should a contemporary Catholic theology of criminal justice assume in this regard?

In chapter 1 we noted that, of all the images that have been used to depict the prisoner across the breadth of Catholic history, the image of Christ as prisoner looms as the most vibrant and resonant. An entire genre of literature found its nourishment in the intimate identification of the imprisoned with the imprisoned Christ. Recall that in the miracle stories of deliverance of captives, there was often no mention of the justice or injustice of the sentence imposed—simply being a prisoner was sufficient to merit divine concern and heavenly intervention to procure release. In the early medieval period a cultural norm of empathy for the captive developed among Christians. Despite the violent tenor of the age, Dunbabin writes that "God remained a source of mercy for captives."[15] She then underscores a phenomenon we observed in medieval Florence: the release of specific prisoners on the patronal feast of a given municipality, a practice she notes that "appears to have been well established."[16] We have already mentioned the yearly lottery in Rome when a condemned prisoner was released and triumphantly paraded through the town on the feast day of the execution of another condemned prisoner, St. John the Baptist.[17] An interesting development of this practice occurred at Treviso in 1315. In recognition of the candidacy for beatification of Henry of Bolzano, the gates of the jail were opened to debtors and to those judged by the citizenry to be fit for release. Dunbabin comments that the rubrics of this ritual provided a "clear assertion that humans could rightly judge where mercy should be shown" and that such moments placed "divine love above human law, at least for one day."[18]

A canon of the Council of Sardica (343 AD) states that "it often happens that those who are suffering from injustice or who are condemned for their offences . . . or, in short, have received some sentence or another, seek refuge with the mercy of the church, such persons should be succored and pardon begged for them without hesitation."[19] The letters of Augustine feature numerous references to the practice of intercession on behalf of the condemned. He also states: "We Christians call rulers happy, if they rule with justice . . . if they fear God, love him and worship him . . . if they grant pardon not to allow impunity to wrong-doing but in the hope of amendment of the wrong-doer."[20] The Constitutions of the Mercedarians, a group founded to seek the ransom of Christians held captive by Muslims, state with regard to imprisonment "that as great as it may be severe so much more does it stand in need of a zeal for charity."[21] Julian of Norwich taught that God does not forgive sin since God cannot be offended. Rather, God gives, graciously and mercifully, despite the frequent hardness of the human heart.[22]

Scripture, particularly the teachings of Christ, announces that mercy must be considered among those elite Christian virtues without which one cannot enter the Kingdom of God. The parable of the unforgiving servant (Mt 18:23–35) reveals that God's justice always favors mercy unless our own justice lacks mercy. This is an extension of the teaching in the Sermon on the Mount in Matthew (5:7) that proclaims the merciful blessed not only because Christians should be merciful, but also because mercy given becomes mercy received. The same doctrine holds true in Luke's portrayal of the Sermon on the Mount (6:36, 37) in which Christ proclaims: "Be merciful as your heavenly Father is merciful . . . . Pardon and you will be pardoned." In the parable of the laborers in the vineyard

(Mt 20:1–16), the common refrain of Jesus—"the last shall be first"—provides the dominant logic. In granting those hired at the end of the day the same wage as those who had labored since early morning, Jesus surprises arithmetic or commutative accounts of justice with a distributive vision based on mercy for those whose résumés would be considered inferior under normal market conditions.

To be faithful to the Catholic tradition, mercy must be an ever-present consideration in both the theory and practice of criminal justice. This holds true not simply because the value of mercy is magnified in the Gospels, but because justice itself cannot be understood or achieved without equity.

Aristotle famously compared the work of legal justice to the measurement of a fluted column: the task cannot be accomplished without a flexible rule. He presented this image and distinction to demonstrate the superiority of equity to strict arithmetical justice in criminal cases. In the latter, similar to the legal positivism and technocratic approach to the resolution of felonies found in many contemporary Western courtrooms, law does not bend to the specific characteristics of the case and the specific conditions in the life of the offender.[23] Aristotle, on the other hand, argued that a subjective and empathetic interpretation of a criminal matter does not undermine the search for a resolution that is just; it enhances it significantly: "Thus equity and justice coincide, and although both are good, equity is superior. What causes the difficulty is the fact that equity is just, but not what is legally just: it is a rectification of legal justice."[24] Aquinas relied upon Aristotle in forming the classic Catholic statement concerning justice. He varied Aristotle's terminology but not his intent when he stated that particular justice is an essential complement to general justice. The latter is excellent in that it takes as its goal the common good, but the former addresses itself to the specific details of the case and, most important, presumes a virtuous regard for the person whose actions are to be evaluated.[25]

This addition of mercy is necessary to the idea and task of justice. It does not change, however, the belief that punishment has an independent, if not primary, value in a Catholic system of justice; nor does it alter the conviction that the way that leads to contrition and reparation is a journey as difficult and ambiguous in its outcome as it is necessary.

SOCIAL REINTEGRATION

Having done one's penance or having completed one's sentence, the second aim of the process of punishment is that the person then rejoin the community from which he or she has been exiled and do so with the full restoration of whatever rights and social standing he or she possessed prior to dismissal. This, despite the lifelong penitential burdens commonly imposed by the church prior to the seventh century, expresses the final intent of the ancient ritual of penance that also formed the basis of the monastic and ecclesiastical prison, as will be shown in the next chapter. From the earliest days of the church the phrase that arises continually is that the punishment must fit the crime. It is found in the earliest conciliar documents, the first handbooks of confessors, and still is invoked in contemporary social documents of the Catholic Church.[26] It is another way of saying that an equivalence can be established between sin and expiation or between crime and full reintegration.

It can be argued that the entire Bible is a long commentary on the dyad of exile and return, whether in foundational stories such as Adam and Eve, Noah, and the captivity in Egypt, or in the persistence of the covenant theme despite episodes of idolatry and its punishment. God's censure is never divorced from what can best be described in the text as a passionate desire for reunion. In Genesis, it is stated: "I am with you and will watch over you wherever you go, and I will bring you back to this land. I will not leave you until I have done what I have promised you" (Gn 28:15). While God proclaims through the prophet Isaiah: "I will say to the north, 'Give them up!' and to the south, 'Do not hold them back.' Bring my sons from afar and my daughters from the ends of the earth" (Is 43:6). Even the stigma attached to Cain as he was being sent into exile for murdering his brother was not meant to distinguish him as a target for recrimination but to announce God's seal of protection given to him as he passed through hostile land on his penitential journey (Gn 4:15).

Christ often employs the metaphor of the "good shepherd" to describe himself and his work on earth. The shepherd not only gives his life for the sheep (Jn 10:11) but leaves everything behind in search of the one who has strayed, and, upon finding the lost sheep, places it upon his shoulders and brings it back to the fold (Lk 15:5).

Despite the ambiguity associated with its interpretation, the suffering and death of Christ, the Atonement, is primarily a work of reconciliation. As Hans Boersma phrases it: "Christ's penal substitution needs to be understood in light of the *goal* of the punishment—restoration of justice and human fellowship with God and each other."[27] Timothy Gorringe sees the reconciling effects of the cross often inverted into a sanction to inflict punishment on the guilty; a tendency he sees emanating from bad Christian theology and poor tutoring on the part of the leaders of the church.[28] No further sacrifices are needed after the sacrifice of Christ, and

Gorringe claims few understood this better than St. Paul, who wrote that Christ's death "had brought about not a new *doctrine* but a new *movement* in which alienated human beings were to be caught up and reconciled."[29]

The theme of finding, reconciling, and reintegrating the offender is not only a theological principle; it is one, due to the ethos of penance, with abundant historical precedent. At the Council of Ancyra (314 AD), the delegates wrote concerning those who had committed adultery that they "be restored to full community" after completing their period of penitential obligation.[30] At the same council, it was stated that "those who have fled and been apprehended" and those who "have been imprisoned" and whose "demeanor" and "humility of life" are demonstrable "are not to be repelled from communion."[31] More sharply stated are the injunctions of church councils that punish, sometimes severely, those who withhold forgiveness to the repentant offender.[32]

Apostate religious during the Middle Ages in England were, by and large, subjected to "medicinal" rather than vindictive punishment, claims one study on the subject. The end was not so much reducing harm to the Christian community as addressing "moral illness." The author states: "the ultimate, professed purpose here was to heal, not hurt, the apostate."[33] Pope Gregory IX, one of the principal architects of the first code of canon law, included the decree "Ne Religiosi Vagndi" (1234) in which religious superiors were enjoined to seek out deserters and, unless severely unruly in their demeanor, reinstate them within their communities.[34] Pope Benedict XII, recalling Christ the good shepherd who was ever vigilant "lest his wandering and straying sheep be devoured by wolves," wrote in the constitution "Pastor Bonus" that superiors must seek out their delinquent members and take back even those who are unwanted.[35] The Dominicans were typical of religious orders in reinstating apostate members after three years of confinement.[36] Edward Peters states that for all of the "concern with criminality" in the early thirteenth century and despite the presence of both torture and the death penalty, there existed in the courts an ethos paying high regard to the dispensation of justice, human and divine; and "justice required strenuous efforts to achieve restoration and the salvation of even the worst criminals."[37]

Stigma

In his reflections on imprisonment, written with a deep measure of sorrow for a beloved friend who had endured terrible suffering as a result of several periods of monastic confinement, Dom Jean Mabillon wrote that the dignity of the fallen must be scrupulously defended. Such a "charitable spirit consists in keeping hidden the faults which are not public . . . . It also consists in managing their reputation with care, in the thought that the shame which remains for these miserable ones after the crime is the most difficult thing in the world to support and the worst temptation to sustain."[38]

Often, the real experience of punishment does not begin until after the completion of sentence. Offenders, having been stigmatized, discover that their incarceration, their alienation from the world, is permanent. Like Cain, they bear an indelible mark of notoriety, what Erving Goffman refers to as an "identity peg."[39] Unlike Cain, however, the intent of the designation is not to ensure protection in a hostile world; rather, it justifies further recriminations that often extend for life, or even beyond, in the eyes of some.

A number of contemporary criminologists have written that the decline in the rehabilitative ideal as a guiding assumption of the penal system has come as a result of an approach that does not correlate penal effectiveness with reducing recidivism. Rather, the goal is social control, occasioned, first, in defining "at risk" individuals in terms of failed access to society's coveted financial and social awards; second, in then calibrating the social definition of crime in such a way that the vast number of those detained come from the same "stigmatized" sectors of the population. Program success, ironically, is seen, in this formula, not in "rehabilitation" but in recidivism itself: re-arrest of the stigmatized attests to the logic of the stigma and, recalling Durkheim, provides the public with the assurance that the "right" people are free and the "wrong" people are where they are ought to be.[40] Traditional criminological theory then explains further that "labeling" an individual as a delinquent, whether or not the designation has been accurately attributed, stimulates a number of social practices that further ensure criminality.[41]

In many ways this approach is reminiscent of the ancient sentence of branding the miscreant, a practice found as early as the Code of Hammurabi. Goffman calls such events "abominations of the body."[42] A derivation of the practice involved wearing a mark of shame upon apparel, as when the Inquisition forced confessed heretics to bear yellow crosses upon their clothing for a specified amount of time.[43] More apropos to contemporary practice was the punitive designation of *infamia* amongst the Romans, in which the mark effecting social isolation and the loss of legal rights was not placed on the body but beside the name of the proscribed individual on the census list.[44] Stigma also has clear resemblance to the anthropological concept of pollution. Shoham argues that the term "sanction" originated not as a warning of legal recrimination for certain actions but as an expiatory act that removed the pollution and accompanying stigma incurred for certain violations.[45]

The long history of stigmatizing the offender, even the repentant one, not only bears witness to the persistence of the desire to make retribution a value in itself; it also uncovers the grim side of deterrence, a practice often justified by many in the church.[46] Punishment not only affects the one being punished; it sends a signal of warning to potential offenders. The question is not whether it is effective; controlled experiments tend to agree that it is. The question is what image of the prisoner is necessary in order to make him or her not the subject invited to suffer the journey to contrition but the object made to serve as an example to others.

The image of the imprisoned and executed Christ, whose public execution was itself meant as a deterrent,[47] requires the acceptance of the punished after the sentence has been completed. As Hans Boersma eloquently points out, "the outstretched arms of Christ on the cross teach us how hospitality is to function."[48] The repentant prisoner condemned with Jesus is accepted "this day" into the reign of God (Lk 23: 43). Unconditional hospitality to the one who has been punished stands in marked contrast to the "phantom acceptance" that Goffman claims awaits the stigmatized individual who must demonstrate "an acceptance of himself and us, an acceptance of him that we have not quite extended to him in the first place."[49]

St. Ambrose, remembering the story of the Prodigal Son, states that repentance must bring forgiveness, regardless of the sin. He proposes that even though Simon Magus committed what the New Testament calls the "unforgivable" sin against the Holy Spirit, had he repented, St. Peter would have "stayed his condemnation."[50] The penal codes of monastic and religious orders often emphasize the need to reintegrate the released brother or sister to their place within the community. The Benedictine Constitutions of Lanfranc give insight into the ritual of reincorporation of the offender. Having completed the sentence imposed, the penitent enters the chapter room and prostrates himself before the abbot, confesses fault, and seeks pardon. "After this the abbot shall say: 'I have been moved by the prayers of our brethren, and by your patience and humility and promise of amendment, and I grant you pardon, that henceforth you may be with the brethren.'"[51]

These examples are not intended to dismiss in any way the violence that has been and is directed to those restrained by ecclesiastical or secular authorities. The injunction to forgive and reintegrate the repentant was at times ignored in cases of sexual deviance and heresy. The stigma attached to sexual misconduct of clerics with children was such that Holy Communion was denied in some instances to the culprit even at the end of life.[52] Once again, it is important to remember the goal of this study: to show that images shape the offender and how the offender is treated. We know that on one hand people were imprisoned, tortured, and sometimes put to death, at least in part, so that a law could then be invoked that relegated their estate and possessions to the church.[53] On the other hand, there were many who perceived the intimate relation between Christ and the criminal and who warmly welcomed him or her on release from captivity.

CONCLUSION

In this chapter we have seen that the end of punishment has both an internal and external meaning: a multifaceted reconciliation through infliction of sentence and acceptance of the person after release. Aquinas stated that the goal of punishment was "the restoration of the equality of justice."[54] He, like Anselm before him, viewed its purpose with the same dyadic tension: a redress of the internal and external disorder associated with the infraction. The process of chastisement sets the order right; its continuation after evidence of reform would be just as criminal as the anterior crime, for it, too, would inaugurate an inequality that would demand restitution. True, there is no way of knowing the sincerity of anyone's declaration of contrition. The tradition, at its best, however, tends to trust the means: solitude, silence, fasting, counsel; its anthropology refuses to acknowledge ontological evil in any form. The risk of recidivism is outweighed by confidence in the power of the rituals, both of excommunication and incorporation. It is outweighed, too, by the dignity conferred upon the confined; a dignity inferred by association with the confined Christ.

NOTES

1. Pius XII, "Crime and Punishment," 374.
2. Current Catholic social teaching affirms these two ends. See Pontifical Council for Justice and Peace, *Compendium of the Social Doctrine of the Church* (Washington, DC: United States Conference of Catholic Bishops, 2005), no. 403.
3. "[T]he etiological myth of Adam is the most extreme attempt to separate the origin of evil from the origin of good; its intention is to set up a *radical* origin of evil distinct from the more *primordial* origin of the goodness of things." Paul Ricoeur, *The Symbolism of Evil*, trans. Emerson Buchanan (Boston: Beacon Press, 1967), 233.

4. The restoration of the Gerasene demoniac to both inner and social peace (Mk 5:1–20) results in his desire to accompany Jesus. On recovering his sight, the beggar Bartimaeus, whose blindness had reduced him to a social recluse, "started to follow [Jesus] up the road" (Mk 10:46–52).

5. St. Cyprian, *The Lapsed*, trans. Maurice Bevenot, S. J. (Westminster, MD: The Newman Press, 1957), ch. 5.

6. St. Ambrose, "On Repentance," bk. II, ch. 1, 5.

7. St. Augustine, *City of God*, bk. XIII, ch. 4.

8. St. Basil, *Letters*, vol. I, trans. Sister Agnes Clare Way, C.D.P. (Westminster, MD: The Catholic University of America Press, 1951), no. 2.

9. St. John Climacus, *Ladder of Divine Ascent*, V, 30.

10. Pugh, *Imprisonment in Medieval England*, 181.

11. Quoted in Shlomo Shoham, *The Mark of Cain* (Jerusalem: Israel Universities Press, 1970), 7.

12. Pius XII, "Crime and Punishment," 379.

13. John DiIulio, *Governing Prisons* (New York: The Free Press, 1987), 2.

14. For a discussion of this dilemma, see Norval Morris and Michael Tonry, *Between Prison and Probation* (New York: Oxford University Press, 1990), 31 ff.

15. Dunbabin, *Captivity and Imprisonment in Medieval Europe*, 138–39.

16. Ibid.

17. Edgerton, *Pictures and Punishment*, 185, 188.

18. Dunbabin, *Captivity and Imprisonment in Medieval Europe*, 139.

19. Henry R. Percival, "The Seven Ecumenical Councils of the Undivided Church," in Philip Schaff and Henry Wace, eds., *A Select Library of Nicene and Post-Nicene Fathers of the Christian Church*, Second series, vol. XIV (New York: Charles Scribner's Sons, 1900), 422.

20. St. Augustine, *City of God*, bk. V, ch. 24.

21. "Quanto ea sit severior, tanto majori studio charitatis indigeat," in Lucas Holstenius, ed., "Constitutiones Fratres B. V. Mariae de Mercede Redemptoris Captivorum," Holstenius, *Codex Regularum* III, cap. xii, c. i.

22. Milbank, *Being Reconciled*, 60.

23. A relevant contemporary example is the practice of "three strikes legislation" in several areas of the United States. A third felony conviction demands a sentence of life imprisonment. The United States Catholic Bishops find this strategy immoral on its face and deeply at odds with a Catholic approach to criminal justice. See Joe Domanick, *Cruel Justice: Three Strikes and the Politics of Crime in America's Golden State* (Berkeley: University of California Press, 2004). The Catholic Bishops of the United States write concerning the "three strikes" policy: "We must renew our efforts to ensure that punishment fits the crime. Therefore, we do not support mandatory sentencing that replaces judges' assessments with rigid formulations." National Conference of Catholic Bishops, *Responsibility, Rehabilitation, and Restoration: A Catholic Perspective on Crime and Criminal Justice* (Washington, DC: United States Catholic Conference, 2000), 15.

24. Aristotle, *Ethics*, bk. V, x. For an insightful discussion of this matter, see Martha Nussbaum, "Equity and Mercy," *Philosophy and Public Affairs* 22 (1993): 83–125.

25. "Legal justice does indeed direct man sufficiently in his relations towards others. As regards the common good it does so immediately, but as to the good of the individual, it does so mediately. Wherefore there is need for particular justice to direct a man immediately to the good of another individual." St. Thomas Aquinas, ST, II-II, q. 58, a. 7.

26. See, e.g., National Conference of Catholic Bishops, *Responsibility, Rehabilitation, and Restoration*, 15; National Conference of Catholic Bishops, "Rebuilding Human Lives," 345.

27. Hans Boersma, "Eschatological Justice and the Cross," *Theology Today* 60 (2003): 196.

28. Gorringe, *God's Just Vengeance*, 68, 103.

29. Ibid., 76-77.

30. It was common custom in the early Church to place penitents in different "stations" within the assembly for a prescribed period of time. See Percival, "The Seven Ecumenical Councils of the Undivided Church," 73.

31. Ibid., 64.

32. The Council of Lerida (c. vii) decreed that anyone who vowed never to pardon a foe was to be forbidden communion for one year, undergo repentance, and be obliged to seek reconciliation. Similar canons were enacted at the councils of Toledo and Mattison. See Joseph Bingham, *Antiquities of the Christian Church*, vol. VI (London: William Straker, 1844), 180.

33. F. Donald Logan, *Runaway Religious in Medieval England* (Cambridge: Cambridge University Press, 1996), 121.

34. Ibid., 122.

35. Ibid., 123–25.

36. "Dispensatio non fiat per eosdem ante tres annos." "Fratrum Praedicatorum," in Holstenius, *Codex Regularum* IV, cap. XX, i–ii.

37. Edward Peters, "Destruction of the Flesh—Salvation of the Spirit: The Paradoxes of Torture in Medieval Christian Society," in Alberto Ferreiro, ed., *The Devil, Heresy and Witchcraft in the Middle Ages* (Leiden: Brill, 1998), 143.

38. Sellin, "Dom Jean Mabillon," 583.

39. Erving Goffman, *Stigma* (Englewood Cliffs, NJ: Prentice Hall, 1963), 56.

40. See Emile Durkheim, *The Division of Labor in Society*, trans. W. D. Halls (New York: The Free Press, 1984), 42–43; Feeley and Simon, "The New Penology"; Garland, *The Culture of Control*, 167–92; John Irwin, *The Jail: Managing the Underclass in American Society* (Berkeley: University of California Press, 1985); Jonathan Simon, "The Emergence of a Risk Society," *Socialist Review* 95 (1987): 61–89.

41. See, e.g., Braithwaite, *Crime, Shame, and Reintegration,* 16–21; Quinney, *Social Reality of Crime*, 20–22.

42. Goffman, *Stigma*, 4.

43. Given, *Inquisition and Medieval Society*, 68–69.

44. Shoham, *The Mark of Cain*, 12.

45. Ibid., 10–11.

46. Deterrence has an obvious "latent function" in the punishment process, as both Augustine and Aquinas pointed out (*City of God*, bk. XIX, ch. 16; St.

Thomas Aquinas, *Petri Lombardi Sententiarum libre quatuor*, III, d. 19, q. 1, a. 3, sol 2. My contention, however, is that it should not be given primary focus as it undermines the goals of retribution and reform that are at the core of the penitential system.

47. See Taylor, *The Executed God*, 70–78.

48. Boersma, *Violence, Hospitality, and the Cross*, 15. It is noteworthy that postmodern writers, following the lead of Levinas, have emphasized the importance of hospitality to the "other," regardless of who the stranger may be. Jacques Derrida writes: "Let us say yes *to who or what turns up*, before any determination, before any anticipation, before any *identification*." See *Of Hospitality*, trans. Rachel Bowlby (Palo Alto, CA: Stanford University Press, 2000), 77.

49. Goffman, *Stigma*, 122.

50. St. Ambrose, "On Repentance," II, iv, 23.

51. Lanfranc, *The Monastic Constitutions of Lanfranc*, trans. David Knowles (London: Thomas Nelson and Sons, 1951), 101.

52. See Bingham, *Antiquities of the Christian Church*, VI, 257.

53. Dunbabin, *Captivity and Imprisonment in Medieval Europe*, 46–48.

54. ST, I-II, q. 87, a. 6.

4

Prison as the Normative Means of Punishment

On this side of eternity hospitality is never extended without the violence of exclusion.

—Hans Boersma

We have investigated aspects of the Catholic tradition to respond to three of the four fundamental questions a theory of criminal justice must seek to address. The first concerned the identity of the prisoner. As social constructs, crime and its perpetrators are ever-malleable creations. Crime emerges as both the obverse of a given society's most deeply held values and as a projection of its most vibrant fears and fantasies; it is the way dereliction and infraction, danger and pollution are made visible in a particular set of images. The criminal is what the culture wants the criminal to be; if it wants a demon, a demon it will have, and the demon will be properly accused and treated in the fashion meriting a fiend. If it envisions a person who is "little less than a god," then, to a commensurate degree, it is God who will be tried, sentenced, and punished. I have suggested that a theory of criminal justice faithful at once to history, scripture, and Catholic social teaching must conclude that Christ himself is and must be treated as the malefactor.

The second question concerned the justification for punishment. Catholic tradition makes two claims in this regard: that forcible restraint of the convicted offender is fitting in acknowledgment of a given society's appreciation of the norms of order and justice, but this action is, ideally, merely the necessary condition to address a second and more primary objective: that detention create the conditions for self-punishment as wrongdoers come to recognize and feel contrition for harm done to others, to the harmony of creation, and to themselves.

The third question concerned the end of punishment. Here we found, once again, that two aims are sought: reconciliation of those held captive, not only to their own better selves, but to those from whom their actions had estranged them; and the hospitable acceptance of chastened offenders upon completion of sentence.

This chapter addresses the fourth question: If the end of punishment is the betterment of the captive, how is such an objective accomplished? The tradition has steadfastly maintained that temporary "excommunication" of the offender from the community, normally to a place of confinement for a specified or unspecified amount of time, is the principal means necessary to accomplish the goal of behavioral reform and, even more fundamentally, of internal conversion.

In the following pages we review how the early church transformed the process of criminal justice, first, by means of its practice of penance, and then by the specific way that penance for socially disruptive infractions was incorporated into the monasteries and, ultimately, into a universally binding penal system. We then discuss the penal environment—the particular way the method of confinement was ordered. In this regard the monastic and inquisitorial prisons are discussed as well as those of religious orders.[1] It is a painful story in many ways, but that, too, is most relevant to the task of tracing the history of the church to find if the benign portrait of the criminal in the New Testament and the social norms honored in its social doctrine informed the creation of those shadowy places reserved for us when we fall.

PENANCE AND THE ORIGINS OF CONFINEMENT

The Catholic understanding of criminal justice and, specifically, its unprecedented use of confinement as a disciplinary and redemptive tool are based principally upon the belief that the rituals involved in the practice of penance have primary significance in the attempt to address the problem of sin and its correction. In the overview that follows the reader will notice that the rudiments of the Western penal system can be traced to the evolving structure of personal amendment found in early Christian experience.

The first Christians were impassioned in their commitment to live, in the words of St. Paul, lives worthy of the calling they had received (Eph 4:1). The first letter of John demonstrates this conviction in its sharply drawn distinction between the sobriety and altruism of the followers of

Christ and the reckless sensuality and misanthropy of the world destined for perdition.[2] In the early second century, St. Polycarp expressed these sentiments in a way common among his contemporaries; he lauded the virtues of the faithful within his congregation while calling those seduced by the "folly of the masses and their false teaching" the "firstborn of Satan."[3]

It did not take long, however, for this moral idealism to crash headlong into the hard reality of serious sin within the walls of the church. Not only do we have the sobering indictments of Christian misconduct in the letters of St. Paul, notably, his condemnation of an incestuous union (1 Cor 5), his veiled recognition of Christians consorting with prostitutes (1 Cor 6:15–18), and his dismay that some gorge themselves with food and get drunk at the Eucharist (1 Cor 11:17–22), but the author of Clement's second epistle goes so far as to describe a sizable proportion of the church as a "den of thieves."[4] Such lapses of discipline were not only a scandal internally, they also had serious repercussions beyond the community. In a time of persecution and ideological onslaught, opponents could find abundant justification for violent attack in the very conduct of those who claimed their faith in Christ had elevated them to a higher moral and spiritual plane.[5]

The teaching of the New Testament, not to mention the hostile political atmosphere, had removed whatever inclination Christians might have had to contend with embarrassing and disruptive conflicts via redress to the Roman legal system.[6] Christians were thus obliged to devise their own method of resolving serious moral lapses within their congregations. The Gospels had furnished a well-known procedure of accusation, exhortation, and communal consultation to combat the lapses of the weak as well as the resistance of the obstinate (Mt 18:15–17; Lk 17:3–4). Furthermore, the church, and specifically its leaders, had received from Christ himself the authority to either banish the evildoer or impart forgiveness (Jn 20:23). Origen gives early witness to the episcopal power underlying the adjudication of fault. He writes that if the penitent "confesses his sins privately before a bishop" and the bishop, in turn, determines that "his sins are really mortal sins and, therefore, have to be submitted to the penance of the Church—and if he is truly sorry, then he is admitted to Church penance proper."[7] Augustine testifies to the unavoidable need to submit to ecclesiastical discipline. To those who claim: "I deal with God privately. God knows and he will forgive me," Augustine states: "So were the keys given to the Church of God for nothing? Are we to nullify the gospel, nullify the words of Christ?"[8]

From the beginning, the discipline imposed upon the wayward Christian was expressed in some form of exclusion from liturgical fellowship.[9]

The serious malefactor was rendered unfit to participate in the celebration of the Mass—a devastating separation in a community whose founding ritual and primary means of salvation was the Eucharistic memorial (Jn 6: 48–51).[10] In the *Didascalia*, a third-century document of the Syrian Church, offenders are to be separated for "some determinate time, according to the proportion of their offence."[11] Joseph Favazza notes that sin was "a rejection of the distinctive mark of Christian 'order' and effected a fundamental alteration in the relationship between the sinner and God, and so within the Church."[12]

The authorization to exclude the sinner was linked to the power of binding and loosing conferred upon the apostles by Christ (Mt 16:19, 8:18). Binding refers to the imposition of a "sentence" by the bishop, or later a priest, upon the guilty; loosing indicates the relaxation of the disciplinary constraint by the same authority upon fulfillment of the penitential obligation.

This biblical warrant provided for the early Christians, with some cultural variation, a recognizable penitential methodology. Exculpatory discipline was obligatory if one had knowingly committed a sin decried as serious in one of the catalogues of vices found in the New Testament.[13] The guilty party first voluntarily implored the church, and specifically its episcopal head, to be sentenced to an ascetical regimen as a result of the transgression. He or she was then consigned to a period of excommunication during which the disciplinary practices were fulfilled; at the end of the exclusionary phase, the chastened penitent was absolved of sin and welcomed back into the fellowship with full rights restored.[14]

All of the early texts cooperate in verifying that this access to forgiveness was in no way constrained by the gravity of the sin; the medicine may have been hard to bear but no sinful patient was diagnosed as incurable. Tertullian writes of those who transgress again after being baptized: "If the indulgence of the Lord favors you with what you need for the restoration of that which you lost, be grateful for His repeated, nay rather, for His increased beneficence."[15] Cyprian, writing at the time of the Decian persecution in the middle of the third century, argued that it was not a question of whether those who had denied their faith in order to escape torture or death were to be forgiven; rather, it was whether they would "seek the slow painful road to recovery" for the "wounds they are dying of."[16] In the *Didascalia*, bishops are encouraged to reject any misguided enthusiasm that might prompt them to withhold the possibility of reconciliation regardless of the offense: "Receive, therefore, without any doubting, him that repents."[17] Concerning those guilty of, and feeling guilty for serious sexual offenses, St. Basil states: "their ignorance pleads their pardon, and their willingness in confirming it; therefore command them to be forthwith received, especially if they have tears to prevail on your tenderness."[18]

In the early church, the first attempt to systematize the three phases in the penitential process can be found in the writings of Tertullian. He intensified the ritual dimension of the process of reparation, centering it within the context of the Eucharist. The penitent, dressed in symbolic attire ("sackcloth") must fall "at the feet of the presbyters, and kneel to God's dear ones, to enlist all the brethren as intercessory legates."[19] The sinner next receives a discipline (*exomologesis*) to demonstrate as well as stimulate humility and self-admonition; this involved ascetical practices such as fasting and coarse penitential attire as well as the command "to sigh and weep and groan day and night to the Lord your God."[20] Tertullian states in regard to this trying regimen: "In proportion as you had no mercy on yourself, believe me, in just this same measure God will have mercy on you."[21] Finally, the burden of penance having been satisfied, the sinner receives divine forgiveness and is fully restored to life within the Christian community. The discipline casts the suppliant down but "it raises him up all the more; when it makes him sordid, it cleanses him all the more; when it accuses, it excuses; when it condemns, it absolves."[22] From this simple formula, the Catholic, and ultimately Western, penal system derives much of its structure and significance.

There was, however, a further evolution in the thinking and practice of early Christians with regard to their own fallen members. By the fourth century, the general guidelines established by Tertullian came more and more under the guidance of local synods and councils. The era of what was termed "canonical penance" saw the practice of "binding" through excommunication frequently expressed in the segregation of delinquent members within the community itself as it gathered to celebrate the Eucharist.[23] This led to the formation of the *ordo paenitentium*, the order of penitents.[24] One was sentenced to this penal community by the bishop, who used the highly significant gesture of the imposition of hands.[25] This latter practice originates in scripture as an act of ordination as well as one of healing. For example, the deacons chosen to aid the apostles received assurance of divine sanction for their election by the imposition of hands (Acts 6:6), and Christ often cured the sick in the same manner (e.g., Mk 5:23, 6:5). Recalling the argument of the second chapter, penance is thus not simply an act of punishment but must be situated within the realm of the sacred and, ultimately, in the transforming power of God within the hearts of the contrite.[26]

Once designated as members of the penitential order, offenders were then given a specific place, the *locus paenitentium*. In the West, this was normally at the rear or narthex of the worship space.[27] In some areas there were different "stations" for penitents, each revealing something of the character of the offense as well as the proximity of the offender to release from his or her penal status, thus anticipating graded prisons and classification levels in secular corrections.[28]

This latter method was practiced in some Eastern churches where there were normally four divisions of penitents and four corresponding stations to which they were consigned. The most serious offenders were the "weepers" who had to gather outside the worship site, sometimes in sackcloth and ashes. St. Gregory Thaumaturgus gives some of the background for the choice of their name: "Weeping takes place outside the door of the church, where the sinner must stand and beg the prayers of the faithful as they go in."[29] Those classified as "hearers" were placed at the entrance. They could hear the scriptures proclaimed as well as the homily but were then dismissed with the catechumens (those preparing to enter the church through baptism). The next designation comprised those called either "kneelers" or "prostrators." They assumed the posture suggested by their name in the nave of the church near the ambo (lectern). These were also permitted to hear the biblical readings and to join in prayers specifically made for them before leaving with the catechumens. Finally, the "co-standers" were allowed to assemble with the rest of the congregation and "hear" the entire Mass, but were restrained from receiving Communion.[30]

A famous case revealing this procedure was that of the Emperor Theodosius (346–395), who, in an act of vengeful justice, murdered the governor and other officials of Thessalonica. According to Augustine, he was then "constrained by the discipline of the Church to do penance in such a fashion that the people of Thesalonica as they prayed for him, wept at seeing the imperial highness thus prostrate."[31]

A canon of the Council of Ancyra during the fourth century states that those who entered a pagan temple with a "pleasing air" and participated "with unconcernedness" must do six years' penance, one as hearer, three as prostrator, and two as co-stander, before being admitted again to Communion.[32] Serious offenses merited long and demanding reparation. For example, St. Basil recommended that one guilty of willful murder be sentenced to twenty years penance: four years with the weepers, five with the hearers, seven as a prostrator, and the final four years as a co-stander.[33]

Similar to the guidelines established by Tertullian, those enrolled in the order of penitents were also frequently given a special garment to wear, reflective of their status; it was known as the *cilicium*. It was mentioned in a canon from the Council of Agda as well as at the First Council of Toledo (398).[34] They were also given a severe disciplinary regimen, exceeding even the rigid asceticism advanced by Tertullian. The penitent was not only to refrain from sexual relations during the period of expiation,[35] in many cases at this historical juncture prohibitions remained in effect long after the act of absolution.[36]

A final element of the order of penitents that anticipates the harmony between its rubrics and the development of both ecclesiastical and secular penal systems, especially the phenomena of probation and parole, is the injunction placed upon the faithful within the community to oversee and monitor the disciplinary sentences meted out. Augustine mentions this practice on several occasions, one being the case of a repentant soothsayer whom he recommended to the community not only for prayer but for watchful supervision: "We must therefore commend him to your eyes and your hearts . . . . This watchfulness is a mercy, for without it the old seducer might drag his heart back again, and assault him. Make yourselves his guardians: do not let the manner of his life or the course he takes be concealed from you."[37] Recalling our chapter on punishment, the purpose of creating such a complex system of correction was not simply to punish but to create the conditions for repentance by making the community an intimate partner in the renewal of the delinquent member.[38]

The fact that the most serious offenses saw the offender still associated with the worshiping community in both liturgical and social aspects reveals that there was little desire among most Christians that expulsion and/or segregation be lifelong penalties. Only the steadfastly obstinate, once again following the lead of the Gospel texts, seem to have been left to their own devices. Their excommunication, however, was not so much an abandonment as a desperate attempt to convince them to reexamine their unwillingness to embrace the penance and, ultimately, forgiveness offered by the church.[39] Polycarp, for example, writes of a fallen presbyter, Valens, and his wife, who had been expelled from the church; their specific sins are not mentioned but can be surmised from the saint's comments on the subjects of chastity, honesty, and avarice. He then states: "Brothers, I am deeply sorry for Valens and for his wife; may the Lord grant them true repentance. As for yourselves . . . . *Do not look on such people as enemies*, but invite them back as frail members who have gone astray."[40]

At the conclusion of the penance, there was a ritual of reincorporation; it was the instance of the "loosing" of penitential discipline and the restoration of the offender to the status once enjoyed in the fellowship. Normally the person was brought to the altar in the same garment worn at the beginning of the period of separation. Then, once again with the imposition of hands, full Communion was restored.[41]

At first, such a procedure could only be done once in the West, and even this concession did not come without dispute. In certain texts (Acts 2:38; Rom 6:1; 1 Cor 6:11) baptism is portrayed as the ritual wherein the sinner receives forgiveness.[42] Such an understanding is stated most forcefully in Hebrews (6:4–6), although it is also suggested in certain passages from St. Paul wherein the "old human" is shed in the baptismal rite and a new life in Christ, presumably now alien to the former sinful existence, is assumed (Col 3:8–10; Eph 4:22–24). The less rigorous interpretation of forgiveness is foreshadowed primarily in the Gospels, and specifically in the compassion of Christ for the despised and the deviant, as well as in texts such as the *Shepherd of Hermas* and the first letter of Clement.[43] This latter view came to prevail, albeit with the proviso that the formal removal of serious sin after baptism could only be sought once in a lifetime. Ambrose sums up the position on repeat confession that held in the West until the early seventh century: "Deservedly are they blamed who think they often do penance, for they are wanton against Christ. For if they went through their penance in truth, they would not think that it could be repeated again; for as there is but one baptism, so there is but one course of penance."[44]

This restriction on the access to forgiveness, coupled with the daunting and frequently lifelong duration of penal asceticism during this period, led to the common practice of postponing confession until the last hour of life. This was done either by choice, particularly among younger congregants,[45] or by constraint, in the cases of those who had recommitted serious sins and were, in the words of Pope Siricius and the Council of Larida, like dogs returning to their vomit.[46]

The Eastern Church did not have similar constraints upon a repetition of the penitential ritual. There, it was held that faith and the merits of the death of Christ provide an inexhaustible source of forgiveness (1 Cor 6:11; Mt 26:28). In the *Didascalia*, bishops are invoked to show the same compassion on repentant sinners as did God who, for their sake, "sent His Son upon earth" and "did not spare Him from the cross" that "he might deliver those from death."[47]

Eventually, through the influence of St. John Cassian (c. 360–435), Eastern Christian practice and the less rigorous position of Clement and the *Shepherd of Hermas* would lead to a repeat access to confession. By the early seventh century, the inflexible restrictions of the canonical period would be supplanted by the introduction of private confession through the implementation of the "penitentials," handbooks for the clergy to guide them in the interpretation of sinful actions with accompanying penances.[48] With this latter development, all of the rudiments of contemporary penance were in place, although the ritual would not become a compulsory sacrament, at least yearly, for all Catholics until the Fourth Lateran Council in 1215.

As far as our overview is concerned, penance provides all of the necessary components for the use of imprisonment by the church as a disciplinary tool, except one: the involuntary incarceration of the socially aberrant. That innovation is described in the next section but, in summary, what is established here is a tradition of handling disciplinary disputes or resolving conflicts that features the unprecedented element of the cure of souls, not simply retribution. In that process, the fundamental characteristics of Western penal systems were established: an elaborate ritual process of sentencing the guilty, a penance exacted in elements of time, a symbolic dress for the penitent, a place where the sentence was to be carried out, a group of overseers to ensure that the sentence was being carried out faithfully, and a ritual that signified the loosing of penal constraint and readmission into the social body.

THE PRISON IN CATHOLIC TRADITION

The Development of the Monastic Prison

It is best, in view of the ambiguity surrounding the act of confinement, to say that the prison came into prominence for conflicting reasons. The best of the tradition transformed the segregation required in penitential rituals into the use of imprisonment in a way that was harmonious with the generous intent of those rituals. However, given the dependence of criminal justice on cultural images and subjective interpretation, one need not look far to find evidence of purely punitive incarceration, particularly after the fourth century.[49] What is not in dispute, however, regardless of how the captive was treated, was the fact that the prison as we know it developed out of Catholic penitential experience and, to great extent, within the context of the monastic tradition. As Norman Johnston, among others, states: "The Catholic Church was the first institution to use imprisonment consistently for any avowed purpose other than detention . . . . Not only was imprisonment calculated to bring about suffering as retribution for sin, but it was hoped that such suffering would better the heart of the 'wrong-doer.'"[50]

How the monastery came to be the crucible from which this new form of confinement would emerge is, upon reflection, somewhat logical to deduce. After all, monasticism itself is a form of voluntary imprisonment. Virtually all communities of monks demand a promise of stability, a vow initially enforced under threat of punitive sanction. Canon four of the Council of Chalcedon (451 AD) states that monks shall "embrace a quiet course of life . . . remaining permanently in the places in which they were set apart."[51] In fact, one of the first uses of imprisonment was precisely as a punishment for runaway monks! But, in a more formative sense, one sees a penal foreshadowing in the very nature of cenobitic life, with its desire for inner perfection through renunciation of the world and worldly values. Johnston phrases it well: "Although this confinement was voluntary, it established a precedent for cellular seclusion and for personal betterment through penitence and contemplation."[52]

Complementing the development of monasticism, indeed preceding it, was the practice of *anchoritism*. Anchorites chose a hermetical life in solitary places. In the Christian era they rarely if ever left the cells in which they chose to dwell. Such cubicles were normally erected alongside a church, monastery, religious hospital, or even a bridge.[53] In some cases they were literally entombed in their quarters. The ascetic man or woman would enter their private prison with a rite that generally featured the prayers and petitions read at funerals. In England, hermits sometimes dwelt over a pit that would serve as their grave. As Johnston notes, "upon death, the cell would be opened, the recluse buried, and the cell cleaned and made ready for a new tenant."[54]

Another key factor in the development of the monastic prison was the requirement, initially instituted by St. Basil in his rule, but adapted later by Western monasticism, that each monk regularly confess his sins.[55] In such cases, the ordinance demanding separation from the worshipping community, rather than being exercised at the weekly celebration of the Eucharist, would be carried out in the monk's own cell or in some designated place of contrition within or in proximity to the monastery.

Finally, the warrant for the use of imprisonment was most convincingly established with the belief, already present in the first extant monastic rule of Pachomius, that confinement itself is a medicine that heals the moral malady, regardless of whether the perpetrator wills it or not. Pachomius (292–346) orders different forms of enforced seclusion for those monks who, having been several times admonished by the superior in the format recommended in the Gospels, steadfastly cling to proscribed behavior. The contemptuous slanderer, for example, is to be "separated from the assembly of the brothers seven days and only receive bread and water until he firmly promises to convert from that sin." For one with the "wicked habit of soliciting his brothers by words and of perverting the souls of the simple," a sentence of isolation outside the monastery is called for "until he is cleansed of his filth." Finally, the mur-

murer should be "considered as one of the sick and put in the infirmary, where he shall be fed and left idle until he returns to the truth."[56]

Here we have the earliest evidence of our contention that the meaning of penal confinement in the Catholic tradition is not fulfilled by the authorities who thrust the wrongdoer into seclusion, but by the conscience of the one so excluded. In Origen's words, "God will accept even those who change from the worst life, if they severely condemn themselves for their past sins." It is not the pain of excommunication that stings offenders in Origen's mind, as much as the "lament for themselves as people who have perished because of their misdeeds."[57]

Aside from the examples from the Rule of Pachomius discussed above, and partly as a result of their influence, we can find quickly developing a rather persistent structure with regard to treatment of threats to communal harmony, informed in great part by the penitential ethos of the wider church. The troublesome monk is first confronted in charity and in secret. Basil states: "All should certainly be compassionate at first . . . as toward an ailing member of the body"[58]; while Benedict adds: "If a brother is found stubborn or disobedient or proud or murmuring . . . let him be admonished by his Superiors once and again in secret, according to the command of our Lord (Mt 18:15–16)."[59] Continued recalcitrance is then met with the penalty most appropriate to curing the malady; often the prescribed treatment was enforced isolation. Basil, for instance, provides a list of cures for various moral illnesses: "vainglory should be corrected by imposing practices of humility, idle talking, by silence . . . murmuring by segregation."[60]

The ecclesiastical justification for confinement can be traced to the period of these very first monastic foundations. In the fourth century, Pope Siricius, in what Walter Ullmann calls the "oldest extant decretal" (papal teaching), sent an important letter to Bishop Himerus. He answered a number of questions and concerns of his colleague, among them the treatment of monks who had broken both civil and ecclesiastical statutes. In his reply, Siricius recommended that such "impure and detestable persons" be consigned to a monastery and there confined in a workroom (*ergastulum*) in continual lamentation that they may melt away their crimes by means of penitential fire.[61] The bearing of the letter upon the validation of the prison is highlighted by the fact that it was reinvoked at the Synod of Tribur in 895 and, especially significant, that it was referenced by Gratian in his *Decretum* of 1140.[62]

Of all of those who contributed to the emergence of confinement as a key element in the understanding of criminal justice in the Catholic tradition, no one is more significant than St. Benedict (480–543). He knew well the writings of his monastic predecessors such as Pachomius and Basil, and much of what he prescribed for his errant monks was a replication of their approaches. There is, however, a particular psychological and spiritual sensitivity to Benedict's reflection, an insight into both the promise and peril of the discipline of segregation, that was to reverberate far beyond the halls of the monastery at Monte Casino, affecting demonstrably the emergence of the prison as we know it in the West. First, Benedict orders that the continually defiant brother must bear the pain of isolation: "Let him work alone at what he is told to do, maintaining all the while a penitential sorrow . . . . He must take his meals alone . . . . No one passing by should bless him, nor food given him."[63] He then complements the stern penal order with a pastoral injunction that intuits much of what we have discussed with regard to the sacral dimension of both confinement and the confined: "The abbot should focus all his attention on the care of the wayward brother, for *it is not the healthy but the sick who need a physician.* Thus he should use all the means that a wise physician would." Benedict also recommends that respected "elderly brothers who know how to comfort the wavering brother" be sent to "*console him so that he be not devoured by too much sorrow.*" He further adds a quote from St. Paul: "*[L]et love for him be reaffirmed and let everyone pray for him.*" Finally, Benedict charges the abbot to imitate Christ, the good shepherd, who "left the ninety nine sheep . . . looking for the one who had strayed . . . . *placed it on his sacred shoulders and carried it back to the flock.*"[64]

The preceding examples helped solidify not only the ecclesiastical sanction for monastic imprisonment but also led to the practice of confining troublesome clerics within monasteries. Gregory the Great writes: "As to lapsed priests, or any others of the clergy . . . . seek out the poorest regular monasteries which know how to live according to God, and consign the lapsed to penance in these monasteries."[65] Regarding women who had fled the monastic enclosure, Gregory writes that "if any of them . . . has been seduced, or should in future be led, into the gulf of adulterous lapse, we will that, after enduring the severity of adequate punishment, she should be consigned for penance to some other stricter monastery of virgins, that she may give herself to prayers and fastings."[66] As to the men who consorted with these "handmaidens" of the Lord, Gregory orders that, if a layperson, he should be deprived of Communion; however, if the offender is a cleric, he states, "let him also be removed from his office, and thrust into a monastery for his ever to be deplored excesses."[67] Church councils also deemed other forms of conduct, such as sedition, sufficient to warrant confinement.[68]

There are numerous reasons that can be proposed for the practice of confining clerics in monasteries. Perhaps the most pressing was the fact that there was no public penance for the clergy. Recall that in the early centuries of the church, all penance was public, beginning often with the imposition of hands by the bishop. The priest, however, could not receive this form of discipline since he had already been ordained by a laying on of hands. Therefore, by the time of Leo the Great (d. 461), one finds the habit of *privata secessio* in which the cleric retires to a monastery, often for life.[69] The practice was to continue, in some places into the second millennium. The *Siete Partidas*, a series of laws instituted by King Alfonso X of Spain in the thirteenth century makes mention of public punishments for criminal offenses and then adds: "It is also called Public Penance where those who perform it are shut up in a monastery, or any other secluded place, to remain there all their lives, on account of some great sin which they committed."[70] Innocent III ordered the Bishop of London first to degrade church clerks convicted of crimes and then imprison them in monasteries.[71]

It was also not uncommon for laypersons to be confined as well. Some chose the monastic life in view of crimes they had committed, or were purported to have committed. We speak here of the right of sanctuary and the ancient privilege granted the church to offer hospitality to those being hunted by the ruling authorities.[72] Others were forced into monasteries for political or moral reasons, often as an alternative to the brutality normally demanded in secular halls of justice. So Pepin the Short, in 751, locked up the last Merovingian king in a monastery.[73] Charlemagne ordered his son, Pepin the Hunchback, as well as his cousin, the Duke of Tassilo, to accept the tonsure and live out their days as monks. Louis the Pious followed a similar course of action with those who had become a political liability.[74] A church council in Rome in 826 stated that entry into a monastery should be voluntary, except in the case of those being punished for a crime.[75] At the Council of Pisa in 1135, Henry of Lausanne, who had been captured by the Bishop of Arles, was ordered to be confined in a local abbey.[76]

As monasteries developed the practice of granting a private cell to each monk, the culprit often served his sentence within its confines. Fructuosus (d. 670) shows not only the influence of Benedict in the way of life he charts for his followers but also how separation had already come to be equated with the geographical atmosphere of the cell. He states that the excommunicated brother should be sent alone into a dark cell and fed a diet of bread and water. There he must dwell in silence and separation from the community, conferring with no one save the monk dispatched to counsel him.[77] St. Columban states that the proud malefactor should be "placed in a cell apart to do penance, until his good will become manifest."[78] However, in many instances, notably the early Benedictine foundations, the monks slept in cubicles and so various types of rooms, often makeshift ones, were utilized for this specific purpose. We already saw in the case of Pachomius that the sullen and malicious gossip was to be locked up in the infirmary. However, with the widespread employment of imprisonment as a disciplinary and reformative technique, individual prison cells were created in monasteries for this specific purpose. A directive in 1229 to the Cistercian monasteries in France ordered the placement of a "solid and secure prison" in each; normally this would have been a room with a barred window under the stairs leading from the cloister to the dormitory.[79] The annals of the monastery at Durham, England, reveal the following entry: "Within the infirmary underneath the master of the infirmary's chamber, was the strong prison called the 'Lying House' which was ordained for such as were great offenders."[80] One history of the Benedictines notes the following: "If one were to visit one of the large and older English monasteries . . . the first building encountered would probably be a rectangular gatehouse set in the boundary wall and having a wide passage leading from the world outside into the monastic precinct . . . . [T]he gatehouse sometimes had a prisoner's cell."[81]

In certain instances, particularly if the monastery was large, an entire prison would be erected for its captives. St. John Climacus (579–649) describes what may have been one of the first prisons of this type at his monastery in Egypt: "At a distance of a mile from the great monastery was a place deprived of every comfort . . . . Here the pastor shut up, without permission to go out, those who fell into sin after entering the brotherhood; and not all together, but each in a separate and special cell . . . . And he kept them there until the Lord gave him assurance of the amendment of each one."[82] The monastery at Iona in Ireland had a dwelling for its wayward brothers, as did the Carthusian abbey at Mount Grace, the latter a two-story house with a covered walk along one wall and a garden.[83]

Aside from the specific structural and theological details we have discussed, as well as the tradition of legitimation from the official church, there were a number of significant developments that systematized the prison within the monastic worldview and prepared the ground for the extension of the prison as a universal place for repentance and conversion. Dom Jean Mabillon, the seventeenth-century Benedictine historian and reformer, reveals that the priors of the Benedictine order gathered at Aix-la-Chapelle in 817 to discuss a response to the frightening abuses of prisoners that had occurred within several of their abbeys. The priors used the opportunity not only to offer guidelines for prisons within the various communities, but also to mandate that facilities conforming to those guidelines be constructed in each foundation. Mabillon notes each habitation was required to be heated and serve as a workroom for its occupant.[84]

A similar force for the expansion of the disciplinary methods we have discussed was the enormous success and influence of the reform instituted by the monastery at Cluny in the century following the reform gathering at Aix-la-Chapelle. In an effort to combat a serious and historically momentous practice of lay investiture, in which civil authorities appointed bishops as well as abbots, the monastery at Cluny organized over 1,000 Benedictine communities under its governance. Each was pledged to order its internal life according to the reform impulse, reinstating the original focus of St. Benedict himself, including his code of discipline and his insistence on the isolation of the sinful brother.[85] In the eleventh century, the Constitutions of Lanfranc, Archbishop of Canterbury, had a similar effect of stabilizing the penal edifice. Serious indeed were the punishments for recalcitrant behavior detailed in the constitutions: "If a brother tries to defend his wrongdoing rather than to admit and amend it . . . then a certain number of the brethren shall . . . lay violent hands upon him, and drag or carry him into the prison appointed for rebels such as he. There confined he shall be punished with all due measure until he lay aside his pride, admit his fault and humbly promise amendment."[86]

Of note in this regard is the fact that with Cluny and Lanfranc we see the origin of multiple forms of imprisonment, a practice that would be reproduced by virtually all of the religious and monastic orders of the Middle Ages as well as by the Inquisition. A less strict form of imprisonment that generally featured short sentences, often in the monk's own cell, was mandated for *culpe graves* (serious faults); *culpe gravior* and *culpe gravissime* (more serious and most serious faults), on the other hand, merited harsher and more demanding confinement in the manner described by Lanfranc.[87] Lighter faults, for example, lateness for choir or talking during proscribed hours, were treated with any number of less stringent disciplinary rulings. As one order's constitutions state: "As there may be diverse faults, so there should be diverse punishments."[88]

THE NORMALIZATION OF THE PRISON
IN THE CATHOLIC WORLDVIEW

The most influential historical development that was to institute the prison as the basic disciplinary apparatus in the church and, by extension, in Western jurisprudence, was the institution of canon law as the attempt by the church to protect its internal life from the influence of secular authorities.[89] Before the work of Gratian, whose collection of decretals (c. 1140) became the foundational work in the creation of what came to be known as the *Corpus Iuris Canonici*, no collection of church decrees or teachings had binding authority. Walter Ullmann gives a concise appreciation of the intent of systematizing the various rulings into a universal body of law: "In a word, the decretal was the vehicle by which the papacy as a monarchic institution attempted to govern Western Europe conceived as the church, and this government concerned the basic requirements of a Christian society. The lively and relevant legislative activity of the papacy most effectively imprinted the idea of the rule of law upon society."[90] For Gregory VII, the church was the literal incarnation of justice and was thus the sole authority capable of encoding laws with universal binding force.[91]

Ironically, the upshot of this momentous shift in the political and ecclesiastical history of the West was the beginning of secularization, the formal uncoupling of church and state, although in practical matters the two remained closely intertwined. However, another development that was mentioned in chapter 2 of this volume also followed necessarily: the church had to create a formal mechanism to evaluate cases and, when necessary, punish its own derelict members. Clergy, even if arrested for civil felonies, could now claim, with even greater justification, benefit of clergy (*privilegium fori*) and have their cases heard in an ecclesiastical court, often a marked improvement over its secular counterpart.[92] Innocent III in 1204 in the decretal "Novit" declared that ecclesiastical courts had full jurisdiction in all cases involving sin.[93]

The legal practice guiding the investigation of misdeeds by clerics marked a turning point in the adjudication of fault in the church and it was to have a dramatic impact on secular law. The time-honored process of judicial procedure in the early Middle Ages was based on accusation. Plaintiff and defendant would appear before a judge or magistrate to each present his or her side of the dispute. The accused, if a common person, could expunge the fault attributed against his or her good name by oath and by the use of oath helpers or compurgators; a member of the clergy and officials of high rank could "purge" themselves by their own word.[94] Where there was a deadlock in the effort to ascertain the truth, authorities often relied on the ordeal to provide a solution.[95] The latter was a process of seeking the veracity of testimony and the innocence or guilt of the accused by investigating, in its most common usage, the appearance of burns caused by rituals such as carrying a hot iron for a number of paces or inserting one's hand into boiling water to recover a stone or a ring; there was also an ordeal of water.[96] In the ecclesiastical laws of King Ethelstan (925) one finds a clause concerning a man suspected of breaking into a church: "If the man appear guilty by the threefold ordeal, let him make satisfaction as the doom-book directs."[97]

Although secular officials often relied upon this method of obtaining proof, it was only legitimate to the degree that a priest was present to offer the proper oration to ensure that the process was divinely sanctioned.[98] The custom fell out of favor with the advent of a legal innovation known as the inquisitorial method, in which lawyers and judges could call witnesses and seek to ascertain certain proof of accusatorial claims.[99] The Dominican Constitutions capture the essence of the approach: the procedure for evaluating a case must involve accusation, denunciation (sufficient cause to investigate the charges being brought), and inquisition; the latter required the examination of at least two witnesses through formal procedure. The Camaldolese add the need to specify, prior to sentence, such factors as persons involved, places, occasions, species, sins, and number.[100] In a judicial tract used by Dominican friars and nuns, the denunciatory element of inquisitory procedure is parsed into twin elements, one evangelical and the other judicial. The evangelical is governed by the Gospel mandate of charity and proceeds by establishing an indictment through secret admonishment. In this process the prelate functions as *pater* (father) not *judex* (judge). The legal investigation then follows in which the judge is governed by equity—both justice and charity ("partim charitati, et partim justitiae").[101] In describing this new approach to law, Harold Berman states: "In the late eleventh and early twelfth centuries . . . . [i]n every country of the West there was created professional courts, a body of legislation, a legal profession, a legal literature, and 'science of law.'" These developments provided perhaps the decisive factor in the separation of sin as a private matter from crime as a public matter.[102]

Once an individual was found guilty, the church then had to decide what punishment was fitting for the culpable. There was ample ideological, if not factual, evidence that compelling offenders to do time often made them better.[103] Yet, at the beginning of the second millennium imprisonment was not commonly utilized in the public life of the church. Dunbabin claims that ecclesiastical officials "had even less need of jails for custodial purposes than had eleventh century secular lords."[104]

Some early examples of ecclesiastical imprisonment can be found in the laws of Theodosius, where one finds a ruling that clerical deserters were to be arrested and placed in church custody.[105] A decree from the first Council of Matison (581) rules that senior clergy charged with indecency or carrying weapons must be incarcerated for thirty days on a diet of bread and water.[106] In the Gelasian Sacramentary (early eighth century), there is a prescription that penitents are to be confined during Lent, beginning on Ash Wednesday, and kept in custody until Holy Thursday.[107] An eighth-century collection of canons written by the Archbishop of York contains a warning that those who question the church's authority to both baptize and forgive sins shall "feel the pain of excommunication, or long bear the confinement of a gaol."[108]

Ecclesiastical prisons as the formal apparatus for dealing with serious "crimes" make their appearance in the thirteenth century. In 1261, Boniface, the Archbishop of Canterbury, decreed the following: "We do with special injunction ordain that every bishop have one or two prisons in his bishopric (he is to take care of the sufficient largeness and security thereof) for the safekeeping of clerks according to canonical censure."[109]

The decisive pronouncement, however, was issued in 1298 by Pope Boniface VIII within the "Liber Sextus," a document that was appended to the first code of canon law. The directive states: "In regard to the detention of the guilty, prison should be primarily understood not as punishment. At the same time we do not reject prison for clerics . . . if they have been convicted of crimes. Taking the nature of their crimes and their persons and other circumstances into prudent consideration, such malefactors could either be confined for a time or for life as you may judge appropriate."[110] Edward Peters writes that Boniface "is the first sovereign authority in the Western tradition to determine that imprisonment as punishment was a legitimate instrument of a universal legal system."[111] This supports the contention that criminal justice as we know it in the West is largely a Catholic innovation that began officially in the late thirteenth century but, in point of fact, began when the first penitent was relegated to a specific place for a period of time in order to accomplish the goal of spiritual and behavioral reform.

Sentences had to be proportional to the fault committed, as in the tripartite taxonomy of serious infractions (grave, graver, gravest) mentioned in the Constitutions of Lanfranc. They also were ideally tailored to the specific disposition of the one about to be imprisoned. Mabillon notes in his observations: "As for the length of imprisonment, it should depend on the nature of the offense and the disposition of the culprit. One would be more punished by six months in prison than another by several years there."[112] All of this echoes the theme of the two previous chapters that the goal of reformation of character had to be at least equal to the intent to punish. One order's constitutions make clear that those guilty of the crimes worthy of the maximum penalty (*poena gravissima*) must be carried off to jail and kept there until grace had accomplished a return to gentleness of spirit.[113]

There were frequently life sentences assigned to monks and clerics. Normally, these would be for crimes that would have merited death in secular courts, such as murder.[114] As noted in the previous chapter, however, such sentences were often rendered for dramatic effect: seven years of confinement or even less was usually the norm, depending on the response of the captive to the experience of confinement.[115] There were also sentences lessened either through supervening interventions over petty or cruel convictions, as when the pope's envoy ordered Abelard to be freed after his theological opponents had confined him in a monastery,[116] or through the compassion of an ecclesiastical official, as when the Archbishop of York in 1314 freed an Augustinian canon from shackles due to the prayers and tears of the captive's mother.[117] Finally, commensurate with our previous observations, the private pain leading to internal conversion was, ideally, the end governing the application of punitive sanction. This approach, never "officially" an end in itself, could therefore be tailored to achieve the desired metanoia of the captive. Furthermore, in that light, charity could prove itself far more effective in achieving the goal of incarceration than judicial severity. Thus, the Second Council of Verneuil (844) ordered that there be no corporal punishment inflicted upon monks who freely returned after having fled their monasteries and that those captured be treated with compassion (*pietas*) and only confined until they showed signs of repentance.[118] Punishment should be carried out "in charity and a spirit of gentleness," say one congregation's statutes; another's state that "as much as [the punishment of incarceration] may be severe so much more does it stand in need of a zeal for charity."[119]

There is also evidence of sentences much longer than seven years (e.g., no less than twenty years confinement for a monk willfully murdering a brother monk),[120] and others in which no amount of leniency would be shown to a certain class of offenders. We will see that this latter judgment often applied to apostates, but there is evidence that a high degree of incorrigibility or a high degree of scandal adhering to an offense could lead to a perpetual imprisonment whose severity not even a provincial chapter or superior general could normally diminish.[121]

Some sentences were feared far more than imprisonment in a monastery or religious convent. One was relegation to the papal galleys or, far worse, those of the king.[122] Some convicts were so terrified of this latter sentence that we have evidence of them accusing themselves of heresy or even, in one case, sodomy with boys and animals in order to be sent to the prisons of the Inquisition.[123] Galleys may or may not have been a fate worse than death, but the fate that invariably ended in death was being handed over to "the secular arm." Since the church forbade

clerics to shed blood, the most dangerous, obstinate, or doctrinally troublesome character would meet his or her fate in the hands of those who
often shed blood liberally and, recalling Norbert Elias's cogent descriptions of medieval life, with little or no cause for alarm.[124]

There would also be a greater sentence imposed on those whose actions
were detrimental to the community at large. This serves as a reminder of
a consistent theme in Catholic social thought: individual human rights
notwithstanding, the needs of the community always take precedence
over those of the individual. Abelard states: "For whatever can redound to
the common ruin or public detriment should be punished with greater
correction and what causes greater wrong deserves among us a heavier
penalty . . . even though a lighter fault has preceded it."[125]

Similarly, there would often be more time imposed on those who were
repeat offenders. Some religious constitutions provide an ascending level
of punishments for the recidivist. For example, the Constitutions for the
Congregation of the Holy Spirit state that if a member of the order is
caught in an act of fornication he should spend a year confined, subsist-
ing on bread and water for six days and with neither meat nor wine for
the length of the sentence. However, a second offense would require two
years of confinement and, as the text says, "may God forbid!" yet another
offense would demand a lifelong imprisonment.[126]

The question that is far more difficult to answer is just how innovative
was the new way once it left the monasteries and became a political requirement. Certainly enough has been presented thus far to substantiate
the claim that it was different in theory. Bear in mind, however, that the
origin of inquisitory procedure dramatically changed the dynamics of judicial investigation. What emerged from its demand to substantiate
charges through legal proof and not simply the oath of friends (or con-
spirators) was the need to detain suspects, many suspects, in penal facilities. Add to this the emphasis on intention rather than action that derived from the thought of Abelard, and one removes the instant clarity of
the "smoking gun" approach to the assigning of guilt that the ordeal, for
example, would furnish, thus further complicating what had normally
been a less taxing and time-consuming legal process.[127]

Certainly one indication of the uniqueness of the "new prison" may
have been the consistent reluctance of church officials to utilize secular
detention centers. Notwithstanding the expected tensions between
church and state in the post-Gregorian era, one can infer that there was,
at least in the eyes of some church leaders, a qualitative difference in the
way offenders were treated in monasteries, religious priories, and ecclesiastical prisons as opposed to the jails of a lord or king. The chapter of
Notre Dame Cathedral, for example, erected its own prison rather than

allow the police officials of Paris to incarcerate delinquent clerics.[128] The more difficult question is whether the best of the monastic model was consistently transported to ecclesiastical prisons or whether the Realpolitik of powerful bishops with land holdings, security needs, and political allegiances led to the sort of abuses common then and now in correctional centers. The pontifical and synodal decrees demanding the construction of prisons in each diocese provided no guidelines as to how they were to be constructed. We have some details about the thirteenth-century prison in the archepiscopal palace at Sens: there were three quarters of varying size adjacent to the courtroom; each had a toilet, a window (from which the occupant could not see out), and anchors on the walls to which chains could be affixed. There was also a trapdoor in an anteroom on the first floor leading to a dungeon located next to the cesspool. The lower cell had a toilet and a small aperture for the admittance of air and light.[129] But with this, as with many similar historical anecdotes, one's imagination is often as good as the fragment of source material in depicting what may actually have transpired there.

It may be wise to side with Dunbabin's theory regarding the ecclesiastical prison: it may have been accepted with reluctance by many prelates as a costly and politically unwise nuisance, but eventually its deeper significance, in many cases, became apparent.[130] With time, the ad hoc nature of church prisons gave way to the construction of facilities that became a model both in architecture as well as in practice for secular prisons throughout much of the world.

By the end of the fifteenth century the Alexian Brothers, following a tradition in which lay associations, guilds, and religious institutes took active concern to work on behalf of inmates, often termed "the poor of Christ," had established "bettering houses" for at-risk youth in some of their foundations in West Germany and the Netherlands.[131] In seventeenth-century Florence, Ipolito Francini undertook a ministry on behalf of street children. Inspired by him, a group of priests from the Oratory of St. Philip Neri, most notably Filippo Franci, established a hospice for these youth and, later, a similar one for unwed mothers. The facility had a correctional department with cells for those who had committed criminal infractions in order to facilitate reformation by means of an isolation whose logic was similar to that orchestrated by St. Benedict. The young inmate was to reflect in silence upon his or her life with the aid of "protectors" who would provide spiritual guidance and care. The institutions grew and thrived and Thorsten Sellin calls Franci "a precursor of modern penology."[132]

Arguably, the most notable of the numerous ecclesiastical penal facilities was St. Michael's in Rome. It opened in 1703 under the aegis of

Pope Clement XI and became a revered symbol of enlightened penal practice. It was a house of detention exclusively focused on seeking the reform of troubled adolescents. Parents or guardians of the young people petitioned the pope directly to have them confined there.[133] The young residents were to work in common and in silence during the day and slept in their own cells by night. Clement's edict mandating the facility can be translated as follows: "And since there are some youngsters and young rascals who disobey their parents and others under whose tutelage and care they now live and who, because of their wicked principles, show strong inclination toward vices, we want and order that they can equally well be kept in custody to correct and emend them in this new house of correction."[134] John Howard, whose work detailing the dreadful squalor of prisons around the world was singularly influential in stimulating public opinion to consider a humane approach to corrections, singled out St. Michael's as worthy of the highest praise. In one room Howard saw an inscription that moved him; he calls it an "admirable sentence, in which the grand purpose of all civil policy relative to criminals is expressed."[135] In fact, he quoted the motto on the title page of the second volume of his study of European prisons: "Repressing villains with punishment is worth little if we do not render them good with discipline."[136] Both of the above quotes, despite the archaic language, give credence to the contention that in a practical as well as official sense punishment was understood as subservient to the greater goal of personal amendment.

Of course, enlightened penology in the early eighteenth century does not always translate easily into contemporary mores. The discipline was strict by any standard: the young men were chained to their desks. The daily regimen at St. Michael's was marked by prayer, work, and, frequently, corporal punishment. Some of the residents remained there until they were of an age where, if the sentences were serious enough, they would then be transferred to Civitavecchia, site of the papal galleys, to complete the remainder of their term at the oars.[137]

The facility remained in operation until 1828, closing, perhaps, under the shadow of scandal: the young men were reported to have had access to prostitutes and there were also accounts of other forms of sexual activity among them. The inmates were then transferred to the Carceri Nuove, constructed with aims similar to that of its predecessor.[138]

It is perhaps best to end this section with the evidence just related. After all, as we have tried to make apparent, there are always serious risks involved in detaining people for any reason; these risks become especially troubling in institutions founded on noble principles. But there is also great risk in allowing destructive social behavior to exist without intervention. We will see that the ambiguity surrounding punishment and imprisonment is further revealed in the penal facilities created by the religious orders.

Prisons of Religious Orders

We have already provided numerous references to the penal regimen practiced within religious congregations. A bit of information that the reader may not know is that the bishop has full authority over the priests of his diocese and over all public ministerial activity within his see. The priories and convents of religious orders, however, have a degree of autonomy in their internal life. Vowed men and women must abide by the constitutions of their congregation and the superior of their local community. That is a way of saying that imprisonment as a disciplinary technique among religious groups would not be, first and foremost, a practice tracing its authority to the pope or local bishop, but must have its own independent validation. We have, however, evidence that in virtually every case, in keeping with the long-standing tradition of incarceration within the church, religious constitutions prescribed imprisonment as punishment for serious infractions after the multiple private warnings encouraged by St. Benedict had failed to remedy the aberrant conduct.[139]

Sentences had to be carried out by due authority. The Augustinians forbid any superior from placing a brother in custody, much less in chains (*in compedibus*) unless expressly in conformity with the constitutional provisions of the order.[140] Similarly, the Dominicans caution their priors not to incarcerate anyone unilaterally but only after due consultation with the provincial.[141] This redounds to the teaching of Aquinas that law is legitimate only when promulgated by due authority.[142]

The Dominican Constitutions urge priors to "punish freely" their lapsed brothers since the "rigor of incarceration is not the same as banishment since it might incite improvement in the delinquent."[143] To that end "secure and strong jails" were to be added in every house.[144] The Mercedarians and Trinitarians, orders founded to raise funds to redeem and care for captives, required that prison facilities be erected in each of their communities.[145] The Trinitarian ordinance states that the place must be secure, "nevertheless not to such a degree that the health of the religious may be imperiled in that place of enclosure." Furthermore, the decree calls for the use of "shackles, chains, and whatever else is necessary to better house the delinquents."[146] Each Augustinian priory was to have a facility secure on all sides and equipped with leg irons, while the Norbertines ordered that at least one, if not two, jails be established in every residence.[147]

There are found in each of the orders' constitutions the same graded list of faults—usually light, medium, and grave—and accompanying penalties similar to those first seen in the monastic rules, with imprisonment always the norm for the most serious infractions. The designation of light (*levi*) fault required a corresponding light and appropriate punishment, such as the recitation of extra psalms in the oratory. More serious (*media*) faults would be met by shaming rituals such as lying at the feet of community members at dinner.[148] Finally, resonant of the monastic legislation, serious breaches of discipline were almost always divided into three classes. Among the Dominicans, for a grave fault (*gravi culpa*), such as receiving, sending, or reading the letter of another, the errant brother was confined for a month. For graver faults (*gravior culpa*), such as sodomy (*concubitus contra naturam*) and murder, the perpetrator was sentenced to prison for life but with the stipulations mentioned previously as to remedial intervention by a general chapter, which could reduce the sentence to twenty years. Among the gravest faults (*gravissima culpa*) were incorrigibility, repeated infractions of the grave or graver categories, and apostasy. The punishment for these faults was generally dismissal from the order, although repentant apostates could either be sent to another house for a period of years or, in some cases, be welcomed back after spending not less than three years incarcerated.[149] If the punishment for the most serious faults appears to the reader to be more desirable than that for the previous designation, consider that to be excommunicated from the order often was a euphemism for being released to the "secular arm."[150]

Punishments among nuns were not far different. The Carmelite Constitutions concerning a grave fault such as repeated conversation about "the affairs of the world" mandate nine days of confinement including a "discipline" in the refectory.[151] The graver fault called for the sister to "bear her shoulders so as to receive the sentence won by her merits" after which she is sent "to the cell designated . . . by the Mother prioress." The practices recommended by St. Benedict are then ordered, including the consolatory acts of mercy and a spiritual advisor. Finally, concerning the gravest fault, St. Teresa writes: "There should be a prison cell set aside where nuns such as these may be held, and no one . . . set free except by the visitor.[152] The apostate nuns should be kept indefinitely in the prison cell as well as she who falls into the sins of the flesh, and she who commits a crime that in the world would merit the death penalty."[153]

The penal facilities themselves varied from house to house and order to order. As with ecclesiastical prisons, sometimes they were makeshift, with storerooms, guest rooms, or infirmaries pressed into service. A good example is the incarceration of St. John of the Cross by his brother Carmelites. He spent nine months confined in the priory in Toledo for his attempts to establish a separate, reformed congregation. After one of the brothers incarcerated with him escaped, he was placed in the lavatory within a suite of rooms reserved for special guests of the friars. It had no windows and only a small hole high up on the wall from which a modicum of light could enter the cell.[154]

In this brief overview the reader sees once again the painful ambiguities involved in attempting to punish and to "correct" the life of another. As we have noted so often, the way infractions and those who commit them are imaged matters most in determining punishments prescribed, environments chosen, and penal regimes imposed. The Catholic Church has provided us with enough evidence to suggest that, even if always the one imprisoned, Christ has often not been treated well when confined. No period in Catholic history testifies to this more than the Inquisition.

The Prisons of the Inquisition

St. John of the Cross was a revolutionary spiritual genius whose good and bad fortune was to splinter one of the oldest religious orders in the church. Crime is a social creation and, more often than not, created by those with the power to determine what is criminal; and what are invariably termed as criminal and deserving of the most severe penalties are perceived threats to internal security and unity.[155]

The Inquisition dates from the decretal *Ad Abloendam*, issued by Pope Lucius IV in 1177, and endured throughout much of Europe into the modern era.[156] As the reader may know, there were areas and time periods in which this institution was quite benign, and others in which it was repressive and violent. This also must be said for individual persons within the authority structure of the church, some of whom believed that persuasion was the most appropriate response to those who dissented from teaching and doctrine, while others responded without pity or regard for those deemed as apostates or heretics.[157] The task here is to provide a snapshot of the prisons run by the Holy Office. While no one needs to be convinced of the inhumanity shown to prisoners across the spectrum of church and state practice, it is important to uncover the degree to which the guiding principles that underlay the creation of the modern prison presented in this chapter also were mirrored in the institutions run by the Inquisition.

The language justifying the prisons of the Inquisition, particularly in those places (France and Spain) most scarred by their violence, does indeed pay an ideological if not a practical debt to the history so far revealed.

In the manual that governed the correctional practices in the French province of Narbonne during the thirteenth century, there is an announced period of "indulgence from imprisonment" in which those who are suspected of heresy may "come voluntarily as penitents" and confess the "full truth about themselves and others."[158] If the accused heretic cooperated with the order to recant and tell all, then we see the influence of the approach to justice discussed in the second chapter. Much as Anselm and Aquinas argued that offenses are injurious not only to the perpetrator and victim but to law itself, and by extension to God, whose creation is safeguarded by duly promulgated laws, so the Inquisitor's manual offers pardon for the capital crime of apostasy and releases the penitent from the judgment of excommunication.[159] The offender, according to the manual of Bernard Gui, then prays aloud from the penitential psalm (Ps 51) after which a prayer is offered by the priest. The inquisitor next reads the formal relaxation of the sentence of excommunication.[160] This action forecloses the sentence of relegation to the "secular arm" and the consequent penalty of death. Despite this, however, what must be atoned for is the actual sin of having "adored," "harboured," and "visited" heretics or "believed in their errors." The penance for such actions was relegation "to the decent and humane prison prepared for you . . . there to make your salutary and permanent abode."[161]

There are, of course, ironies as well: "[The] Lord will gloriously and wonderfully be made manifest" not only "if prisoners are adequately provided with necessities" but also "if their property [and goods are] surely confiscated."[162]

As we have seen with life sentences ordered in monastic and religious communities, only rarely was a sentence of that magnitude actually served. The practice of perpetual sentences placed upon heretics became customary after the bull "Excommunicamus" was issued by Gregory IX in 1229. He stated that those who converted from what appeared to be fear of death at the hands of secular authorities should be confined for life.[163] Dunbabin claims, however: "In most cases of heresy, abjuration of error, followed by an act of penance, was sufficient to secure release from prison sooner or later."[164] Henry Kamen echoes this contention in his study of the Inquisition in Spain: "A 'lifetime' sentence was more commonly completed in ten years."[165]

What do we know of the prisons themselves? There was no intention, at first, to erect separate institutions for the culpable but, particularly in France and Spain, the large number of prisoners overwhelmed monastic and ecclesiastical centers of detention.[166] By the middle of the thirteenth century, there were inquisitorial prisons in France at Carcassone, Bezier, and Toulouse.[167] Finances were a major factor in all of this. Lea suggests that in the face of episcopal hesitation to defray the expense of prison construction, often the royal exchequer provided the capital, although rulers were not always cooperative.[168] Therefore, following a decree of Pope Innocent III, it became the custom to use the funds confiscated from those who repented toward the construction of facilities. Kamen claims that due to the number of prisoners and the cost of building and maintaining prisons, the conditions, at least in Spain, were often rather lax. He notes that sentences were normally served in the home or, if that was not feasible, then in a monastery or hospital.[169]

Financial pressures and regional variation notwithstanding, we do know that, as in many monasteries, there were two classes of inquisitorial prisons, what were termed *murus largus* and *murus strictus*. The former, patterned on monastic life, established a precisely regulated daily regimen within the penal enclosure. The latter called for a much more severe confinement in a single cell.[170]

Depending on the facility involved, the type of incarceration ordered, and the way offenders were viewed by those in control, the experience of confinement could be salutary, as befits a true philosophy of punishment, or an experience of cruelty and terror. As to the first, recall the claim that prisoners assigned to the galleys of the Spanish king would declare themselves heretics in order to be confined by the Inquisition. In 1571, a French painter "tried to pass himself off as an atheist, blasphemer or a Jew" in order to be tried before the Holy Office.[171] Another account states that the cruelty associated with the Spanish Inquisition of the seventeenth century was more the work of the state and that "the Inquisition was the first tribunal in Europe to abolish the torment and instruments of torture" and that the punishments imposed were of a penitential character: recanting, exile, suspension of responsibilities, fasting, or penitential clothing.[172] Monter would agree with this analysis. He states: "Torture simply does not correlate with inquisitorial punishments."[173] Edward Peters writes that when, in the early fourteenth century, Pope Clement V was informed by a delegation he had sent to inspect the inquisitorial prisons in Southern France that they were not only in poor condition but poorly run, he issued "apparently successful orders for improvement. From the fourteenth century on, Inquisitorial prisons were probably the best-maintained in Europe."[174]

These accounts must be presented with contrasting evidence. The words of the inquisitor's manual that a "decent and humane" prison awaits the repentant heretic must be balanced against the sort of conditions the delegates of Clement V found in the prison of Carcassone: prisoners were forced into confession by torture and by the sordidness of the facility, which provided few beds and meager rations.[175] In a village in

Narbonne during the thirteenth century, residents complained and then staged a riot against the tactics used by inquisitors within the local prison.[176] Despite the prohibition against the shedding of blood by clerics, exceptions in defense of torture are found in the *Corpus Iuris Canonici* both in the decretals of Gratian and in the "Liber Extra" of Pope Gregory IX.[177] Torture was certainly employed against the Catholic order of knights, the Templars, many of whom were arrested in 1307 by Philip IV in the name of the Inquisition. Although the reason for their suppression was probably more financial than either moral or doctrinal, they were charged with denying the divinity of Christ, spitting on the crucifix, homosexual conduct, and idol worship.[178] In the nightmare that followed they were induced to confession by means of sleep deprivation, rations consisting of bread and water, and physical humiliation. They were tortured on the rack or with the strappado, although some had flames applied to the soles of their feet.[179] Those who confessed were released to the secular arm for execution. In 1310, fifty-four Templars were handed over to French officials by the Archbishop of Sens and were burnt alive in a field outside of Paris.[180]

While guilt could be proven by two witnesses despite the lack of a confession, the difficulty in procuring witnesses led inquisitors to seek what was called "the queen of proofs," torture. Dunbabin writes that its use "was based on the assumption that the accused would not have been arrested unless there were good grounds for thinking him guilty, and that a confession was worth obtaining by any possible means."[181]

All of this again gives us a split portrait. Clearly the intervention of Clement V and the relative moderation of the inquisitorial discipline throughout much of Europe reveal that the need for order and doctrinal coherence was never meant to excuse maltreatment nor to dispense with the understanding of punishment as a pretext for conversion (despite the theological and moral reservations many may have about the meaning of conversion in this case). In contrast, there is strong evidence that the conditions of intimidation and coercion under which these prisons were instituted supervened in many cases any convincing connection with the sort of familial discipline often found in accounts of the prisons in monastic and religious communities. Ironically, the inquisitorial method was often suspended by the Inquisition in its examination of suspected apostates. The "Manual for Inquisitors" reveals this in referencing Gregory IX's relaxing the stipulation that those arrested for heresy be allowed to face their accusers.[182]

Regarding the prisons, Given's account of detention facilities, though largely dismissing the sinister portrayals often associated with this period, derides what he sees as the prevailing philosophy of benign neglect that overshadowed the judicial mechanism: "[S]uspects were apparently not kept under lock and key or isolated from one another. Instead, they were allowed to wander about, almost at pleasure, within the walls of the prison . . . little effort was made to isolate them from outsiders." Similarly, in his account, administrators largely dismissed whatever noble points the Catholic tradition may have brought to the idea of confinement: "The most striking feature of life in the inquisitorial prisons was its largely unstructured nature . . . . virtually no effort was made to establish a penitential regime."[183] This is corroborated to some degree in Kamen's study of the Inquisition in Spain where, in some tribunals, "prisoners were free to come and go, providing they observed basic rules."[184] Finally, as Monter suggests, bishops in realms with imperial aspirations had no qualms about sending many of the prisoners to man the king's galleys, despite all the demonstrable "differences" between church prisons and those of the realm.

CONCLUSION

It has been stated frequently in the preceding pages, but it bears repeating, since it is the theme of this volume, that the image employed in penal history determines more than any other factor how the prisoner was and is treated. As the eloquent objections of Lactantius against cruelty to prisoners read: "For if we all derive our origin from one man, whom God created, we are plainly of one blood; and therefore it must be considered the greatest wickedness to hate a man, even though guilty."[185] A sixteenth-century Spanish synod of bishops released an exhortation to those overseeing jails and prisons, including those of the Inquisition, that prisoners be treated with gentleness and love (*benignidad y amor*), that they be provided with their necessities, and, above all, that they live happily and in a Christian manner while confined.[186]

It has not been the intention of the preceding pages to diminish in any way the fact that prisoners in Catholic institutions often did not "live happily." Mabillon writes that "a frightful kind of prison, where daylight never entered, was invented, and since it was designed for those who would finish their lives in it, it received the name *Vade in pace* [go in peace]." A similar fate in a prison with the same title awaited a monk of St. Alban's who was "solitarily imprisoned in fetters, and dying was buried in them."[187] Rulings, such as the one enacted at the Council of Rheims (1157) that those young women swayed by the influence of a heretical Manichaean group were to be put to the ordeal of the hot iron and, if found guilty, branded on the forehead and cheek and then banished, were by no means rare.[188] The warden of a house of detention for women wrote that there must be chains, bolts, gags, and various sorts of discipline because if the jail is meant to terrorize and cause fear then it stands to reason that it should be rigorous.[189] Nor should we forget that, in 1256, despite the ancient tradition condemning the shedding of blood by clerics, inquisitors were permitted to absolve each other of sin if they participated in torturing their prisoners.[190]

Dunbabin claims that examples such as the preceding reveal that one must pronounce the emphasis on imprisonment as a means to achieve justice, if not conversion, a failure, especially given "the body of evidence for high mortality, callousness, and venality in medieval prisons."[191] The strength of this criticism can be seen in instances where the end seemed to justify the means: penance can certainly be induced if there is enough suffering inflicted. The inquisitor Bernard Gui quipped: "I have often seen those vexed and detained for many years confess not only recent faults but even deeds committed long ago."[192] The frequently ominous nature of the legislation enacted suggests that charity had to be exercised in the face of the constant prospect of mistreatment.

Still, I strongly contend that there is evidence to sustain a commitment, verified in hard reality and not simply in romantic speculation, to the understanding of imprisonment as a moment to ponder the empathic love bestowed by God in Christ to the prisoner; a love that has and can continue to summon a thankful piety among the captives and stifle a will to hurt among the captors. It is no more than the vision of inner and social renewal that lies at the heart of the Gospel and of the Catholic social tradition. It was spoken of by Carlo Luigi Morichini, an eighteenth-century Italian cardinal, who wrote first of the monastic prison with its "cloistered life of penitents in separate cells, with a small adjacent vegetable garden to cultivate, accompanied by silence and prayers." He then reasoned that the same should inform penal techniques with all offenders in the general populace: "Therefore, why not treat—against their will—those who were truly sinners not only before God but also before men in the same way? . . . returning the offender to society, after he had served his sentence, a man completely different from what he was when he entered prison?"[193]

NOTES

1. The term *religious orders* in the church refers to communities of "active" men and women, as opposed to contemplative monastic orders and the diocesan clergy associated with a particular diocese and under the authority of its bishop.

Religious orders must receive papal approval for their rule of life, which explains and justifies the specific task or *charism* that marks their raison d'être. Orders are organized into provinces, under the leadership of an elected provincial, and all of the provinces are under the authority of a superior general.

2. For an analysis of the countercultural overtones of this epistle, see H. Richard Niebuhr, *Christ and Culture* (New York: Harper & Row, 1951), 45–48.

3. St. Polycarp, "Letter to the Philippians," in *Early Christian Writings*, trans. Maxwell Stanforth (London: Penguin, 1968), I, 7.

4. St. Clement, "Second Letter to the Corinthians," in Cyril C. Richardson, ed., *Early Christian Fathers* (New York: Macmillan, 1970), ch. XIV.

5. Of the extant polemical texts attacking the Christian faith, perhaps the best known is that by Celsus, which prompted Origin's classic apology. See Celsus, *On the True Doctrine: A Discourse against Christians*, trans. Joseph Hoffman (New York: Oxford University Press, 1987); Origen, *Contra Celsum*, trans. Henry Chadwick (Cambridge: Cambridge University Press, 1953).

6. Realpolitik aside, by the third century, classical Roman jurisprudence had become, in the words of Fritz Schultz, "so undefined, arbitrary, and authoritarian, that any juristic construction of concepts and principles would have been devoid of any significance." Quoted in Peters, "Destruction of the Flesh—Salvation of the Spirit," 134. Even after the fall of Rome and the dramatic weakening of the Roman political and military establishment, Christians were still urged to avoid presenting cases in secular courts. The Council of Chalcedon threatened penalties for those who would violate this norm. See "The Council of Chalcedon," in Percival, *The Seven Ecumenical Councils*, c. ix.

7. Quoted in Karl Rahner, "Penance in the Early Church," in *Theological Investigations* XV, trans. Lionel Swain (New York: Crossroad, 1982), 10.

8. St. Augustine, "Sermons," in *The Works of St. Augustine*, pt. III, vol. 10, trans. Edmund Hill, O.P. (Hyde Park, NY: New City Press, 1965), no. 392.

9. Cyril Vogel, "Sin and Penance," in Philippe Delhaye et al., *Pastoral Treatment of Sin* (New York: Desclee Company, 1968), 193.

10. Joseph Favazza, *The Order of Penitents* (Collegeville, MN: The Liturgical Press, 1988), 241; Bernhard Poschmann, *Penance and the Anointing of the Sick*, trans. Francis Courtney, S. J. (New York: Herder & Herder, 1964), 88; Rahner, "Penance in the Early Church," 8.

11. "Constitutions of the Holy Apostles," in Rev. Alexander Roberts and John Donaldson, eds., *The Ante-Nicene Fathers*, vol. VII (New York: Charles Scribner's Sons, 1925), II, iii, 16.

12. Favazza, *Order of Penitents*, 238–39.

13. Catalogues of sins are found in both the Gospels and Epistles. For example, Jesus states: "Wicked designs come from the deep recesses of the heart; acts of fornication, theft, murder, adulterous conduct, greed, maliciousness, deceit, sensuality, envy, blasphemy, arrogance, an obtuse spirit. All these evils come from within and render a man impure" (Mk 7:21–23). Other catalogues are found in the following verses: Mt 15:19; Lk 18:11; Col 3:5; Rom 1:29, 13:13, 16:17; Gal 5:20; 1 Cor 6:9; 2 Cor 12:20; Eph 4:19; 1 Tm 1:10; 1 Thes 4:5; 1 Pt 2:1.

14. Vogel, "Sin and Penance," 192–93.

15. Tertullian, "On Penitence," in *Treatises on Penance*, trans. William P. Le Saint, S. J. (Westminster, MD: The Newman Press, 1959), ch. 7.

16. St. Cyprian, *The Lapsed*, trans. Maurice Bevenot, S. J. (Westminster, MD: The Newman Press, 1957), ch. 15.

17. "Constitutions of the Holy Apostles," II, xiv.

18. Percival, "Seven Ecumenical Councils," 604–5.

19. Tertullian, "On Penitence," ch. 9.

20. *Exomologesis* came to represent both the open acknowledgment of minor failures in Christian comportment at the Eucharistic assembly, formalized in the rite of penance at the beginning of the liturgy, as well as the process of personal amendment done in response to grave sin. Discipline in the first instance did not require public penance and was generally mild (prayer, fasting, almsgiving), but the gravest of sins normally required heroic manifestations of personal and social debasement in order to be absolved. See Vogel, "Sin and Penance," 202.

21. Ibid.

22. Ibid.

23. Favazza, *Order of Penitents*, 247.

24. Poschmann, *Penance and the Anointing of the Sick*, 87. Favazza claims that "this exclusion was the premier sign of an order of penitents before the fourth century." See *Order of Penitents*, 243.

25. A canon of the Council of Agda states, "Poenitentes tempore, quo poenitentiam petunt, impositionem manuum et cilicium super caput a sacerdote consequantur." See "Concilium Agathense," in Johannes Dominicus Mansi, ed., *Sacrorum Conciliorum*, VIII (Paris, Leipzig, 1901), c. 15 [originally published 1762).

26. Rahner, "Penance in the Early Church," 4.

27. Vogel, "Sin and Penance," 232.

28. Poschmann, *Penance and the Anointing of the Sick*, 88.

29. Percival, "Seven Ecumenical Councils of the Undivided Church," 25.

30. Percival, 26. McNeill and Gamer note that the "kneelers" were required to kneel, often in sackcloth and ashes, while the rest of the congregation was standing. See *Medieval Handbooks of Penance*, 7–8. Poschmann believes that the practice was not widely used in the early church, confined mostly, he claims, to Asia Minor. See *Penance and the Anointing of the Sick*, 91.

31. St. Augustine, *City of God*, V, 26.

32. Bingham, *Antiquities of the Christian Church*, VI, 8–9.

33. Percival, "Seven Ecumenical Councils," 608.

34. "Poenitente vero dicimus de eo, qui post baptismum, aut pro homicidio, per diversis criminibus, gravissime que peccatis publicam poenitentiam gerens, sub cilicio, divino fuerit reconciliatus altario." "Concilium Toletanum I," in Mansi, *Sacrorum Conciliorum*, III, c. 2. For the canon from the Council of Agda, see "Concilium Agathense," in Mansi, *Sacrorum Conciliorum*, VIII, c. 15.

35. St. Ambrose, "On Repentance," bk. II, ch. 10.

36. Vogel, "Sin and Penance," 239–40.

37. St. Augustine, "Exposition of the Psalms," in *The Works of St. Augustine*, pt. III, vol. 17, trans. Maria Boulding, O.S.B. (Hyde Park, NY: New City Press, 1995), ps. 61, v. 23.

38. Favazza reads St. Paul's injunction concerning the man in Corinth living with his stepmother as directed to the community to "effect the sinner's isolation." In keeping with the theme presented in the second chapter, Paul would be suggesting that the work of repentance is primarily between the sinner and God and only indirectly a function of communal aggressiveness. Thus, Favazza terms the attitude of the early Christians in such matters as imposing "an indirect coercive penance of isolation." See *Order of Penitents*, 77–79.

39. Vogel states the texts of the patristic period "say nothing of a definitive excommunication." See "Sin and Penance," 194.

40. St. Polycarp, "Letter to the Philippians," ch. 9.

41. "Concilium Toletanum I," in Mansi, *Sacrorum Conciliorum*, III, c. 2; See also Logan, *Runaway Religious*, 146.

42. Rahner, "Penance in the Early Church," 5.

43. Clement writes to rebuke a rebellious faction within the Church at Corinth: "You, then, who are the instigators of the schism, submit yourselves to the presbyters and be corrected unto repentance, bending the knees of your heart." In the *Shepherd of Hermas* it is stated: "But those whom they have rejected and cast aside, who are they? These are they who have sinned and are willing to do penance. For this reason they have not been cast far aside from the tower, because they will be of use for the building, should they do penance." See "Sacraments and Forgiveness," in *Sources of Christian Theology*, vol. II, ed. Paul F. Palmer, S. J. (Westminster, MD: The Newman Press, 1959), 10, 12–13.

44. St. Ambrose, "On Repentance," Bk. II, ch. 10.

45. Vogel writes of the dilemma of the "vigorous" in the face of such strict regulations: "We know, however, that because of very precise legislation, and also owing to the conditions of extreme severity placed upon its accomplishment, penance was inaccessible both by law and in fact to those very individuals for whom it would have been most profitable, namely vigorous persons in the middle of life." See "Sin and Penance," 246.

46. "Concerning those . . . who having completed penance, have become like dogs and pigs going back to their vomit and filth by reentering military service, seeking forbidden sexual unions and new marriages . . . . they cannot receive penance again . . . they must be kept from the Lord's table . . . . We want them to be comforted when they come to pass to the Lord by receiving viaticum and re-establishing communion." ("De his vero . . . qui Acta poenitentia, tamquam canes ac sues ad vomitus pristinos et volutabra redeuntes, et militiae cingulum, et ludicras voluptates, et nova conjugia . . . . non habent poenitendi . . . a Domincae autem mensae convivio segregentur. . . . Quos tamen . . . viatico munere, cum ad Dominum coeperint proficisci, per communionis gratiam volumus sublevari") Pope Siricius, "Epistola ad Himerium Episcopum Tarraconensem," in J. P. Migne, ed., *Patrologia Latina* (Paris, 1845), 13, col. 1137. Likewise, Gratian reproduces the canon from the Council of Larida that speaks of repeat sinners "velut canes ad vomitum." See "Concordia

Discordantium Canonum," in *Corpus Iuris Canonici* (Lyon, 1616), dist. I, c. lii. On the forgiveness implied in the reception of Communion at the final hour, see Vogel, "Sin and Penance," 247–59.

47. "Constitutions of the Holy Apostles," II, iii, 24.

48. See McNeill and Gamer, *Medieval Handbooks of Penance*.

49. Favazza notes that during the fourth century some of those enrolled in the order of penitents "were saddled with certain lifelong consequences." Some of these deferred to the practice of a single confession but there were also certain "juridic restraints" placed upon the reconciled. See *Order of Penitents*, 247–48. Compagnoni is more forceful in his reminder that it was during the fourth century that the church initiated its long acquaintance with both torture and the death penalty. See "Capital Punishment and Torture in the Tradition of the Catholic Church," 41, 47–48

50. Johnston, *Forms of Constraint*, 17.

51. Percival, "Seven Ecumenical Councils," 270.

52. Johnston, *Forms of Constraint*, 17.

53. Ibid., 18.

54. Ibid.

55. Poschmann, *Penance and the Anointing of the Sick*, 120.

56. St. Pachomius, "Precepts and Judgments," in *Pachomian Koinonia, vol. 2: Pachomian Chronicles and Rules*, trans. Armand Veilleux (Kalamazoo, MI: Cistercian Publications, 1981), 1, 4, 5 (pp. 175–76).

57. Origen, *Contra Celsum*, III, 71.

58. St. Basil, "The Long Rules," in *St. Basil: Ascetical Works*, trans. Sister M. Monica Wagner (New York: Fathers of the Church, 1950), q. 28.

59. St. Benedict, *Benedict's Rule*, trans. Terrence G. Kardong (Collegeville, MN: The Liturgical Press, 1996), ch. 23.

60. St. Basil, "The Long Rules," q. 51.

61. Pope Siricius, "Epistola ad Himerium Episcopum Tarraconensem," col. 1137; Walter Ullmann, *Law and Politics in the Middle Ages* (Ithaca, NY: Cornell University Press, 1975), 122.

62. See Peters, "Prison Before the Prison," 28.

63. St. Benedict, *Benedict's Rule*, ch. 25.

64. Ibid., Ch. 27.

65. Gregory the Great, "Epistles," trans. Rev. James Barmby, in Philip Schaff and Henry Wace, eds., *A Select Library of Nicene and Post-Nicene Fathers of the Christian Church*, vol. XII (Grand Rapids, MI: Eerdmans, 1956), I, 41, 42.

66. Ibid., IV, 9

67. Ibid.

68. The Second Council of Arles (452 AD) ordered those to be imprisoned who, in opposition to ecclesiastical decree, attempted to free those who were in servitude. See "Concilium Arelatense II," in Mansi, *Sacrorum Conciliorum*, VII, c. 33. See also Gratian, "Concordia Discordantium Canonum," c. XX, q. 4, c.3.

69. Poschmann, *Penance and the Anointing of the Sick*, 111–12.

70. Robert I. Burns, S. J., ed., *Las Siete Partidas*, vol. I, trans. Samuel Parsons Scott (Philadelphia: University of Pennsylvania Press, 2001), tit. iv, xx.

71. Frederick Pollock, *The History of English Law Before the Time of Edward I*, vol. I (Cambridge: Cambridge University Press, 1899), 442–43.

72. Concerning sanctuary, see "The Council of Sardica," c. 7, in Percival, "Seven Ecumenical Councils," 422; Ives, *A History of Penal Methods*, 25; Burns, a canon in *Las Siete Partidas* states: "A church and its cemetery possess an exemption . . . for every man who takes refuge in them, on account of any offense which he has committed, or debt that he owes," pt. I, tit. xi, ii.

73. Pieter Spierenburg, *The Prison Experience* (New Brunswick, NJ: Rutgers University Press, 1991), 14.

74. Dunbabin, *Captivity and Imprisonment in Medieval Europe*, 25.

75. Spierenburg, *Prison Experience*, 14.

76. R. I. Moore, *The Formation of a Persecuting Society* (London: Basic Blackwell, 1987), 24.

77. "Cum excommunicatus aliquis pro culpa, mittantur solitarius in cellam obscuram, in solo pan et aqua . . . . Absque ullo solatio vel colloquio fratrum sedeat, nisi quem Abbatis, vel Praepositi cum eo praeceperit auctoritas ut loquatur." "Regula S. Fructuosi," in Holstenius, *Codex Regularum*, I, cap. xiv.

78. See John Ryan, S. J., *Irish Monasticism: Origins and Early Development* (Dublin & Cork: The Talbot Press, 1931), 281.

79. Johnston, *Forms of Constraint*, 22.

80. Ibid., 23.

81. Lowrie J. Daly, S.J., *Benedictine Monasticism* (New York: Sheed and Ward, 1965), 194.

82. St. John Climacus, *Ladder of Divine Ascent*, 4, 40.

83. McNeill and Gamer, *Medieval Handbooks of Penance*, 34; Johnston, *Forms of Constraint*, 19.

84. Sellin, "Dom Jean Mabillon," 584.

85. See Berman, *Law and Revolution*, 89.

86. Lanfranc, *Monastic Constitutions of Lanfranc*, 102.

87. The Camaldolese, in their constitutions (c. 1023), recommend no less than twenty days of silence in their cell for brothers guilty of a graver fault ("Illi igitur, qui culpam graviorem prepetraverint, hunc in modum Patres puniri volunt . . . . Assigneturque talibus cella propia pro carcere, et silentium eis indicatur non minus quam viginti dierum"). See "Constitutiones Congegationis Camaldulensis," in Holstenius, II, cap. xxv. See also Pugh, *Imprisonment in Medieval England*, 375–76.

88. "Et cum diversae sint culpae, et poenae debent esse diversae," "Constitutiones Congregationis Montis Oliveti," in Holstenius, V, pars. III, cap. x.

89. The code was compiled in the twelfth and thirteenth centuries and was published by Gregory IX in 1234. The latest addition dates from 1317. It remained in force until 1918. See Gabriel LeBras, "Canon Law," in C. G. Crump and E. F. Jacobs, eds., *The Legacy of the Middle Ages* (Oxford: The Clarendon Press, 1926), 321.

90. Ullmann, *Law and Politics in the Middle Ages*, 141. Frederick Pollock notes of the body of canon law after the added volume of Gregory IX in 1234: "This was an authoritative statute book; all decretals of a general import that had not

been received into it were thereby repealed, and every sentence that it contained was law." See *History of English Law Before the Time of Edward I*, 113–14.

91. Walter Ullmann, *The Growth of Papal Government in the Middle Ages* (London: Methuen & Co., 1955), 275.

92. There are a number of references in Gratian to justify *privilegium fori*. See Chodorow, *Christian Political Theory and Church Politics in the Mid-Twelfth Century*, 219–23.

93. Peters, "Prison Before the Prison," 30.

94. "Let the priest purge himself by his own veracity, by saying thus in his holy vestment, before the altar: 'I say the truth in Christ, I lie not.' Let the deacon purge himself in the same manner." "Let the common man purge himself by four of his equals, at the altar." "King Withred's Dooms Ecclesiastical (AD 696)," in Johnson, *Collection of Laws and Canons of the Church of England*, I, c. 17, 18, 21.

95. See Vaux, *Ancient Israel: Its Life and Institutions*, 155–57; Edward Peters, *Torture* (Philadelphia: University of Pennsylvania Press, 1996), 41.

96. Thomas Head, "Saints, Heretics, and Fire: Finding Meaning Through the Ordeal," in Sharon Farmer and Barbara H. Rosenwein, eds., *Monks and Nuns Saints and Outcasts: Religion in Medieval Society* (Ithaca, NY: Cornell University Press, 2000), 223–24; Johnson, *Collection of the Laws and Canons of the Church of England*, I, 341–42, n. e.

97. "King Ethelstan's Laws Ecclesiastical," in Johnson, *Collection of the Laws and Canons of the Church of England*, I, 341.

98. See Robert Bartlett, *Trial by Fire and Water* (Oxford: The Clarendon Press, 1986), 1; Dunbabin, *Captivity and Imprisonment in Medieval Europe*, 107.

99. Berman, *Law and Revolution*, 50, 64.

100. See "Fratrum Praedicatorum," in Holstenius, IV, cap. xviii, v; II, cap. xxv.

101. "Tractatus De Judiciis," in Holstenius, IV, cap. iii.

102. See Laura Ikins Stern, *The Criminal Law System of Medieval and Renaissance Florence* (Baltimore, MD: Johns Hopkins University Press, 1994), 21. See also Edward Peters, *Inquisition* (New York: The Free Press, 1988), 52.

103. Gabriel LeBras states that an important result of the formation of canon law was the transformation of imprisonment from a "purely preventive" measure to a "true punishment" involving "solitary confinement in a dungeon for the moral safeguarding of the prisoners as well as enforced inaction for the purifying of their souls." See "Canon Law," 357.

104. Dunbabin, *Captivity and Imprisonment in Medieval Europe*, 146.

105. Bingham, *Antiquities of the Christian Church*, VI, 184.

106. "[Clericus] cum indecenti veste, aut cum armis inventus fuerit, a seniore ita coerceatur, ut triginta dierum inclusione detentus, aqua tantum et modico pane diebus singulis sustentur," See "Concilium Matisconense," in Mansi, *Sacrorum Conciliorum*, IX, c. v.

107. Poschmann, *Penance and the Anointing of the Sick*, 136–37.

108. "Ecgbriht's Excerptions," in Johnson, *Collection of the Laws and Canons of the Church of England*, I, 193.

109. "Constitutions of Boniface, Archbishop of Canterbury," in Johnson, *Collection of the Laws and Canons of the Church of England*, II, c. 21.

110. "Quamvis ad reorum custodiam non ad poenam carceri specialiter deputatus esse noscatur: Nos tamen improbamus seu convictos eorum excessibus et personis, caeterisque circumstantiis provida deliberatione pensatis in perpetuum vel ad tempus prout videris expidere, carceri mancipes ad peinitnetiam peragendam." Boniface VIII, "Liber Sextus," in *Corpus Iuris Canonici* (Lyon: 1616), lib. V, tit. ix, cap. iii.

111. Peters, "Prison Before the Prison," 29.

112. Sellin, "Dom Jean Mabillon," 590–91.

113. "Constitutiones Congregationis Somasche," in Holstenius, III, lib. IV, cap. vi, c. iv.

114. "Quicumque crimen . . . pro quo in saeculo foret injungenda poena mortis, in perpetuam carcerem detrudantur." See "Constitutionum Coelestinorum Tractatus I," in Holstenius, IV, cap. xv, xviii. See also "Constitutions of Boniface," in Johnson, *Collection of the Laws and Canons of the Church of England*, II, c. 21.

115. In most cases, an edict by a provincial chapter or superior general could free the captive at any time, regardless of the severity of the sentence. So, after the statute justifying lifelong imprisonment for the incorrigible offender, the Constitutions of the Holy Spirit then state that a chapter has the power to mitigate the punishment: "Et sit in potestate praeceptus cum consilio capituli aliquando, si necesse fuerit, poenam mitigare." See, e.g., "Regula Ordinis S., Spiritus in Saxia," in Migne, *Patrologia Latina*, ccxvii, 1144. This practice dates back to the earliest church councils. See, e.g., "The Council of Nicea," c. xii; "The Council of Chalcedon," c. xvi, in Percival, "Seven Ecumenical Councils."

116. After his conviction in a ruling by the Council of Soissons, Abelard wrote: "Thereupon as if I had been a convicted criminal, I was handed over to the Abbot of St. Medard, who was there present, and led to his monastery as to a prison." See Peter Abelard, *The Story of My Misfortunes*, trans. Henry Adams Bellows (Glencoe, IL: the Free Press, 1958), ch. 10.

117. Logan, *Runaway Religious in Medieval England*, 154.

118. Sellin, "Dom Jean Mabillon," 585.

119. "Licet in charitate, et spiritu mansuetudinis, et non in virga ferrea religiosi regi debeant." "Constitutiones Congregationis Montis Oliveti," in Holstenius, V, pars. III, cap. x. "Cum poena carceris sit frequens in Constitutionibus nostris, et quanto ea sit severior, tanto majori studio charitatis indigeat." "Constitutiones Fratres B. V. Mariae de Mercde Redemptionis Captivorum," in Holstenius, III, dist. V, cap. xii, c. i.

120. "Si autem . . . Monachus aliquis alium occiderit . . . carceri perpetuo adjudicetur . . . nec possit ullo pacto liberari, nisi forte post vigesimum annum de consilio, et consensu Deffinitorum." Camaldolese Constitutions, in Holstenius, II, cap. lxx.

121. "Criminus vero, qui delicta gravia commiserunt, item scandalosi, et incorrigibiles . . . secundum criminum qualitatem in his Constitutionibus specificantur, quae nec per Abbatem Generalem, nec per Capitulum minui possint." Ibid., cap. xxi, iv.

122. Henry Kamen, *The Spanish Inquisition: A Historical Revision* (New Haven, CT: Yale University Press, 1997), 201.

123. See William Monter, *Frontiers of Heresy* (Cambridge: Cambridge University Press, 1990), 32.

124. Elias, *Civilizing Process*, I, esp. 193 ff. The prohibition against bloodshed is found in several early councils but received its formal and universal legitimacy when a canon of the Second Council of Toledo was incorporated into Gratian's *Decretum*: "His a quibus Domini sacramenta tractanda sunt, iudicium sanguinis agitare non licet." See "Concordia Discordantium Canonum," c. XXIII, q. viii, c. xxx.

125. Abelard, *Peter Abelard's Ethics*, 43.

126. "Et si forte, quod Deus avertat! tali facinore fuerit iterum deprehensus, omni vita sua absque remedio ibi habitet." "Regula Ordinis S. Spiritus In Saxia," in Migne, *Patrologia Latina* ccxvii, cap, xxxi (1144).

127. Abelard stated: "For God thinks not of what is done but in what mind it may be done, and the merit of glory of the doer lies in the intention, not in the deed." See *Peter Abelard's Ethics*, 28–29.

128. Dunbabin, *Captivity and Imprisonment in Medieval Europe*, 43.

129. Johnston, *Forms of Constraint*, 25.

130. Dunbabin, *Captivity and Imprisonment in Medieval Europe*, 144–45.

131. Thorsten Sellin, *Pioneering in Penology* (Philadelphia: University of Pennsylvania Press, 1944), 18–19.

132. Thorsten Sellin, "Filippo Franci—A Precursor of Modern Penology" *Journal of the American Institute of Criminal Law and Criminology* 17 (1926): 104–12.

133. Luigi Cajani, "Surveillance and Redemption: The Case di Correzione of San Michele a Ripa in Rome," in Norbert Finzsch and Robert Jutte, eds., *Institutions of Confinement* (Washington, DC: German Historical Institute, 1996), 314.

134. Quoted in Cajani, "Surveillance and Redemption,"314.

135. John Howard, *Prisons and Lazarettos* (Montclair, NJ: Patterson Smith, 1973), I, 114 [originally published 1789].

136. Cajani, "Surveillance and Redemption," 301.

137. Cajani, "Surveillance and Redemption," 314.

138. Ibid., 323–24.

139. "Expectatus per deim et noctem, et exhortatus primo, secundo, et tertio" ("having hoped day and night and having exhorted a first, second, and a third time"). See "Constitutiones Ordinis Fratrrm Eremitarum S. Augustini," in Holstenius, IV, pars. VI, cap. i, xiv.

140. Ibid., pars. VI, cap. vvii, vii.

141. "Fratrorum Praedicatorum," in Holstenius, IV, cap xviii, v.

142. St. Thomas Aquinas, ST, I, II, q. 95.

143. "Rigor carceris exterminium non pariat, sed ad meliora provocet delinquntem: Item declaramus . . . qud Prelati Ordinis nosti . . . possint libere punire, et corrigere fratres delinqunetes." "Constitutions of the Order of Preachers," in Holstenius, *Codex Regularum Monasticarum*, IV, cap xviii, v.

144. "In omnibus Conventibus suae Provinciae sint firmi, et fortes careceres. . .". Ibid.

145. Concerning the ransoming orders, especially the Mercedarians, see Brodman, *Ransoming Captives in Crusader Spain.*

146. "In omnibus nostris conventibus . . . sit locus securus . . . non tamen adeo rogorosus, ut in discrimen veniat salus Relisiosorusm in ibi insclusorum, et sint in eo compedes, vincula, aliaque noecssaria ad peinam, et majorem custodiam delinquentium." "Constitiones Fratres Trinitariorum," in Holstenius, VI, cap. xxi, iv, i.

147. For the Augustinians, see Holstenius, IV, pars. VI, cap. xvii, i; for the Norbertines (Premonstraterians), see Holstenius, V, dist. III, cap. xiv, x.

148. "Culpae levi . . . poena levis correspondeat. Imponatur scilicet aliquis psalmus recitandus, vel oratio." Poena media . . . poena etiam media plectatur . . . exosculatio terrae penes cujusue accumbentis pedes." See "Constitutiones Congregationis Somasche," Holstenius, III, lib. IV, cap. ii, c. 1, iii.

149. "Constitutiones Fratrum Praedicatorum," in Holstenius, IV, cap. xvi (*levi culpa*), cap. xvii (*gravi culpa*), cap. xviii (*graviori culpa*), cap. xix (*gravissima culpa*), cap. xx (*de aapostatis*). See also Logan, *Runaway Religious in Medieval England*, 149–50.

150. See, e.g., "Statua Ordinis Praemonstratensis," in Holstenius, V, dist. III, cap. ix, 3.

151. What was known as the "circular discipline" was a common practice in all of the religious communities of that era. Self-flagellation for penitential purposes was normally mandated for all religious, male and female. Those who violated the behavioral norms, however, would bare their shoulders, usually in the refectory, and receive the discipline from the community with a rope made of knotted cords. See St. Theresa of Avila, "The Constitutions," in *The Collected Works of St. Teresa of Avila*, trans. Kieran Kavanaugh, O.C.D., and Otilio Rodriguez, O. C. D. (Washington, DC: ICS Publications, 1985), III, 455, n. 25.

152. The nuns such as the Carmelites were under the authority of the prior general of the Carmelite men. He would either visit the houses himself or, as in the case of the Carmelites with many convents, send a visitator.

153. St. Teresa of Avila, "The Constitutions," III, 18, 52, 55.

154. Federico Ruiz, O. C. D., et al., *God Speaks in the Night: The Life, Times, and Teaching of St. John of the Cross* (Washington, DC: ICS Publications, 1991), 163.

155. Gratian, who otherwise follows the tradition that force should not be used to induce belief, nevertheless made exception when it came to preserving the integrity of the believing community. See "Concordia Discordantium Canonum," in *Corpus Iuris Canonici*, dist. 45, c.4, c. 5.

156. Peters, *Inquisition*, 48.

157. On the use of *persuasio* and coercion, see Peters, *Inquisition*, 44–52.

158. "A Manual for Inquisitors," in Walter L. Wakefield, *Heresy, Crusade and Inquisition in Southern France* (Berkeley: University of California Press, 1974), 251.

159. Among those whose theological views supported the sentence of death for those convicted of heresy was Aquinas: "[I]f the heretic still remains pertinacious the church, despairing of his conversion, provides for the Salvation of others by separating him from the church by the sentence of excommunication and then leaves him to the secular judge to be exterminated from the world by death." See ST, II. II, q. 11, a.3.

160. "Ego, auctoritate Dei et officii inquisiationis heretice pravitatis qua fungor, vos absolvo a sententiis excommunicationis quas incurristis proper illa que commisistis contra officium inquisitionis de quibus estis confessi in judicio coram nobis, si tamen de corde bono et fide non ficta ad Ecclesiae redieritis unitatem et si plenam et meram confessi estis de vobis de aliis judicio veritatem." See Bernard Gui, *Manuel De L'Inquisiteur*, trans. G. Mollat (Paris: Librairie Ancienne Honoré Champion, 1926), II, 138.

161. Wakefield, "Manual for Inquisitors," 254.

162. Ibid., 257. It was a common practice to confiscate the goods of heretics and even to allow the latter to be held as slaves. See Burns, *Las Siete Partidas*, pt. I, tit. ix, xxxviii.

163. Johnston, *Forms of Constraint*, 26.

164. Dunbabin, *Captivity and Imprisonment in Medieval Europe*, 157.

165. Kamen, *Spanish Inquisition*, 201. Monter suggests that lifelong incarceration was normally seven years. See *Frontiers of Heresy*, 128–29.

166. Innocent issued the decretal Cum ex officii nostri in 1207. See Peters, *Inquisition*, 49.

167. Johnston, *Forms of Constraint*, 26.

168. Henry Charles Lea, *A History of the Inquisition of the Middle Ages* (New York: Harper & Brothers, 1888), I, 334, 342; Dunbabin, *Captivity and Imprisonment in Medieval Europe*, 154–55.

169. Kamen, *Spanish Inquisition*, 201.

170. *Murus* is the Latin word for wall. Since, often, prisons were constructed along the walls of monasteries, the term became a synonym for prison in medieval usage. On the two types of facilities, see Peters, *Inquisition*, 66.

171. Monter, *Frontiers of Heresy*, 32.

172. Isabel Barbeito, ed., *Carceles y Mujeres En El Siglo XVII* (Madrid: Editorial Castalia, 1991), 26.

173. Monter goes on to write that "among the 2,000 *conversos* tried at Valencia before 1530, only twelve were tortured, although hundreds of them were executed." See *Frontiers of Heresy*, 75.

174. Peters, *Prison Before the Prison*, 31.

175. Lea, *History of the Inquisition of the Middle Ages*, I, 420–21.

176. Walter Wakefield, "Friar Ferrier, Inquisition at Cannes, and Escapes from the Prison at Carcassone," *The Catholic Historical Review* 58 (1972): 222.

177. See Peters, *Torture*, 52.

178. Malcolm Barber, *The Trial of the Templars* (Cambridge: Cambridge University Press, 1978), 1, 57–58.

179. A person was tied to the rack and the joints of the ankles and wrists were contorted until dislocated. The strappado featured the hands tied behind the back and attached to a rope that was then hoisted and allowed to fall; "at times a weight was attached to the feet or the testicles to add to the shock of the fall." Ibid., 56.

180. Ibid., 2–3.

181. Dunbabin, *Captivity and Imprisonment in Medieval Europe*, 108.

182. "To no one do we deny a legitimate defense nor do we deviate from established ecclesiastical procedure, except that we do not make public the names of witnesses, because of the decree of the Apostolic See, wisely made by Lord Gregory." See "A Manual for Inquisitors," in Wakefield, *Heresy, Crusade and Inquisition*, 253.

183. Given, *Inquisition and Medieval Society*, 62, 82.

184. Kamen, *Spanish Inquisition*, 201.

185. Lactantius, "The Divine Institutes," in Rev. Alexander Roberts and John Donaldson, eds., *Ante-Nicene Fathers*, vol. VII (New York: Charles Scriber's Sons, 1925), bk. VI, ch. 10.

186. Quoted in Barbeito, *Carceles y Mujeres En El Siglo XVII*, 14.

187. See Sellin, "Dom Jean Mabillon," 585; Thomas Dudley Fosbroke, *British Monachism*, third edition (London: M. A. Nattali, 1843), 261.

188. "Sequaces vero itidem confessi vel convicti, his exceptus qui abeis seducti correptique facile resipiscant, ferro calido frontem et facies signat, pellantur." See "Remense Concilium," in Mansi, *Sacrorum Conciliorum*, XXI, c. i. The sentence recommended for women who fled captivity in seventeenth-century Spain also was branding. See Barbeito, *Carceles y Mujeres En El Siglo XVII*, 81.

189. "Ha de haber en esta Galera todo genero de prisiones, cadenas . . . y mordazas, cepos y disciplina de todas hechuras, de cordeles y hierro; que de solo ver instrumentos se atemoricen y espanten, porque como esta ha de der como una carcel muy penosa, conviene que haya grande rigor." Barbeito, *Carceles y Mujeres En El Siglo XVII*, 79.

190. Dunbabin, *Captivity and Imprisonment in Medieval Europe*, 153.

191. Ibid., 158, 173.

192. Quoted in Given, *Inquisition and Medieval Society*, 54.

193. Quoted in Cajani, "Surveillance and Redemption," 318.

5

The Prison and Secular Society

The ideals of reform and cellular isolation in church prisons were not reflected in secular prisons . . . . It was only at the close of the eighteenth century that civil authorities, searching for a substitute for the usual penalties of death, mutilation, or exile, began to use imprisonment on a large scale as punishment, often inspired by church teachings.

—Norman Johnston

The last chapter concluded with the question of whether imprisonment as conceived and practiced within the Roman Catholic tradition was an innovation worthy of praise or recrimination. That question is for the reader to decide. What is not in question is whether the approach taken was considered worthy of imitation. In this chapter we look at the impact of the Catholic understanding of criminal justice on the world around its monasteries, churches, and prison walls. We begin where we left off and ask: Assuming that the method of imprisonment developed by the church was in many ways a model for secular society, to what degree was it also a model *of* the social environment? We then describe briefly some of the dominant themes and practices in the history of civil prosecution of criminal offenses and detail the specific ways these were influenced by the church.

SECULAR JUSTICE AND THE CHURCH

It was mentioned in the first chapter that the early Christians did all in their power to distinguish themselves from those who did not share their faith. For them, the world was composed of, at least in ideological terms, light and darkness, or, using Augustine's imagery, the world was characterized by two cities: one bound for eternal glory and one destined for eternal damnation. We saw, however, that sectarian impulses of difference and separation were frequently compromised by factors such as spatial proximity and shared language, and that formerly "pagan" individuals did not automatically lose all of their formative influences once they converted to Christianity.

We further saw in chapter two that, beginning with the writings of Augustine, and especially those of Aquinas, there was recognition and acceptance within the Catholic Church, a formal acceptance that remains to this day, that the earthly and ecclesial realms are companions in the social project, each with a vital and, we might add, divinely appointed function. There has been an extensive body of theological literature that has reflected upon this mixed marriage, and in every age voices have been raised declaring the union unholy and requiring permanent dissolution. Despite this, the teachings of the official church and the majority of those in the field of Catholic social ethics still insist that part and parcel of the church's mission, particularly since Vatican II, is the need to engage and learn from the world as much as to teach and evangelize it.[1]

Nor has this church–world exchange lacked reciprocity if one takes a historical view. Certainly, as Ullmann among others has pointed out, the translation of the Bible into Latin by St. Jerome brought notions of Roman law into Christian consciousness along with the teachings of Jesus.[2] Recall also that much of the legislation in canon law dealing with persons and property, especially as these relate to marriage, contracts, and crime, borrowed generously from Roman law, specifically the influential Florentine manuscript of the Digest of Justinian, which had been discovered around 1070 by an Italian canonist.[3] One legal historian states unequivocally: "a world without the Digest would not have been the world we know."[4] Thus, despite the theocratic assertions of Pope Gregory VII in the "Dictatus Papae" and Pope Boniface VIII in Unam Sanctam that the "two swords" spoken of in the Bible (Lk 22:38) regarding spiritual and temporal power both belonged to the pope, canon law, beginning with the work of Gratian and the Bolognese school, accepted the classic formulation of Pope Gelasius I (492–496) that the two powers existed in a cooperative independence.[5]

Furthermore, history bears witness to corrupt ecclesiastical officials being chided and schooled by the moral perceptiveness and moral courage of laypeople, both of high and low rank. Secular rulers intervened on a number of occasions on behalf of monks who were tortured and abused by their own brothers: Charlemagne responded to the pleas of some of the monks of the monastery at Fulda to put an end to torture of the prisoners confined there and, a "horrified" King John, having been apprised of the *Vade in Pace* prisons, ordered all priors and religious superiors to visit their prisoners at least twice a month and delegate two monastic ombudsmen similarly to visit the confined and ensure that they were treated humanely.[6] In the late thirteenth century, the consuls of Carcassone addressed a complaint to the warden of the inquisitorial prison in their locality. They stated that the prison "could be called with good cause a hell." The "little cells" held "miserable wretches with shackles" unable to move who were left to "defecate and urinate on themselves." Although the complaint may have been exaggerated, it represents what was not an uncommon example of lay opposition to and influence upon ecclesiastical penal practice.[7]

SECULAR JUSTICE AND SECULAR PRISONS

A principal reason why the prison emerged in the Catholic tradition was the incompatibility of secular justice with Christian principles. As noted in the opening chapter, prisons were rarely used by civil rulers in the first millennium, and only in a restricted sense for much of the second. Not only were they costly to maintain, but there was no justification for their employment aside from the need to detain suspects prior to trial and the guilty prior to execution of sentence.[8] As late as the twelfth century, many counties in England still lacked both jails and prison cells.[9] Not surprisingly, imprisonment receives virtually no recognition in early collections of law. For example, in the Lombard Laws of the seventh and eighth centuries there is only one instance of confinement for the purpose of punishment.[10] Similarly, a code of laws dating from the time of King Alfred (849–899) contains only a single reference to imprisonment: one who fails to adhere to a pledge is to be confined in a royal manor.[11] The most common punishments in the ancient codes were fines, and in more serious cases, either death or mutilation. An example of the latter is found in the Laws of Cnut. Concerning a culprit who was found "foul" after the ordeal, the ordinance states: "[Let] his hands be cut off or his feet, or both, according as the deed may be and, if then, he have wrought yet greater wrong, then let his eyes be put out, or his nose and his ears and the upper lip be cut off, or let him be scalped . . . so that punishment be inflicted and also the soul preserved."[12]

Dunbabin notes that the literary evidence for imprisonment begins to accumulate precisely at the time that castles were being built throughout Southern France. This corresponds to the evidence presented in the last chapter that the early prisons were most often located in gatehouses, towers, or dungeons.[13] Newgate prison in England, dating from the early twelfth century, was originally constructed adjacent to the city gate, but by 1236 was located in one of the turrets of the gate.[14] In the literature on the miraculous redemption of prisoners, much of it dating from the twelfth and thirteenth centuries, Our Lady of Rocamadour frees a knight from "the dungeon at the bottom of the tower," and Ste. Foy rescues one held in coercive confinement in "the dark foul depths of the tower," and another bound in chains "in a chamber outside the tower."[15]

As the repercussions of the legal revolution initiated in the pontificate of Gregory VII began to alter the face of church and society, clearer comparisons could be drawn between the ecclesiastical and secular approaches to justice. The latter was far more severe. As we saw in the last chapter, clerics arrested for civil offenses could claim benefit of clergy, often to the dismay of their captors, and even if tried and found guilty in the king's court, would normally receive their sentence from an ecclesiastical tribunal and be detained in church-run facilities. However painful a stint in the bishop's prison may have been, it would have been preferable to "brutal corporal punishment or death," which increasingly became the normal fate of the convicted in the secular realm.[16]

In the early Middle Ages, one notes a shift from the payment of fines to payment in blood. This can be traced to the evolution of the term *felony*. Deriving from the Latin verb "to fail" (*fallere*), it was initially used in France and Normandy in conjunction with "the most heinous of all crimes": the betrayal of one's lord or, simply put, treason. However, Maitland points out that in England by the end of the twelfth century felony took on a dramatically broader meaning: every crime of great gravity became a capital offense.[17] France was little different in its application of the sword to a host of offenses. The Laws of Saint Louis never took on official status but were widely copied and, according to a number of scholars, revealed the customary mindset of thirteenth-century life. Concerning brigands who loot travelers on the highway or in the forest, the law states that "all those who commit this offense must be hanged and drawn." Another law reads as follows: "[A] person who burns down a house by night loses his eyes. A person stealing something from a church . . . should lose his ear for the first offense, for the next theft he loses a foot, and at the third theft he is to be hanged."[18] In Florence, a law was passed in 1325 concerning persons committing sodomy with young boys: the violator was to have his testicles cut off and the house where the act was perpetrated was to be burned down.[19]

If the convicted had little hope of avoiding the noose or the knife, life in the jails of the Middle Ages did little to diminish the pending sense of doom. Henry Lea dubs them "frightful abodes of misery." Lords and municipal governments were unwilling to divert public funds to their upkeep and, as for the debtor, "the worse he was treated the greater effort he would make to release himself."[20] Detainees of the common classes were almost always placed in chains; the environment was usually dark, damp, and infested with disease; and the fact that they were of lowly means did not, in most instances, summon compassion from the keepers: inmates were expected to pay for their food.[21] While punitive imprisonment was not often employed, it was certainly a common occurrence at Newgate. Whether from vengeance or out of a strategy of selective incapacitation, many of the detainees only left their cells to be buried. Small wonder that, as one historian claims, "Newgate acquired a sinister reputation."[22]

Florentine criminal justice essentially prepared the convict for a life in hell by approximating hell in its jails and dungeons.[23] Machiavelli experienced this justice firsthand, having been arrested, incarcerated, and tortured due to a slanderous assertion that he was an accomplice in a conspiracy to assassinate a political official. He endured six turns on the rack and, in the poems he penned while confined, he depicts the torture of others, including the use of the infamous strappado.[24]

The prosecution of criminal acts struck a similar tone in Siena. Aside from the cold, dark, and foul atmosphere, the commune that administered the city initiated a phenomenon popular once again in our own day: hiring private companies to oversee penal operations. The results were dire, as the entrepreneurs strove to recover their investment and make a profit by doing as little as humanly possible for the prisoners. When the city council decided in 1327 to forgo the practice of subcontracting criminal justice and erect communal prisons, it was noted in the proceedings that sixty persons had perished in detention in only two years as a result of the wretched conditions.[25]

The sixteenth century saw the elevation of the state into the realm of the sacred and the consequent public festivals of torture for assailants upon the "body politic."[26] The new sense of social identity and social solidarity required the expression of "public anger" through ritual reproduction; there was "an integrating element in punishment," and it was stimulated by the repression of that "outrage to morality" that we know as crime.[27] In view of this, secular frustration at felonious clerics circumventing rightful punishment at the hands of the state had moral legitimacy, even if the way punishment was exercised did not. In England in 1351, magistrates expressed that very complaint, arguing that roguish clerics were, quite literally, getting away with murder. Trevor Dean explains: "Church courts lacked the power to impose 'penalties of blood': their only punitive option was imprisonment. Moreover, their greater aim, dictated by Christian charity, was to heal the hurt of crime through penance and reconciliation. Lay people might find this unsatisfactory."[28]

When the power of lay authorities was sufficient to overcome ecclesiastical mandate the results were not surprising. In Siena, the municipal officials spared no expense, and even endured threats of excommunication, to try a priest accused of homicide at the end of the thirteenth century. The priest was found guilty and subsequently decapitated.[29] An interesting footnote to the dispute is that an agreement was reached between the bishop and the commune in 1297. The magistrates conceded that clerics deserving the death penalty would be sentenced to life imprisonment, but were granted the provision that the guilty serve their sentence in the communal prison rather than in one run by the church.[30] The execution of Prior Bertulf, authorized by the King of France in 1127, was another matter entirely:

> He was stripped except for his trousers . . . being pelted with rocks and filth and struck with sticks as he passed. When he reached the gallows, his arms were outstretched . . . and his neck placed in a fixed noose so that he could just reach the ground with his tiptoes. His trousers were then pulled down around his feet. When his executioner . . . gave the command, the people . . . rushed upon Bertulf, striking him with clubs and bailing hooks, and kicking his feet from under him so that he swung by the neck. As he was dying, the guts of a dog were tied around his neck and its muzzle stuffed in his mouth. His body was then tied to a cart wheel and hung from a tall tree for everyone to ponder on.[31]

These admittedly anecdotal references reflect what most historians of this subject attest: the church and civil society had fundamentally different approaches to criminal justice until the idea of the penitentiary suddenly transformed the landscape and ideology of criminal justice at the end of the eighteenth century.

CATHOLIC EFFECTS ON SECULAR JUSTICE

The amelioration of the deplorable conditions in which most prisoners dwelt throughout much of Western history can be tied to the embodiment of the ideals of criminal justice that originated within the church. Ralph Pugh observes that penal improvements in the Christian West may be seen in relation to the commitment to incarcerate not primarily for custody's sake, nor for financial or vindictive motives, but to "furnish opportunities for reflection upon past misdeeds and change of heart."[32]

As we have noted, the formal separation of church and state led to the creation of the first legal system, canon law, but also the first secular legal systems. Given the fact that the two realms existed in the same social space and had such a long history of mutual influence, emerging secular juridical concepts proceeded from the same religious metaphors that guided the creation of canon law: the four last things (death, judgment, heaven, hell) as well as the ritual of penance. Berman states: "It is impossible to understand the revolutionary quality of the Western legal tradition without exploring its religious dimension."[33]

We saw that the inquisitorial procedure transformed the structure of law and the manner of its use. Among the elements adopted by canon law and to which both modern criminal procedure and legal practice are indebted was the reliance on the "minute and detailed analysis of the circumstances of sin." As noted, this became particularly relevant when crime and sin were formally separated with the creation of canon law.[34] There also arose in secular jurisprudence at this time the judicial inquest and the "judicial pilgrimage." The latter became a part of the civil law of Europe due to its regular employment by the church, particularly by the Inquisition, which began to use it as a penance for minor offences in the early years of the thirteenth century.[35]

Slowly the shape of punishment in the West came to reflect the belief that time could be an agent not only in retributive justice but also in the amelioration of the behavior of the convict. Early evidence of this innovation in secular thinking can be seen in Le Carceri delle Stinche in Florence where, despite the "ominous end" in store for traitors and those guilty of capital crime, "the idea of imprisonment as a form of punishment *per se* without subsequent flogging, mutilation, or branding became an integral part of Florentine penal law."[36] Even more noteworthy was the creation of the workhouse, "the Bridewell," in England and in many areas of the continent in the late sixteenth century. Based on a family model, the idea was to instill diligence and industry in the residents through productive labor and a "paternal" sense of care for the inhabitants.[37] As one Dutch magistrate phrased it, the aim of the institution was to make the prisoners "healthy, temperate eaters, used to labor, desirous of holding a good job, capable of standing on their own feet, and God-fearing."[38] Many have correctly noted that the workhouse is a precursor of modern secular penology, but both its philosophy and structure owe their inspiration to the monastic and ecclesiastical prisons. As Sellin notes: "Many of the features of the English workhouse . . . were not

English innovations at all, but had earlier counterparts on the Continent."[39] Johnston states that "there clearly was a Christian influence upon the later workhouse movement . . . . Certainly it can be said that the Church dogma of the reformation of prisoners left a strong imprint upon later thought and social theory."[40]

Various monarchs relied not only on imprisonment as shaped by Christian tradition, they also began to employ a penitential vocabulary in relation to it. Inmates, after their sentence and in some cases before its termination, would occasionally be granted pardon. Letters of pardon, such as those issued in France in the latter half of the fourteenth century, used "the vocabulary of penance, apparently inspired by canon law and ecclesiastical models" and were "issued on important Christian festivals such as Easter." In fifteenth-century Castille, King Juan II issued a decree that all petitions for clemency should be kept until "the day of pardon," Good Friday. On that day, on the advice of his confessor, he would then select an appropriate number to be released. In Siena, at the groundbreaking of the city's penitentiary, all of the clergy were present to lead the people in psalms and prayers.[41]

The most substantial evidence, however, of the influence of Catholic practice on the shape of secular criminal justice came with the creation of the penitentiaries in England and especially in the United States. America developed two prototypical penitentiaries with conflicting theological and organizational bases. In one, at Auburn in New York, the innovations at St. Michael's and many ecclesiastical facilities provided the inspiration for the "separate system": work in common and in silence during the day, separate cells at night. The innovations of Mabillon, and the general monastic prison culture that he promoted, became the basis of the silent system at the Eastern State Penitentiary in Philadelphia.[42] These penitentiaries were very much at the forefront of public consciousness for several decades and their variations on penal organization were vociferously debated, in the United States and around the world. The debate was fostered by the desire to change the meaning and structure of criminal justice. One of the reasons for the strength of the American influence was the caliber of ambassadors who came from around the world to study its "experiment" in corrections. Authors such as Alexis de Toqueville and Charles Dickens visited and commented upon the new prisons—de Toqueville wrote *Democracy in America* while on this investigative journey.[43] It would take too long to go into the history and specific methodologies of these facilities in detail but, though reflecting variations on the two types of church prisons previously described, each believed, as did their ecclesiastical forebears, that the combination of work, silence, prayer, and spiritual counsel could mend what was wrong in the human heart. Johnston asserts that these prisons "must be regarded as the indirect outgrowth of the uses of imprisonment by the Christian church."[44] Sellin, referencing the work of Karl Kraus, states, concerning Mabillon's reflections:

> Aside from their revolutionary ideas on penal treatment, they throw light on the real sources of our entire penitentiary system for the correction of delinquents. These sources must be looked for in the Church and particularly in those bodies which regarded silence, isolation, and self-inflicted mental and physical pain as the road to salvation. In a sense, therefore, Mabillon was but the mouthpiece of that 'old ecclesiastical spirit of penance out of which grew the penitentiary system, which was later and in another form applied to the worldly prisons.[45]

These revolutionary penal developments, undertaken in significant part by Protestant clergy, were not conceived with a specific emphasis on the image of Christ the prisoner; but these reformers were still expressing the idea that the meaning of confinement, and the penitentiary as its expression, has a fundamentally religious dimension and that punishment, as we noted in the second chapter, does not accomplish its intended meaning until it is willed by the offender and used as a medicine leading to his or her own reform.

Other familiar concepts and practices that had their origin in innovations undertaken within church circles include parole, day release, separate institutions for juveniles, and judicial discretion in sentencing. We have noted the work of Filippo Franci and his contemporaries in the detention and reform of troubled adolescents. Inquisitors in France instituted a form of probation for those whose views were not considered dangerous, while an early form of parole was instituted for those whose "perpetual sentences" were reduced and they were provided freedom contingent upon certain behavioral and especially ideological constraints.[46]

The ecclesiastical vocabulary of corrections influenced and continues to exercise influence on the penal and legal format instituted within secular polities. Words like cell, penitentiary, and reformatory trace themselves to the ancient origins of confinement in the church. When, at the end of the nineteenth century, religious language was edited in favor of the optimistic secularized language of the Progressive Era, the "old wine" was in many ways poured into "new wineskins" (Mt 9:17). The penal welfare model that ensued, and lasted almost without interruption into the last decades of the twentieth century, was dominated by secular synonyms for a correctional methodology dating back to the dawn of the Christian era: intervention, diagnosis, treatment, and rehabilitation. As one author states:

> An earlier era reckoned there was something wrong with an offender's soul or spiritual life and a change had to be affected through penitential solitude . . . . The more recent version reckons something is awry with an offender's mind or psychological and social adjustment . . . . A change in language accompanies the treatment model of imprisonment: prisoners become "residents" . . . guards become "correctional officers," solitary confinement cells become "adjustment units."[47]

Finally, we should mention the "official" ecclesial recognition in the thirteenth century of purgatory (the prison in the next life). It is not without consequence, given the reliance of legal concepts and metaphors on spiritual commitments, that incarceration in purgatory emerged at precisely the same time that the prison was normalized as the means of both expressing societal disapproval and encouraging the purification of the soul's sinful elements. Purgatory altered the way the geography of the cosmic world is shaped and, in turn, revolutionized the way time has been understood in precise fragments, measured against the reality of judgment for our deeds and their necessary recompense in this life or the next.[48]

The legacy of the Catholic practice of criminal justice has loomed large in the development of the Western penal system. However, despite the architectural remnant of the old penitentiary, despite linguistic metaphors still reproduced or transmuted into more contemporary forms of discourse, and despite the persistence of time as an expression of both social dissatisfaction and the meaning of confinement, that influence has been dramatically reduced. Or to put it differently, the structure of criminal justice has never been farther from what the early architects of the penal system intended it to be. Whether we are better off now than then is open for debate. Our final task is to summarize what has been presented thus far and offer, within the constraints of the method selected, a Catholic theory of criminal justice.

NOTES

1. See *Catechism of the Catholic Church,* (New York: Doubleday, 1995), nos. 2234–46; Pontifical Council for Justice and Peace, *Compendium of the Social Doctrine of the Church* (Washington, DC: United States Conference of Catholic Bishops, 2005), nos. 425, 427; Walter M. Abbot, S. J., ed., "Pastoral Constitution on

the Church in the Modern World," in *The Documents of Vatican II* (New York: Guild Press, 1966), no. 44. See also Himes and Himes, *Fullness of Faith*; David Hollenbach, S.J., *The Common Good and Christian Ethics* (Cambridge: Cambridge University Press, 2002), chs. 4, 5.

2. Ullmann, *Law and Politics in the Middle Ages*, 42–45.

3. See LeBras, "Canon Law," 323. See also Stephen Kuttner, "The Revival of Jurisprudence," in Robert L. Benson and Giles Constable, eds., *Renaissance and Renewal in the Twelfth Century* (Cambridge, MA: Harvard University Press, 1982), 299–323.

4. Pollock, *The History of English Law Before the Time of Edward I*, I, 10.

5. LeBras, "Canon Law," 336–37. Gratian wrote that when a relevant church law does not cover a specific case then full obedience must be given to secular law. See Chodorow, *Christian Political Theory and Church Politics in the Mid-Twelfth Century*, 215.

6. Sellin, "Dom Jean Mabilllon," 584–86.

7. See Given, *Inquisition and Medieval Society*, 64.

8. Johnston, *Forms of Constraint*, 1; Pugh, *Imprisonment in Medieval England*, 2.

9. See Ives, *History of Penal Methods*, 10; Pollock, *History of English Law Before the Time of Edward I*, I, 49.

10. "In connection with thieves, each judge shall make a prison underground in his district. When a thief has been found, he shall pay composition for his theft, and then the judge shall cease him and put in prison for two or three years, and afterwards shall set him free." See *The Lombard Laws*, trans. Katherine Fischer Drew (Philadelphia: University of Pennsylvania Press, 1973), no. 80. It may be of some consequence that the sovereign, Liutprand, was a Catholic.

11. Pugh, *Imprisonment in Medieval England*, 1–2.

12. Quoted in Ives, *History of Penal Methods*, 8.

13. Dunbabin, *Captivity and Imprisonment in Medieval Europe*, 23, 36.

14. Margery Bassett, "Newgate Prison in the Middle Ages," *Speculum* 18 (1943): 234.

15. See Bell, *Miracles of Our Lady of Rocamadour*, 153–54; Sheingorn, *Book of Sainte Foy*, 149–50, 164.

16. Johnston, *Forms of Constraint*, 22.

17. Maitland, *Constitutional History of England*, 110.

18. *The Establissements de Saint Louis*, trans. F. R. P. Akehurst (Philadelphia: University of Pennsylvania Press, 1996), xii, bk. I, nos. 28, 32.

19. Dean, *Crime in Medieval Europe*, 61.

20. Lea, *History of the Inquisition of the Middle Ages*, I, 488.

21. Dunbabin, *Captivity and Imprisonment in the Middle Ages*, 121–22; Ralph Pugh, *Imprisonment in Medieval England*, 316.

22. Bassett, "Newgate Prison in the Middle Ages," 233–34.

23. Samuel Edgerton notes that it was "uncompromising, harsh, and eschatologically anchored to the proposition that just as the sinner's immortal soul will suffer forever in hell, so his living body must be punished on earth." See *Pictures and Punishment*, 13.

24. Wolfgang, "A Florentine Prison," 150–51.

25. William M. Bowsky, *A Medieval Italian Commune: Siena Under the Nine* (Berkeley: University of California Press, 1981), 117.

26. "The metaphor of the body politic helps us to read more clearly the presence of that other body at an execution, that of the condemned. Its occurrence reminds us that the punishment of the offender's body had as much to do with a language of community as it did with the mechanics of pain." See McGowen, "The Body and Punishment in Eighteenth-Century England," 654. See also Dean, *Crime in Medieval Europe*, 130.

27. Durkheim, *Division of Labor in Society*, 47, 57–58.

28. Dean, *Crime in Medieval Europe*, 109.

29. Bowsky, *A Medieval Italian Commune*, 110–111.

30. Ibid., 111.

31. Herman of Tournai, *The Restoration of the Monastery of St Martin of Tournai*, trans. Lynn H. Nelson (Washington, DC: Catholic University of America Press, 1996), 203, n. 11.

32. Pugh, *Imprisonment in Medieval England*, 18.

33. Berman, *Law and Revolution*, 165.

34. LeBras, "Canon Law," 357.

35. See Peters, *Torture*, 44; Jonathan Sumption, *Pilgrimage: An Image of Medieval Religion* (London: Faber & Faber, 1975), 104.

36. Wolfgang, "A Florentine Prison," 156, 164.

37. See Pieter Spierenburg, "The Body and the State," in Norval Morris and David Rothman, eds., *The Oxford History of the Prison* (New York: Oxford University Press, 1995), 68–72; Sellin, *Pioneering in Penology*, 17.

38. Sellin, *Pioneering in Penology*, 27.

39. Sellin, *Pioneering in Penology*, 22.

40. Johnston, *Forms of Constraint*, 27.

41. Dean, *Crime in Medieval Europe*, 134–35.

42. There is a vast body of literature discussing the rise of the penitentiary and particularly the two prototypical penitentiaries at Auburn and Philadelphia. Historical overviews are provided by W. David Lewis, *From Newgate to Dannemora* (Ithaca, NY: Cornell University Press, 1965) and Negley K. Teeters and John D. Shearer, *The Prison at Philadelphia Cherry Hill* (New York: Columbia University Press, 1957). There are other well-known works that tell the story well but do not uncover, or simply dismiss, the religious dimension of these facilities. See, e.g., Blake McKelvey, *American Prisons: A History of Good Intentions* (Montclair, NJ: Patterson Smith, 1977); David Rothman, *The Discovery of the Asylum* (Boston: Little Brown, 1971). An account of the British penitentiaries and a critical appraisal of the role of religion in their development is provided by Michael Ignatieff. See *A Just Measure of Pain* (New York: Pantheon, 1978). See also my own account of this period: Andrew Skotnicki, *Religion and the Development of the American Penal System* (Lanham, MD: University Press of America, 2000).

43. Gustave de Beaumont and Alexis de Toqueville, *On the Penitentiary System in the United States and its Application in France*, trans. Francis Lieber (Philadelphia: Carey, Lea, and Blanchard, 1833); Charles Dickens, *American Notes* (Greenwich, CT: Fawcett, 1961) [originally published 1843].

44. Johnston, *Forms of Constraint*, 27.

45. Sellin, "Dom Jean Mabillon," 600–601.

46. Given, *Inquisition and Medieval Society*, 61, 67; Sellin, "Filippo Franci—A Precursor of Modern Penology."

47. Griffith, *The Fall of the Prison*, 40–41. See also Graeme Newman, *Just and Painful* (New York: Harrow and Heston, 1995), 82–83.

48. See Richard Fenn, *The Persistence of Purgatory* (Cambridge: Cambridge University Press, 1995); Jacques Le Goff, *The Birth of Purgatory*, trans. Arthur Goldhammer (Chicago: University of Chicago Press, 1984; Andrew Skotnicki, "God's Prisoners: Penal Confinement and the Creation of Purgatory," *Modern Theology* 22 (2006): 85–110.

6

A Catholic Theory of Criminal Justice

As I go about in these chains, invested with a title worthy of a god . . .

—St. Ignatius of Antioch

Remember that I am a prisoner.

—Colossians 4:18

"A mutation in morals bewilders," writes John Noonan.[1] His words provide a more than apt starting point for reflecting upon what could well be called the bewildering overview of how the church has confronted the challenges posed by sin and crime.

The approach taken in this volume has been to respond to the four foundational questions that any theory of criminal justice addresses: Who is the one deserving of punishment? By what justification is he or she punished? What is the purpose or end of the punitive action? By what circumstances can this end be brought about? In this final chapter, I summarize the evidence presented heretofore and note its consistency with the fundamental ideas about punishment that have become apparent in our survey of Catholic penal history: its harmony with a Gospel vision of Christ identifying with the least of our fellow humans, particularly the confined, and with the normative emphases in Catholic social thought. It can be stated at this point that a strong current exists within the tradition to support the conclusions about to be presented, although parallel and contradictory patterns exist as well. After this summary, I address two further points: the disturbing trends in contemporary corrections and the value of the Catholic position in relation to those trends.

ELEMENTS OF THE THEORY

If criminologists are correct in asserting that crime is a social fabrication, a fact borne out repeatedly in the history we have surveyed, then the limits and breadth of a given culture's moral imagination have as much to do with crime as do the actions of its citizens. Anything is potentially unlawful or, in the words of Nils Christie, "Acts with the potentiality to be seen as crimes are like an unlimited natural resource."[2]

The importance of the image imparted to the fallen, regardless of how universal the penchant to fall, has been a consistent theme throughout this volume. The contention argued and now repeated here is that the path to criminal justice cannot be traveled faithfully until Christ is imaged as the prisoner. Just as Christ cannot change the circumstances of his birth to lowly parents in a barn in Bethlehem, so he cannot change the manner of his death as a condemned criminal. Christ is a prisoner. It is a significant part of his story; it is inscribed in the scars upon his body.

The second contention presented here concerns the keepers of the kept. What image should they strive to imitate? The faithful witness of the tradition is one that utilizes a parental or familial model with a commitment to the liberation of the one being disciplined from any internal or external punitive constraint.

There is much evidence in the history of the church to recommend the veracity of both portraits. There have been many like St. John Climacus, who made himself a prisoner to share the burden and hope of his captive brothers, and St. Teresa of Avila was not alone in her very human warning that no prisoner find grounds for legitimate complaint: "I am afraid the devil will be subjecting these sisters to fresh temptations now, and telling them they are disliked and being ill-treated. I should be extremely annoyed if they were given any excuse for thinking that."[3] In more recent times, Pope Pius XII summarized the best of the tradition when he stressed that three attitudes must mark our thinking about the imprisoned: sincere pardon, belief in the good of other people, and love like that of the Lord;[4] while a key document of the Second Vatican Council states: "In our times a special obligation binds us to make ourselves the neighbor of absolutely every person."[5]

Some of the force behind the rejection of the death penalty and torture by the church can be attributed to the accommodation of its moral doctrine to a vision of Christ confined. As many are aware, the church long justified the death penalty in conjunction with its commitment to the primacy of the common good: killing cannot be a legitimate end but one can kill a threat to the well-being of the social body.[6] Recently, however, the church has amended its teaching in favor of a commitment similar to the one enunciated by Ambrose: "God, who preferred the correction rather than the death of the sinner, did not desire that a homicide be punished by the exaction of another homicide."[7] Current doctrine maintains that it is virtually impossible that any single person could undermine the viability and integrity of society and, in conjunction with its emphasis on the ontological sanctity of the human person and the unbreakable relation between nature and grace, the church has for all intents and purposes condemned the use of capital punishment.[8]

Torture was condemned by the early Christian community,[9] but was given formal sanction in some of the lamentable strategies utilized to eradicate heresy in the Middle Ages. In recent decades, the church has formally embraced an unequivocal renunciation of torture for any end, including the greater good. It was proscribed in the writings of Pope Pius XII, in the Vatican ratification of the United Nations declaration against torture, and in many subsequent documents. Pope John Paul II summarizes this position: "Christ's disciple refuses every recourse to such methods, which nothing could justify."[10]

Concerning the second element of the theory, the rationale for punishing the one labeled as a criminal, we traced the ascending and interrelated nature of three concepts integral to the Catholic theological tradition: order, justice, and atonement. If anything, as Augustine pointed out, order is the default value in an ethic of criminal justice. Crime, however, is not simply a violation of order. In the Catholic tradition, law upholds the natural harmony of creation; violations of the statutes promulgated by legitimate authority are not simply infractions against the behavioral constraints imposed by a given society but acts of resistance to the order established by God. Therefore, repressing criminal activity is linked to justice in this fundamental sense. Pius XII states that crime is a "violation of the laws of being and of moral duty, laws rooted in the nature of things" and therefore repression of criminal activity "constitutes an intervention in favor of the imminent principles, ontological and moral . . . whose internal structure crime threatens and whose vital force crime saps."[11] The Catholic Bishops of the United States write: "We cannot and will not tolerate behavior that threatens lives and violates the rights of others . . . . The community has a right to establish and enforce laws to protect people and to advance the common good."[12]

These commitments justify the forcible constraint of those who violate the law. Recalling the argument of Hans Boersma, they reinforce the claim that on this side of eternity divine hospitality cannot be exhibited without some degree of violence.[13] Although environment powerfully shapes how reality is perceived, free will cannot be effaced: "Without discounting the many powerful forces at work in our society, we believe that the *individual* makes basic choices about personal action."[14] As the tradition has maintained since Anselm, the person in each facet of his or her being commits the crime and so each relevant dimension of the self must be addressed through the punishment process.[15] However, the fact that criminals are wrong in what they do and should be "brought to justice" in no way diminishes, even among those who commit the most heinous of crimes, the divine claim to their persons and the possibility of metanoia. This assertion reveals to us the redemptive dimensions associated with the doctrine of the Atonement: Christ assumes the garb and persona of the criminal to efface the rupture in the divine covenant caused by human rebellion and to demonstrate how the imprisoned are to bear their confinement.[16] Punishment, then, as we have stated, is not primarily to assuage the thirst for vengeance among the captors, nor simply to repair sinful damage to the shattered order of creation, but to create "a humble contrite heart" (Ps 51:19). Like the rampaging "demoniac" now "sitting, clothed, and in his right mind" (Mk 5:15), the truest reparation is to be reacquainted with one's best self. This lies at the heart of the penitential system dating back to the very beginning of Christianity

As to the degree of punishment merited by crime, the tradition, which rarely produces unambiguous clarity, has been consistently clear on the fact that punishments must be suited to the culpable offense and to the life circumstances of the offender. This recalls the Aristotelian and Thomist contention that justice is constrained without equity, as well as the scriptural teaching that those who are just must also be kind (Ws 12:19).[17] Ambrose stated that as soon as crime has been established mercy must come into play.[18] Pius XII wrote that the risk invited by merciless judgment is that "law in its highest form" may well lead to "injury in its highest form."[19]

The end of the punitive process was discussed in chapter 3. There it was suggested that the true meaning of criminal justice cannot be separated from the final end of all human life: the beatific vision.[20] The transcendent spiritual goal implies and is contingent upon the imminence of the proximate end: a harmonious and equitable social project. There is symmetry between this Thomist formulation and the two aims of punishment: spiritual and relational healing and social reintegration. In effect, then, the purpose of criminal justice can be summed up in the concept of liberation: internal freedom to assent to God's will for both the offender and the rest of creation, accompanied by external liberation from captivity and social stigma. This echoes the prophetic vision of justice as liberation of the oppressed from captivity and Mary's joyful refrain in the *Magnificat* that God's cosmic plan aims at the "lifting up of the lowly" (Lk 1:52).

In conjunction with this liberating goal of punishment, there is a growing movement, with abundant precedent in the Catholic tradition, to induce the perpetrators of crime to make restitution to the victims of their misbehavior. Since both law and persons are violated by crime, the legal payment of criminal debt with increments of time does little to address the harm done to the victim. Pius XII notes this when he states that, by the "law of retaliation" alone, "the one injured . . . would not receive reparation or have his rights restored." Therefore, the culprit "at his own expense" ought to address this inequality "from his personal being, property and ability, for the benefit of another."[21] The spirit of this assertion is found in our own day in the unprecedented growth in many countries of restorative justice: an approach to criminal misdeeds that seeks to create a mediated interchange between victims and offenders in which the former can express not only their sentiments over the violation done to them and seek explanation from those who aggrieved them, but the two parties can then seek to reach a cooperative and consensual agreement over how a just recompense may be offered for the offense. One of the criminologists most identified with promoting the practice has stated that when the Catholic Church instituted private confession in the seventh century, it "institutionalized" restorative justice.[22]

What then is to be done with those who can no longer justly be detained but whose comportment poses a foreseeable threat to others? One might recall that in the history of penance, although full reinstatement of the penitent was the goal, and although in a spiritual and moral sense the offense had received full pardon, there were still communal constraints placed upon those whose specific offenses were held to require continual supervision.[23] Such restrictions were common with regard to repentant heretics, particularly in the Middle Ages.[24] As the U.S. bishops note, full acceptance of the criminal offender is always the desired end of punishment, but given the risk to the wider society, this reintegration "may not be possible in certain cases."[25] One sees this today in the measures restricting former felons from certain venues that could trigger the excesses and the harm that characterized their former life. A particularly poignant contemporary example of constraints after absolution is the common practice among many religious communities to place members guilty of sexual abuse under a permanent form of house arrest: they may not leave the cloister without supervision and are permanently banned from public ministry.[26]

A critical issue that surfaces regarding pardon and release is the impact of culture and socialization upon the determination of a standard by which rehabilitation can properly be judged. All too often, as numerous critical thinkers in both criminology and Christian ethics have pointed out, it is to the sober, sensible, and compliant values of bourgeois respectability that conversion and rehabilitation have been measured.[27] Therefore, when, for example, Pius XII notes that the goal of criminal justice is liberation understood in a voluntary "submission and conformity to the ethical order,"[28] one can rightly be suspicious of the degree to which the moral ideals of the Gospel have fallen in homage to an all-too-worldly set of powers. However, the ethical order of which Pius speaks is that conditioned by the natural law. This, of course, brings its own set of questions, but at least from a Catholic perspective, the normative conditions for a just social order—for example, respect for life, human rights, and the common good—have consistently produced a qualitatively different conception of the good life than that offered by Western liberal democracies. Also, at least since Aquinas, it has been consistently affirmed that law must not be understood in a positivist, but in an ontological sense; one has no obligation to obey directives that violate conscience or the natural law.[29]

We thus conclude our third component by re-emphasizing the twin goals of criminal justice: reform of the captive and his or her acceptance into the community, ideally with no sense of recrimination.

Finally, accomplishment of the end of criminal justice is contingent upon the creation of an adequate set of structures that provide the means for its realization. We have noted in the first element of our theory that a set of cultural images are first required to enable one to "see" Christ as the prisoner. Now we recall that the practical format best suited to the accomplishment of the goals of criminal justice is the monastic or penal cell.

Dom Jean Mabillon has been an important figure in this volume, largely because he understood so well the ethical ground upon which the just and humane prison must be constructed. His historical notes have not only provided a critical snapshot of the "real" monastic prison, its cruelty and beneficence, but also his reflections on the "culture" of care that must guide the correctional project at every level sum up much of what is best in the Catholic tradition and have had significant impact on the translation of that ethos into a wider social context. As Sellin notes: "As to his ideas on the internal regime of prisons, all that can be said is that we are still striving to put some of them into practice."[30] Mabillon's outline of the ideal penal facility serves as a model for the means best suited to meet the ends intended in Catholic tradition for those undergoing punishment. It is really an extension of the ideas of the founder of Mabillon's order, St. Benedict, to whom must be paid a formidable debt for so carefully linking the environment of correction with a communal sense of both sternness and compassion. But Mabillon too should be revered, for while Benedict linked the concepts of work and prayer in the monastery, Mabillon, recalling the monastic prison of which St. John Climacus speaks, was convinced that prayer and fasting needed to be balanced with work, fresh air, and, in his idea of a little garden for each prisoner, a sense of beauty and an opportunity for the captive to nurture life in a concrete way. In examining this question of the best means in the tradition to attain criminal justice, I provide some of the details that Mabillon wished to see and comment on them separately.[31]

Concerning those who have been judged guilty, Mabillon, echoing Benedict's sense of moderation, was insistent that care must define not only the treatment of the one undergoing punishment but also the manner in which the offender's reputation is managed. It takes more than rules to weaken the effect of gossip, rumor, and slander on human personalities and communal solidarity; sociologists and anthropologists tell us that the identity of both communities and the persons within them proceeds from the organizational principle of a group and the moral norms seen as essential to its fulfillment. Mabillon's directive points to the social stance necessary to inhibit the temptation to inflict harm by word and deed.[32]

The cell was first established for those voluntary prisoners, initally monks and later contemplative nuns, living lives of prayer and asceticism. In one of her letters, St. Teresa spoke of "the convent and its inmates."[33] The prison and the prisoner are not only cultural depictions and, in the case of the latter, a social class, they are also metaphors for the monastic life. Silence, solitude, prayer, fasting, and labor are spiritual as well as human goods. They need no elaborate justification to warrant their practice, as they form much of the paradigmatic core of the disciplines essential for human integrity, in a psychological as well as spiritual sense. The cell is a place for people serious about finding their true identity and rooting out the influences and impulses that lead to alienation from self, from others, from nature, and from God. As Ambrose stated, God banished Cain that he might have "time for reflection" that would "inspire him to change his ways."[34]

As we saw, confinement in monastic communities was established for those guilty of serious infractions or repeatedly guilty of minor ones. Much like the early penitential discipline, the tradition of exomologesis was common in the monastic setting and has continued unabated: minor faults are addressed by asceticism and shaming rituals, one of which continues in the Mass today as members of the congregation pray an act of contrition and beat their breasts to acknowledge they alone are responsible for the wrong they have committed. Shaming rituals common in monastic and religious communities were loss of place (seats in chapel and other locales were assigned according to seniority), loss of the right to vote, public asceticism such as praying the penitential psalms with arms extended, restricted rations, as well as eating on the ground and bowing to others as they left the refectory or chapel.[35] Some of these rituals have a sadistic ring to them and, as we have seen, depending on the level to which Christian compassion had permeated the hearts of the community, they *were* sadistic in both spirit and practice. But contemporary criminology has rediscovered the importance of shaming as a vital element in an ethic of reintegration. John Braithwaite argues that shaming is at the core of familial discipline: children are not punished for punishment's sake; rather, they are reprimanded so as to summon a sense of personal remorse for having violated basic principles necessary for familial harmony. Part and parcel of this approach is that the child is never made to feel that the love of the parents has in any way been diminished, even though it is they who impose the deprivation.[36]

For the serious offender, however, confinement in a cell is as time-honored as monasticism and the values that sustain it. As we have noted, the cell is not so much a place for inflicting punishment but the environment best suited for the painful process of self-examination and self-transformation. It must be seen as a place for penance, a place for doing one's time, making time an agent of healing even as it necessarily becomes one of painful memory. This sacred place must have an air of silence to match the solitude of the cell. Catholic anthropology does not only locate the imminent God in the created world, but also in all created beings: "in him everything continues in being" (Col 1:17). Phrasing it in philosophical terms, not to mention spiritual ones, God is speaking, but the "Word" can only be apprehended by one who listens in silence.[37]

Mabillon recalls the ascetic tradition in suggesting that the prisoner's food "be simpler and coarser and the fasts more frequent."[38] The parsimonious environment he recommended, however, is not one without healthy food or medical care, but one where the penal experience is consistent with the culture of penance.[39] One English bishop interpreted confinement as serious enough to warrant a substantial, but by no means total, reduction in the ration of beer for prisoners, only allowing a small draught on Monday, Tuesday, Thursday, and Saturday, but with a more substantial ration on feast days.[40] Despite the fact that clean water may have been in short supply, this example serves to remind us that the true meaning of punishment cannot be determined by the deprivation imposed by those who punish.

Finally, the prisoner must be given the opportunity to receive encouragement and counsel from wise and caring people who know the prisoners and visit them regularly. As St. Teresa states, concerning one of the nuns in captivity, "If she is alone all the time it would be very bad for her."[41]

Imprisonment is then not the only means to bring the offender back to personal well-being and normal social interaction but, criticisms and misuse notwithstanding, it is clearly the preferred means to accomplish the ends of criminal justice unique to the Catholic tradition. Pius XII states: "Up to a certain point it may be stated that imprisonment and isolation, properly applied, is the penalty most likely to effect a return of the criminal to right order and social life."[42]

The question that undoubtedly arises in the mind of the reader is whether the theory outlined here and discussed in detail in the preceding chapters can work in practice. The material presented, given the filters established for verifying reliable evidence, suggests that if the idea of confinement cannot work, then the entire monastic system, as well as Catholic anthropology and spirituality, is in question, not to mention its penitential ethos. Therefore, it is one thing, and an important one, to protest the cruelty, racism, and neglect often exhibited in the correctional system; it is quite another, both short-sighted historically and incorrect theologically, for people generally and the Catholic Church particularly to call for an end to the prison.[43] Certainly alternatives to prison have great appeal and should be sought.[44] As we now know, only those guilty of the most serious offenses were required to undergo forced confinement. But it is significant that penal alternatives are exactly what those who have designed and implemented the "new penology" also want, but for an entirely different set of reasons than those valued by the church. This takes us to our final area of investigation: the contemporary correctional apparatus and what relevance, if any, the Catholic tradition might provide for it.

THE CATHOLIC CHURCH AND
CONTEMPORARY CORRECTIONS

The era of rehabilitation has passed in both the philosophy of punishment and its programmatic implementation. The early 1970s saw a sense of bitter disappointment with rehabilitation, not only among criminologists, whose research frequently revealed that "nothing works," but also among religious groups, most notably the Quakers, who saw (correctly) that judicial discretion and its complement in prison treatment programs disguised injustice based on class and racial stereotypes, and who saw (incorrectly) that a strict, "agnostic" sentencing structure based on "just desserts" would be more just than the previous rehabilitative paradigm.[45]

The reason, I would like to suggest, why treatment programs failed to work cannot be tied to the impracticality of the programs themselves—what happened to their subjects *during* their participation—and even less to the misanthropic view of many that criminals are irredeemably disposed to malevolence, but to what happened *before* anyone was treated. I am referring to the systematic undermining of an environment conducive to the very things for which the time sentence and the cell were originated in the first place and which provide the context in which a given offender might well seek to be treated. Although the roots of the collapse of a conversion model of criminal justice, and the institutional climate necessary for its implementation trace themselves to developments originating in the latter half of the nineteenth century, it was the emergence of specific cultural forces a century later that finally severed whatever frail threads linked the correctional milieu to its former meaning. David Garland outlines the substance of this shift:

> [W]e are developing an official criminology that fits our deeply divided and increasingly anxious society. Unlike the rehabilitative welfare ideal, which, for all its faults, was linked into a broader . . . vision of social justice, the new policies have no broader agenda . . . no means for overcoming inequalities and social divisions. They are, instead, policies for . . . policing the divisions created by a certain kind of social organization—and for preserving the political arrangements which lie at its centre.[46]

Contemporary prisons and jails are in most cases anything but the quiet and meditative locales they were originally intended to be. With double-celling the norm, and dormitory and makeshift sleeping arrangements a not infrequent occurrence, the culture that conditions the experience of incarceration now provides a set of incoherent symbols, leaning toward the sort of restrained chaos that was perhaps overstated in the description of several contemporary prisons in the third chapter, but one that nonetheless harmonizes with violence and feelings of frustration.

The abandonment of what Garland has called "penal welfare" in favor of more aggressive programs of punishment and social control has become a self-fulfilling prophecy in another aspect: now that it is no longer believed that inmates should "get better" as a result of confinement, and *a fortiori* that the environment be altered so as to stimulate the anticipated betterment. The emerging paradigm has despaired of positive changes happening in the "life course" of the inmate and instead has focused on controls built into the fabric of everyday life, the selective incapacitation of "the real bad ones," and a justification for pursuing retribution for its own sake.[47]

As early as the late 1960s a movement in criminal justice was inaugurated that focused on observation and targeting projected troublemakers rather than apprehension of criminals. This approach rediscovered why imprisonment as social policy was so late in developing in the West: social control is a lot cheaper than prison construction and maintenance.[48] At this juncture, one of the "forks" of the new approach, now termed "technological corrections," made its appearance. Briefly, the thinking is as follows: those deemed dangerous or simply offensive can be effectively monitored and controlled by electronic means and social programs, rather than draining overused state and federal budgets.[49] Combined with the commitment to incapacitate by means of punitive restraint the most egregious, high-profile offenders, a quiet revolution came about not only in the meaning of crime control but also in the meaning of imprisonment within its realm.[50]

Just who are the bad guys? In some ways the answer to this question has never substantially changed. Recall the use of "honorable captivity"—often house arrest or the chance simply to relocate "anywhere but here"—that has been standard practice for high-end offenders dating back to the early Greeks, and the whips, chains, and mutilation that normally awaited the ordinary misfit. Today we still often see the same disparity of destinations based on social class; but that is not the crux of the matter. The current strategy has come to emulate the same systems-management approach to social organization that has so significantly altered the meaning and quality of daily life in many areas of the developed world. As with achieving access to insurance, credit, health care, and elite institutions of higher education, the task of identifying criminals depends on isolating the trustworthy, the healthy, and the promising from that sector of the populace whose social forecast is permanently cloudy. In other words, recalling the discussion on the social nature of crime, the most common offense in the new penology is not fitting into the financial, educational, and professional determinant of upward mobility.[51] The euphemism coined for this approach to classifying individuals is "risk," a term with precise ramifications in actuarial methodology. Each person is aggregated into a given pool; membership is dictated solely by objective and quantitative methods of analysis. One's personal history or character has little or nothing to do with how one's worth is judged. Those at the low end of the risk pool are, simply put, not a risk and will in most instances be "passed over" by the avenging penal angel should an unfortunate incident occur. Those at the deep end, who commit serious offenses or are guilty of what are often judged as "nuisance crimes"—acts that interfere with the visual, social, and consumer comfort of the favored—can expect to be enrolled in the central computers of the criminal justice apparatus, into its jails and prisons and, with increasing frequency, into the broad list of alternatives to prison geared not to "rehabilitation" but to a permanent and low-cost form of social control.[52] The incapacitation of the most dangerous and threatening also provides the stage for the satisfaction of the public's punitive hunger.[53] Tutored by an entertainment industry with an insatiable fascination with criminal atrocities and abetted by a "governance through crime" strategy in which current and potential political officials ratchet up the rhetoric on the need to "protect the public," public lust has never been more refined for retributive violence, or at least its equivalent in "hard time." All of this is occurring in a period, at least in U.S. history, when every indicator of serious crime has been in decline for two decades.[54]

The ideological nexus of protecting society and isolating the "predators" also justifies the infusion of social control and panoptic surveillance into minute corners of social life. These "criminologies of everyday life," brilliantly foreseen by Foucault, have provided "security" at the expense of making everyone a suspect and reveal that society itself has become a penal metaphor, with the entire "legal" framework underwritten by and dwelling in the perpetual shadow of the threat of lethal force.[55]

This punitive current, deeply suffused with demonstrable racial and class biases,[56] recalls the thesis of Rene Girard that violence is mimetic; and because a social psychology based in covetousness and envy no longer is mitigated by religious prohibitions and rituals, there is a growing thirst for violence against scapegoats: "Victimage is still present . . . , of course, but in degenerate forms that do not produce the type of mythical reconciliation and ritual practice exemplified by primitive cults. This lack of efficiency means that there are often more rather than fewer victims. As in the case of drugs, consumers of sacrifice tend to increase the dosage when the effect becomes more difficult to achieve."[57] Gorringe, commenting on Girard's work, sees this clearly. He states that dating from the early modern period, a new scapegoat was found to appease the violence formerly directed to the Jews: "the idle, the vagabonds, the criminal class—the poor."[58]

The stark contrast between current penal directives and the intentions underlying early penance and monasticism is borne out at virtually every level of comparison. Yet, because of a large degree of methodological and terminological confusion in contemporary Catholic reflection on the penal system there are actually areas where the two approaches imitate and legitimate one another. A case in point is with regard to penal alternatives, or what is often termed "diversion." Given the strong preference to emphasize social control and invasive surveillance in lieu of confinement, calls by Catholic officials for alternatives to imprisonment need far more nuance than is currently being provided.[59]

There is also a misunderstanding in some recent church statements concerning the hierarchy of methodological approaches to punishment. There are four basic organizational principles that can govern correctional practice: retribution, deterrence, incapacitation, and rehabilitation. Precise clarity is required concerning which of these methods to emphasize; otherwise a Catholic theory of criminal justice can fall into hopeless thematic confusion, unwittingly canonize former errors, and, most seriously, underwrite the punitive and socially repressive current now stimulating contemporary penal directives. The preceding chapters have sought to emphasize that only two methods—retribution and rehabilitation—belong in a necessary and inviolable tension. Deterrence and incapacitation cannot be given primary emphasis in a Catholic system faithful to the Gospel and to its own social tradition as they not only objectify the inmate—making him or her respectively a "lesson" to others or a threat to the social order—they are the precise motivations that underlie a false and violent penology that has in all but name declared war on poor racial minorities. Deterrence was a frequent justification for penal treatment by Catholic theorists in the past, and there is no hiding the fact that most current justifications for a Catholic approach to criminal justice have inserted "social defense" as a primary Catholic penal value.[60] Even more confusing are recommendations in some documents that all four ends be held in a balance.[61] The twin values of retribution and rehabilitation are at the heart of the penal system and the revolutionary experiments in imprisonment that emerged as its result. Deterrence and incapacitation can only function as secondary or latent functions in the theory I am presenting, a fact understood by Pius XII but not always by his episcopal successors.[62]

The work of some current criminologists recalls the idea of Erving Goffman that the suspicion and fear that permeate the culture of a "total institution" like the prison can only be mitigated by the creation of "islands" of civility that help alleviate "the psychological stress engendered by assaults upon the self."[63] They have proposed that the creation of virtue is a necessary goal of criminal confinement and requires an institutional commitment to a set of coherent and humane symbols and practices.[64]

Other criminologists and philosophers of punishment have argued that while the state cannot replicate the monastery or the penitential ethos of Catholicism, it can communicate to inmates that they are being punished in order to reacquaint them to the moral truth from which they have become alienated.[65] Their work recalls the communicative dimension of the penitential ritual and its instrumental role in shaping criminal justice policy in the West.

In the second chapter it was noted that, since the time of Augustine, the vital importance of order has bequeathed a legacy of interchange and cooperation between church and state that Catholic social thought has always upheld despite the tensions and contradictions this association has so often caused. What is to be the relation between the church and the state in regard to the correctional and legal network that owes so much to its ecclesiastical origins? Certainly, Catholic claims concerning the ontological sacredness of the human person, the justification for punishment, the end of the penal process, and the means for its realization should be orchestrated in the public square. The demands of the Gospel and the fate of the imprisoned Christ require nothing less.

CONCLUSION

Christian theology proclaims that all is grace and all is gift. Despite the shock of violence and preventable human suffering, the triumph of the cross is that Christ transformed rejection, confinement, and execution at the hands of the powerful into the means by which the world is redeemed. Nothing and no one within creation stands outside the divine reach and thus, in a doubly evocative way, grace and gift apply themselves to all who are imprisoned.[66]

While law can proscribe torture and maltreatment, no rule or legal ordinance can train the eye to see the true nature of those who dwell in the jails and detention centers spread across the globe. Therefore, despite the elegant denunciation by Pius XII of those penal regimes that "now in savage passion, now in cold reflection [bring] unspeakable sufferings, misery, and extermination," criminal justice cannot finally be achieved by juridical decree, but from the recognition that the person detained bears a noble, even divine countenance.[67]

We began the chapter with the reminder that moral consistency over time, particularly in an institution as old as the Catholic Church, is a hopeless ideal. All the facts collide. There are too many pronouncements, too much historical data, too many justifications. There is enough to praise, enough to acquit, and enough to condemn. Only one constant remains: Christ confined, then and now, whose penal seclusion graces all who are confined and whose liberation from captivity anticipates the liberation intended for all captives. That is the real challenge for the church: to be faithful to those times and places when it *was* consistent in its image of who is locked in the prison cell, in whatever place, for whatever reason.

NOTES

1. Noonan, "Development in Moral Doctrine," 676.
2. Christie, *A Suitable Amount of Crime*, 10.
3. St. Teresa, *The Letters of St. Teresa*, II, no. 274.
4. Pius XII, "Prisoners, Punishment, and Pardon," 174.
5. "Pastoral Constitution on the Church in the Modern World" (Gaudium et Spes), in Walter M. Abbott, S.J., ed., *The Documents of Vatican II* (New York: Guild Press, 1966), 27.
6. Compagnoni, "Capital Punishment and Torture in the Tradition of the Catholic Church," 47–50. Brugger summarizes the tradition, arguing that the "plain face" teaching is an invocation of the principle of "double effect": the intent to kill is immoral but not the intent to defend the common good. See *Capital Punishment and Roman Catholic Moral Tradition*, 9–37.
7. St. Ambrose, "Cain and Abel," II, 9, 38.
8. In *Evangelium Vitae* Pope John Paul II writes: "Modern Society in fact has the means of effectively suppressing crime by rendering criminals harmless without definitely denying them the chance to reform." Quoted in Pontifical Council, *Compendium of the Social Doctrine of the Church*, no. 405.
9. Lactantius provides a classic summation: "Torture and piety are widely different; nor is it possible for truth to be united with violence, or justice with cruelty." Lactantius, "Divine Institutes," V, 20.
10. "The judicial investigation must exclude physical and psychic torture." Pius XII, "International Penal Law," *The Catholic Mind* 52 (Feb. 1954): 111. The quote from John Paul II is found in Pontifical Council, *Compendium of the Social Doctrine of the Church*, no. 404.
11. Pius XII, "The Criminologist and His Important Service to Society," *The Pope Speaks* 1 (1954): 364.
12. The Catholic Bishops of the United States, *Responsibility, Rehabilitation, and Restoration*, 16.
13. Boersma, *Violence, Hospitality, and the Cross*, 43–51.
14. United States Catholic Conference, "A Community Response to Crime," *Origins* 7 (1978): 598.
15. See, e.g., Pius XII, "Crime and Punishment," 365, 373.
16.

[If] the supernatural benefit of Christ's sacrifice alone remits guilt, penitential practice is both contained in and overcome by the motion of Christ's redeeming act; if grace, then, allows for a penitential return of the sinner, it does so solely because prayerful humility is the fitting form of a redeemed life . . . . In one stroke, Anselm has done away with the notion that penance is a punitive discipline intended to satisfy God's wrath, and shown it to be simply a thankful piety that responds to . . . an unmerited and transforming grace.

See Hart, "A Gift Exceeding Every Debt," 340–41.

17. See Nussbaum, "Equity and Mercy."

18. "Once the crime is admitted . . . then the divine Law of God's mercy should be immediately extended . . . . God in His providence gives this sort of verdict so that magistrates might learn the virtue of magnanimity and patience, that they may not be unduly hasty in their eagerness to punish." See St. Ambrose, "Cain and Abel," II, 9, 38.

19. Pius XII, "Crime and Punishment," 381.

20. St. Thomas Aquinas, ST I–II, q. 3, a. 7.

21. Pius XII, "Crime and Punishment," 376.

22. John Braithwaite, *Restorative Justice and Responsive Regulation* (Oxford: Oxford University Press, 2002), 5. There is a very large and growing corpus of literature on this subject. Several volumes that treat this development from a Christian perspective are Christopher Marshall, *Beyond Retribution* (Grand Rapids, MI: Eerdmans, 2001) and Howard Zehr, *Changing Lenses* (Scottdale, PA: Herald Press, 1990). For my own views, see Skotnicki, "How Is Justice Restored?" *Studies in Christian Ethics* 19 (2006): 187–204. While there are many elements of restorative justice that bear respectful imitation, they miss, I think, the "painful road to recovery" implied in character change and/or spiritual renewal.

23. See Vogel, "Sin and Penance," 239–40.

24. Given notes that once a person was caught in the "nets" of the inquisitorial authorities it was very difficult to return to life as normal, even if acquitted or released for one's offense. See *Inquisition and Medieval Society*, 84–85. The Mercedarian Constitutions order that apostates be placed under a perpetual form of house arrest, serving in the archives of the order ("servari in archivo communi") even after the sentence has been served. See Holstenius, *Codex Regularum*, III, dist. V, cap. 6, c. 8.

25. Catholic Bishops of the United States, "Statement on Capital Punishment," 375.

26.

If a religious has abused a child or adolescent, he is not only subject to civil and criminal law, but, according to the *Charter for the Protection of Children and Young People* adopted by the U.S. Conference of Catholic Bishops, he also cannot be reassigned to public ministries or be involved with young people . . . . We abhor sexual abuse. We will not tolerate any type of abuse by our members. Our tradition of fraternal correction requires us to hold one another accountable. In addition to being a crime, sexual abuse of this type violates our most fundamental values as religious. Bearing our responsibility, we place these men under severe restrictions after treatment and those with the greatest danger to the public are carefully supervised to avoid occasions where they can engage in abuse again.

Conference of Major Superiors of Men, "Improving Pastoral Care and Account-ability in Response to the Tragedy of Sexual Abuse," Proceedings of Annual Meet-ing, Philadelphia, PA, 2002.

27. See Griffith, *The Fall of the Prison*, 49. Rusche and Kirchheimer, *Punishment and Social Structure*; T. Richard Snyder, *The Protestant Ethic and the Spirit of Pun-ishment* (Grand Rapids, MI: Eerdmans, 2001).

28. Pius XII, "Crime and Punishment," 378.

29. *Catechism of the Catholic Church*, no. 2235; Pontifical Council, *Com-pendium of the Social Doctrine of the Church*, no. 400.

30. Sellin, "Dom Jean Mabillon," 593.

31. Ibid., 592.

32. Ibid., 583.

33. St. Theresa, *The Letters of St. Theresa of Jesus*, I, 26.

34. St. Ambrose, "Cain and Abel," II, 9, 35.

35. The Constitutions of the Camaldolese, for example, offer the following shaming devices for grave fault: loss of active and passive voice (*privationes vo-cis tam activae, quam passive*); loss of place, rank, and office (*privatio loci, gradus, officii*); prostrations and exile (*prostrationes, exilium*). See Holstenius, *Codex Regularum*, II, cap. 25. For faults of the first order, the Constitutions of the Barnabites order the offender into the choir with arms extended (*"In choro brachiis extentis"*). While there he is to recite some or all of the penitential psalms (*"Recitare aliquem ex Psalmis poenitentiales, aut omnes"*). See "Canones Poenitentiales," in "Constitutiones Barnibatum," Holstenius, *Codex Regu-larum*, V.

36. Braithwaite, *Crime, Shame, and Reintegration*, 54–68.

37. Martin Heidegger, *Being and Time*, trans. John Macquarie and Edward Robinson (New York: Harper & Row, 1962), 205–10.

38. Ibid.

39. The Catholic Bishops of the United States maintain Mabillon's spirit in writing that prisoners "have a right to proper food, health care and recreation and opportunities to pursue other human goods as education and the cultiva-tion of their skills." See "The Pastoral Letter on Moral Values," *Origins* 6 (1976): 367.

40. See "Archbishop Islep's Constitutions," in Johnson, ed., *Collection of Laws and Canons of the Church of England*, II, 414–15.

41. St. Theresa, *Letters of St. Theresa of Jesus*, no. 274.

42. Pius XII, "Crime and Punishment," 369.

43. Lee Griffith writes: "The Bible does not present the prison as simply one of many social institutions . . . . prisons are *identical in spirit* to the violence and murder that they pretend to combat." See *Fall of the Prison*, 106. The American Catholic bishops, in their rightful critique of the injustices of the penal system and their desire to further alternative punishments, have on several occasions leaned in the direction that Griffith suggests. See, U.S. Catholic Conference, "A Community Response to Crime," 598; Catholic Bishops of the United States, "Rebuilding Human Lives," 345.

44. See, e.g., Pius XII, "Crime and Punishment," 369; U.S. Catholic Conference, "A Community Response to Crime," 598; Catholic Bishops of the United States, *Responsibility, Rehabilitation, and Restoration*, 39–40.

45. Two classic studies that galvanized discontent with rehabilitation are Robert Martinson, "What Works? Questions and Answers About Prison Reform," *The Public Interest* 35 (1974): 22–54; and the American Friends Service Committee, *Struggle for Justice: A Report on Crime and Punishment in America* (New York: Hill & Wang, 1971). For a historical overview of this disaffection, see Francis A. Allen, *The Decline of the Rehabilitative Ideal* (New Haven, CT: Yale University Press, 1981).

46. Quoted in Duncan B. Forrester, *Christian Justice and Public Policy* (Cambridge: Cambridge University Press, 1997), 70.

47. An analysis of a "life course" approach to criminal justice is found in Robert J. Sampson and John H. Laub, *Crime in the Making* (Cambridge, MA: Harvard University Press, 1993). The criminal theorist attributed with pioneering the movement to "selective incapacitation," James Q. Wilson, argued, not without merit, that the large percentage of common crime is committed by a relatively small percentage of the population. It was his innovation to concentrate on apprehending those "career criminals," imprison them for a long time, and find other ways to castigate the occasional or one-time offender. See *Thinking About Crime*, revised edition (New York: Vintage, 1985), esp. ch. 8 [originally published 1975].

48. In 1967 a task force called "The President's Crime Commission on Law Enforcement and the Administration of Justice" suggested that "intensive supervision" before crime is committed, and not due process or rehabilitative programs after the fact, was the key variable in the repression of criminal activity. See Diana Gordon, *The Justice Juggernaut* (New Brunswick, NJ: Rutgers University Press, 1996), 98.

49. See April Pattavina, ed., *Information Technology and the Criminal Justice System* (Thousand Oaks, CA: Sage, 1996).

50. David Garland writes that what the growing and contradictory hegemonic patterns (risk management and punitive harm) have in common is social control: "a much darker vision of the human condition" than was found in the era of penal welfare. See *The Culture of Control*, 15–19.

51. See Feeley and Simon, "The New Penology"; Simon, "The Emergence of a Risk Society."

52. Writing in the mid-1990s of two community-based correctional programs in the Northeast, Gordon notes: "In purporting to supervise offenders who would otherwise have been imprisoned had the programs not existed, these programs represent the bellwether of transformation to a penal system that places as much emphasis on observation as on capture and imprisonment." See *The Justice Juggernaut*, 97. The analysis of "nuisance crimes" is found in John Irwin, *The Jail: Managing the Underclass in American Society* (Berkeley: University of California Press, 1985), 19–41. Disparities in sentencing based on socioeconomic status are discussed in Morris and Tonry, *Between Prison and Probation*, chs. 3–4.

53. John Irwin, *The Warehouse Prison* (Los Angeles: Roxbury, 2005).

54. On "governance through crime," see Jonathan Simon, "Governing Through Crime," in Lawrence M. Friedman and George Fisher, eds., *The Crime Conundrum* (Westview Press, 1997), 171–89. On the "myths" that create and sustain criminal justice policy, see Victor E. Kappleler and Gary W. Potter, *The Mythology of Crime and Justice*, 4th ed. (Long View, IL: Waveland Press, 2005).

55. Foucault writes of the diffusion "of penal techniques into the most innocent disciplines . . . placing over the slightest illegality, the smallest irregularity, derivation or anomaly, the threat of delinquency." See *Discipline and Punish*, 301. On the "criminologies of everyday life," see Gordon, *The Justice Juggernaut*, 42; Garland, *The Culture of Control*, 182–83. On political communities and the violence that ensures the rule of law, see Max Weber, *Economy and Society*, vol. II, Guenther Roth and Claus Wittich, eds. (Berkeley: University of California Press, 1978), 901–3.

56. "Based on current rates of first incarceration, an estimated 32% of black males will enter State or Federal prison during their lifetime, compared to 17% of Hispanic males and 5.9% of white males." U. S. Department of Justice, Bureau of Justice Statistics, Criminal Offenders Statistics, 9/6/06. See also Jerome G. Miller, *Search and Destroy: African-American Males in the Criminal Justice System* (Cambridge: Cambridge University Press, 1996).

57. Rene Girard, "Mimesis and Violence," in James G. Williams, ed., *The Girard Reader* (New York: Crossroad, 1996), 17.

58. Gorringe, *God's Just Vengeance*, 26.

59. Catholic Bishops of the United States, *Responsibility, Rehabilitation, and Restoration*, 36–40.

60. *Compendium: Catechism of the Catholic Church*, no. 2266; Catholic Bishops of the United States, *Responsibility, Rehabilitation, and Restoration*, 27–28.

61. Catholic Bishops of the United States, "Rebuilding Human Lives," 346.

62. Pius XII, "International Penal Law," 117, 118.

63. Erving Goffman, "Characteristics of Total Institutions," in *Asylums* (Garden City, NY: Anchor Books, 1961), 69–70.

64. See Francis Cullen, Jody Sundt, and John Wozniac, "The Virtuous Prison," in Henry Pontell and David Shichor, eds., *Contemporary Issues in Criminal Justice* (Saddle River, NJ: Prentice Hall, 2000).

65. See R. A. Duff, *Punishment, Communication, and Community* (Oxford: Oxford University Press, 2001); Jean Hampton, "The Moral Education Theory of Punishment," in A. John Simmons et al., eds., *Punishment* (Princeton, NJ: Princeton University Press, 1995), 112–42.

66. Milbank, *Being Reconciled*, xi.

67. Pius XI, "International Penal Law," 108.

Bibliography

Abbott, Walter M., S. J., ed. *The Documents of Vatican II*. New York: Guild Press, 1966.

Abelard, Peter. *Peter Abelard's Ethics*. Trans. D. E. Luscombe. Oxford: Clarendon Press, 1971.

———. *The Story of My Misfortunes*. Trans. Henry Adams Bellows. Glencoe, IL: The Free Press, 1958.

Allen, Francis A. *The Decline of the Rehabilitative Ideal*. New Haven, CT: Yale University Press, 1981.

Ambrose, St. "Cain and Abel." Trans. John J. Savage. In *The Fathers of the Church*, vol. 42. New York: Fathers of the Church, Inc., 1961, 359–437.

———. "On Repentance." In *St Ambrose: Select Works and Letters*. Trans. Rev. H. De Romestin. Vol. X of Philip Schaff and Henry Wace, eds., *A Select Library of the Nicene and Post Nicene Fathers, Second Series*. 14 vols. New York: The Christian Literature Company, 1890.

American Friends Service Committee. *Struggle for Justice: A Report on Crime and Punishment in America*. New York: Hill & Wang, 1971.

Anselm of Canterbury, St. *Proslogion*. Trans. M. J. Charlesworth. Oxford: The Clarendon Press, 1965.

———. *Why God Became Man*. Trans. Joseph M. Colleran. Albany, NY: Magi Books, 1969.

Aquinas, St. Thomas. *On the Governance of Rulers*. Trans. Gerald B. Phelan. London: Sheed & Ward, 1938.

———. *On the Truth of the Catholic Faith*. Trans. Vernon J. Burke. Garden City, NY: Image Books, 1956.

———. *Petri Lombardi Sententiarum libre quatuor*. Excudebat Migne, 1841.

———. *Summa Theologica*. Trans. Fathers of the English Dominican Province. New York: Benziger, 1947.

——. *Truth.* 3 vols. Trans. James V. McGlynn. Chicago: Henry Regency, 1953.

Aristotle. *Ethics.* Trans. J. A. K. Thompson. Harmondsworth, UK: Penguin, 1955.

——. *The Politics.* Trans. T. A. Sinclair. Harmondsworth, UK: Penguin, 1981.

Augustine, St. *The City of God.* Trans. Henry Bettenson. Harmondsworth, UK: Penguin, 1984.

——. "Exposition of the Psalms." In *The Works of St. Augustine,* pt. III, vol. 17. Trans. Maria Boulding, O.S.B. Hyde Park, NY: New City Press, 1995.

——. *The Lord's Sermon on the Mount.* Trans. John J. Jepson. Westminster, MD: The Newman Press, 1948.

——. "On the Trinity." In *Basic Writings of Saint Augustine,* vol. II. Trans. A. W. Haddan. New York: Random House, 1948.

——. *The Problem of Free Choice.* Trans. Dom Mark Pontifex. Westminster, MD: The Newman Press, 1955.

——. "Sermons." In *The Works of St. Augustine,* pt. III, vol. 10. Trans. Edmund Hill, O.P. Hyde Park, NY: New City Press, 1965.

Barbeito, Isabel, ed. *Carceles y Mujeres En El Siglo XVII.* Madrid: Editorial Castalia, 1991.

Barber, Malcolm. *The Trial of the Templars.* Cambridge: Cambridge University Press, 1978.

Bartlett, Robert. *Trial by Fire and Water.* Oxford: The Clarendon Press, 1986.

Basil, St. *Letters,* vol. I. Trans. Sister Agnes Clare Way, C.D.P. Westminster: The Catholic University of America Press, 1951.

——. "The Long Rules." In *St. Basil: Ascetical Works.* Trans. Sister M. Monica Wagner. New York: Fathers of the Church, 1950.

Bassett, Margery. "Newgate Prison in the Middle Ages." *Speculum* 18 (1943): 233–246.

Bauman, Richard. *Crime and Punishment in Ancient Rome.* London and NY: Routledge, 1996.

Beaumont, Gustave de, and Alexis de Toqueville. *On the Penitentiary System in the United States and its Application in France.* Trans. Francis Lieber. Philadelphia: Carey, Lea, and Blanchard, 1833.

Bell, Marcus, ed. *The Miracles of Our Lady of Rocamadour.* Trans. Marcus Bell. Woodbridge, UK: Boydell Press, 1999.

Benedict, St. *Benedict's Rule.* Trans. Terrence G. Kardong. Collegeville, MN: The Liturgical Press, 1996.

Berman, Harold. *Law and Revolution.* Cambridge, MA: Harvard University Press, 1983.

Bernstein, Alan E. *The Formation of Hell.* Ithaca, NY: Cornell University Press, 1993.

Bingham, Joseph. *Antiquities of the Christian Church,* vol. VI. London: William Straker, 1844.

Boersma, Hans. "Eschatological Justice and the Cross." *Theology Today* 60 (2003): 186–99.

——. *Violence, Hospitality, and the Cross.* Grand Rapids, MI: Baker Academic, 2004.

Boniface VIII, Pope. "Liber Sextus." In *Corpus Iuris Canonici.* Lyon: 1616.

Bowsky, William M. *A Medieval Italian Commune: Siena Under the Nine.* Berkeley: University of California Press, 1981.

Braithwaite, John. *Crime, Shame, and Reintegration.* Cambridge: Cambridge University Press, 1989.

———. *Restorative Justice and Responsive Regulation.* Oxford: Oxford University Press, 2002.

Brodman, James William. *Ransoming Captives in Crusader Spain.* Philadelphia: University of Pennsylvania Press, 1986.

Brugger, E. Christian. *Capital Punishment and Roman Catholic Moral Tradition.* Notre Dame, IN: University of Notre Dame Press, 2003.

Burns, Robert I., S. J., ed. *Las Siete Partidas.* Trans. Samuel Parsons Scott. Philadelphia: University of Pennsylvania Press, 2001.

Cajani, Luigi. "Surveillance and Redemption: The Case di Correzione of San Michele a Ripa in Rome." In Norbert Finzsch and Robert Jutte, eds. *Institutions of Confinement.* Washington, DC: German Historical Institute, 1996, 301–24.

Carter, Stephen L. *The Culture of Disbelief.* New York: Anchor Books, 1993.

Catechism of the Catholic Church. New York: Doubleday, 1995.

Catholic Bishops of the United States. "The Pastoral Letter on Moral Values." *Origins* 6 (1976): 357–70.

———. "Rebuilding Human Lives." *Origins* 3 (1973): 344–50.

———. "Statement on Capital Punishment." *Origins* 10 (1980): 373–77.

———. *Responsibility, Rehabilitation, and Restoration: A Catholic Perspective on Crime and Criminal Justice.* Washington, DC: United States Catholic Conference, 2000.

Celsus. *On the True Doctrine: A Discourse against Christians.* Trans. Joseph Hoffman. New York: Oxford University Press, 1987.

Chodorow, Stanley. *Christian Political Theory and Church Politics in the Mid-Twelfth Century.* Berkeley: University of California Press, 1972.

Christie, Nils. *A Suitable Amount of Crime.* London and New York: Routledge, 2004.

Chrysostom, St. John. "Homilies on the Gospel of Saint Matthew." In Philip Schaff, ed. *A Select Library of the Nicene and Post Nicene Fathers,* vol. X. New York: The Christian Literature Company, 1888.

Clear, Todd. *Harm in American Penology.* Albany: State University of New York Press, 1994.

Clement, St. "Second Letter to the Corinthians." In Cyril C. Richardson, ed. *Early Christian Fathers.* New York: Macmillan, 1970.

Climacus, St. John. *The Ladder of Divine Ascent.* Trans. Archimandrite Lazarus Moore. London: Faber & Faber, 1959.

Compagnoni, Francesco. "Capital Punishment and Torture in the Tradition of the Catholic Church." *Concilium* 120 (1979): 39–53.

Compendium: Catechism of the Catholic Church. Washington, DC: United States Conference of Catholic Bishops, 2006.

Conference of Major Superiors of Men. "Improving Pastoral Care and Accountability in Response to the Tragedy of Sexual Abuse." Proceedings of Annual Meeting, Philadelphia, PA, 2002.

Cullen, Francis, Jody Sundt, and John Wozniac. "The Virtuous Prison." In Henry Pontell and David Shichor, eds. *Contemporary Issues in Criminal Justice*. Saddle River, NJ: Prentice Hall, 2000.

Cyprian, St. *The Lapsed*. Trans. Maurice Bevenot, S. J. Westminster, MD: The Newman Press, 1957.

———. *The Letters of Saint Cyprian of Carthage*. Trans. G. W. Clarke. New York: Newman Press, 1984.

———. *Letters*. Trans. Sister Rose Bernard Donna, C.S.J. Washington, DC: Catholic University of America Press, 1964.

Daly, Lowrie J., S.J. *Benedictine Monasticism*. New York: Sheed and Ward, 1965.

Dean, Trevor. *Crime in Medieval Europe 1200–1500*. Harlow, UK: Longman, 2001.

Derrida, Jacques. *Of Hospitality*. Trans. Rachel Bowlby. Palo Alto, CA: Stanford University Press, 2000.

Dickens, Charles. *American Notes*. Greenwich, CT: Fawcett, 1961 [originally published 1843].

Dilulio, John. *Governing Prisons*. New York: The Free Press, 1987.

Domanick, Joe. *Cruel Justice: Three Strikes and the Politics of Crime in America's Golden State*. Berkeley: University of California Press, 2004.

Drapkin, Israel. *Crime and Punishment in the Ancient World*. Lexington, MA: Lexington Books, 1989.

Duff, R. A. *Punishment, Communication, and Community*. Oxford: Oxford University Press, 2001.

Dunbabin, Jean. *Captivity and Imprisonment in Medieval Europe, 1000–1300*. Houndmills, UK: Palgrave Macmillan, 2002.

Durkheim, Emile. *The Division of Labor in Society*. Trans. W. D. Halls. New York: The Free Press, 1984.

———. *The Elementary Forms of the Religious Life*. Trans. Karen E. Fields. New York: The Free Press, 1995.

Edgerton, Samuel Y. *Pictures and Punishment*. Ithaca, NY: Cornell University Press, 1985.

Elias, Norbert. *The Civilizing Process*. 2 vols. Trans. Edmund Jephcott. New York: Urizen Books, 1978 [originally published 1939].

The Establissements de Saint Louis. Trans. F. R. P. Akehurst. Philadelphia: University of Pennsylvania Press, 1996.

Eusebius. *The History of the Church*. Trans. G. A. Williamson. Harmondsworth, UK: Penguin, 1965.

Favazza, Joseph A. *The Order of Penitents*. Collegeville, MN: The Liturgical Press, 1988.

Feeley, Malcolm, and Jonathan Simon. "The New Penology: Notes on the Emerging Strategy of Corrections and its Implications." *Criminology* 30 (1992): 449–74.

Fenn, Richard. *The Persistence of Purgatory*. Cambridge: Cambridge University Press, 1995.

Forrester, Duncan B. *Christian Justice and Public Policy*. Cambridge: Cambridge University Press, 1997.

Fosbroke, Thomas Dudley. *British Monachism*. 3rd ed. London: M. A. Nattali, 1843.

Foucault, Michel. *Discipline and Punish*. Trans. Alan Sheridan. New York: Vintage Books, 1979.

Freud, Sigmund. *The Future of an Illusion*. Trans. W. D. Robson-Scott. Garden City, NY: Anchor Books, 1964.

Garland, David. *The Culture of Control*. Chicago: University of Chicago Press, 2001.

——. *Punishment and Modern Society*. Chicago: University of Chicago Press, 1990.

Garnsey, Peter. *Social Status and Legal Privilege in the Roman Empire*. Oxford: Clarendon Press, 1970.

Girard, Rene. "Mimesis and Violence." In James G. Williams, ed. *The Girard Reader*. New York: Crossroad, 1996, 9–19.

——. *Things Hidden Since the Foundation of the World*. 3 vols. Trans. Stephen Bann (vols. 2 & 3) and Michael Metteer (vol. 1). Palo Alto, CA: Stanford University Press, 1987.

Given, James B. *Inquisition and Medieval Society*. Ithaca, NY: Cornell University Press, 1997.

Goebel, Julius, Jr. *Felony and Misdemeanor*. Philadelphia: University of Pennsylvania Press, 1976 [originally published 1937].

Goffman, Erving. "Characteristics of Total Institutions." In *Asylums*. Garden City, NY: Anchor Books, 1961, 1–124.

——. *Stigma*. Englewood Cliffs, NJ: Prentice Hall, 1963.

Gordon, Diana. *The Justice Juggernaut*. New Brunswick, NJ: Rutgers University Press, 1996.

Gorringe, Timothy. *God's Just Vengeance*. Cambridge: Cambridge University Press, 1996.

Gratian. "Concordia Discordantium Canonum." In *Corpus Iuris Canonici*. Lyon: 1616.

Gregory the Great, Pope. "Epistles." Trans. Rev. James Barmby. In Philip Schaff and Henry Wace, eds. *A Select Library of Nicene and Post-Nicene Fathers of the Christian Church*, vol. XII. Grand Rapids, MI: Eerdmans, 1956.

Gregory of Tours. *The History of the Franks*. Trans. Lewis Thorpe. London: Penguin, 1974.

Griffith, Lee. *The Fall of the Prison: Biblical Perspectives on Prison Abolition*. Grand Rapids, MI: Eerdmans, 1993.

Gui, Bernard. *Manuel De L'Inquisiteur*. Trans. G. Mollat. Paris: Librairie Ancienne Honoré Champion, 1926.

Guibert. *The Autobiography of Guibert: Abbot of Nugent-Sous-Coucy*. Trans. C. C. Swinton Bland. London: Routledge & Sons, 1925.

Hampton, Jean. "The Moral Education Theory of Punishment." In A. John Simmons et al., eds. *Punishment*. Princeton, NJ: Princeton University Press, 1995, 112–42.

Hart, D. Bentley. "A Gift Exceeding Every Debt." *Pro Ecclesia* VII (1998): 333–49.

Head, Thomas. "Saints, Heretics, and Fire: Finding Meaning Through the Ordeal." In Sharon Farmer and Barbara H. Rosenwein, eds. *Monks and Nuns Saints and Outcasts: Religion in Medieval Society.* Ithaca, NY: Cornell University Press, 2000, 223–24.

Heidegger, Martin. *Being and Time.* Trans. John Macquarie and Edward Robinson. New York: Harper & Row, 1962.

Herman of Tournai. *The Restoration of the Monastery of St. Martin of Tournai.* Trans. Lynn H. Nelson. Washington, DC: Catholic University of America Press, 1996.

Himes, Kenneth R. *Responses to 101 Questions on Catholic Social Teaching.* New York: Paulist Press, 2001.

Himes, Michael J., and Kenneth R. Himes. *Fullness of Faith.* New York: Paulist Press, 1993.

Hollenbach, David, S. J. *The Common Good and Christian Ethics.* Cambridge: Cambridge University Press, 2002.

Holstenius, Lucas, ed. *Codex Regularum Monasticarum et Canoniciarum.* Graz: Akademische Druck–U. Verlagsanstalt, 1957 [originally published 1759].

Howard, John. *Prisons and Lazarettos.* Montclair, NJ: Patterson Smith, 1973 [originally published 1789].

Ignatieff, Michael. *A Just Measure of Pain.* New York: Pantheon, 1978.

Irenaeus of Lyons, St. "Against Heresies" In Rev. Alexander Roberts and John Donaldson, eds. *Ante-Nicene Fathers,* vol. I. New York: Charles Scribner's Sons, 1900.

Irwin, John. *The Jail: Managing the Underclass in American Society.* Berkeley: University of California Press, 1985.

———. *The Warehouse Prison.* Los Angeles: Roxbury, 2005.

Ives, George. *A History of Penal Methods.* Montclair, NJ: Patterson Smith, 1970 [originally published 1914].

John of Salisbury. *The Statesman's Book of John of Salisbury (Policraticus).* Trans. John Dickinson. New York: Russell & Russell, 1963.

John Paul II, Pope. *The Gospel of Life (Evangelium Vitae).* Boston: Pauline, 1995.

——— . "Homily in the Trans World Dome." *Origins* 28 (1999): 599–601.

——— (Karol Wojtyla). *Person and Community.* Trans. Theresa Sandok. New York: Peter Lang, 1993.

Johnson, John, ed. *A Collection of the Laws and Canons of the Church of England.* Oxford: John Henry Parker, 1850.

Johnston, Norman. *Forms of Constraint.* Urbana: University of Illinois Press, 2000.

Kamen, Henry. *The Spanish Inquisition: A Historical Revision.* New Haven, CT: Yale University Press, 1997.

Kappleler, Victor E., and Gary W. Potter. *The Mythology of Crime and Justice,* 4TH ed. Long View, IL: Waveland Press, 2005.

Kuttner, Stephen. "The Revival of Jurisprudence." In Robert L. Berson and Giles Constable, eds. *Renaissance and Renewal in the Twelfth Century.* Cambridge, MA: Harvard University Press, 1982.

Lactantius. "The Divine Institutes." In Rev. Alexander Roberts and John Donaldson, eds. *The Ante-Nicene Fathers,* vol. VII. New York: Charles Scribner's Sons, 1925, 9–258.

Lakoff, George, and Mark Johnson. *Metaphors We Live By.* Chicago: University of Chicago Press, 1980.

Lanfranc. *The Monastic Constitutions of Lanfranc.* Trans. David Knowles. London: Thomas Nelson and Sons, 1951.

Lea, Henry Charles. *A History of the Inquisition of the Middle Ages.* New York: Harper & Brothers, 1888.

LeBras, Gabriel. "Canon Law." In C. G. Crump and E. F. Jacobs, eds. *The Legacy of the Middle Ages.* Oxford: The Clarendon Press, 1926, 321–61.

Le Goff, Jacques. *The Birth of Purgatory.* Trans. Arthur Goldhammer. Chicago: University of Chicago Press, 1984.

Leonardus, Sanctus. *Acta Sanctorum.* 6 Novembris, Tomus III. Brussels: 1910, 139–208.

Lewis, W. D. *From Newgate to Dannemora.* Ithaca, NY: Cornell University Press, 1965.

Logan, F. Donald. *Runaway Religious in Medieval England.* Cambridge: Cambridge University Press, 1996.

The Lombard Laws. Trans. Katherine Fischer Drew. Philadelphia: University of Pennsylvania Press, 1973.

Lovin, Robin, ed. *Religion and American Public Life.* New York: Paulist Press, 1986.

Mahoney, John. *The Making of Moral Theology.* Oxford: Clarendon Press, 1987.

Maitland, F. W. *The Constitutional History of England.* Cambridge: Cambridge University Press, 1968 [originally published 1908].

Mansi, Johannes Dominicus, ed. *Sacrorum Conciliorum.* Paris, and Leipzig: 1901 [originally published 1762].

Maritain, Jacques. *The Person and the Common Good.* Trans. John J. Fitzgerald. Notre Dame, IN: University of Notre Dame Press, 1966.

Marshall, Christopher. *Beyond Retribution.* Grand Rapids, MI: Eerdmans, 2001.

Martinson, Robert. "What Works? Questions and Answers About Prison Reform." *The Public Interest* 35 (1974): 22–54.

Masur, Louis P. *Rites of Execution.* New York: Oxford University Press, 1989.

McGowen, Randall. "The Body and Punishment in Eighteenth-Century England." *The Journal of Modern History* 59 (1987): 651–79.

McKelvey, Blake. *American Prisons: A History of Good Intentions.* Montclair, NJ: Patterson Smith, 1977.

McNeill, John T., and Helena M. Gamer. *Medieval Handbooks of Penance.* New York: Columbia University Press, 1938.

Meeks, Wayne A. *The Origins of Christian Morality.* New Haven, CT: Yale University Press, 1993.

Megivern, James J. *The Death Penalty: An Historical and Theological Survey.* New York: Paulist Press, 1997.

Milbank, John. *Being Reconciled: Ontology and Pardon.* London: Routledge, 2003.

———. *Theology and Social Theory.* Oxford: Blackwell, 1990.

Miller, Jerome G. *Search and Destroy: African-American Males in the Criminal Justice System.* Cambridge: Cambridge University Press, 1996.

Monter, William. *Frontiers of Heresy.* Cambridge: Cambridge University Press, 1990.

Moore, R. I. *The Formation of a Persecuting Society.* London: Basil Blackwell, 1987.

Morris, Norval, and Michael Tonry. *Between Prison and Probation.* New York: Oxford University Press, 1990.

Mounier, Emmanuel. *Personalism.* Trans. Philip Mairet. Notre Dame, IN: University of Notre Dame Press, 1970.

Musurillo, Herbert, ed. and trans. *The Acts of the Christian Martyrs.* Oxford: Clarendon, 1972.

Neuhaus, Richard John. *The Naked Public Square.* Grand Rapids, MI: Eerdmans, 1986.

Newman, Graeme. *Just and Painful.* New York: Harrow and Heston, 1995.

New York State Bishops Conference. "Reforming the Criminal Justice System." *Origins* 12 (1983): 569–73.

Niebuhr, H. Richard. *Christ and Culture.* New York: Harper & Row, 1951.

Noonan, John T. "Development in Moral Doctrine." *Theological Studies* 54 (1993): 662–77.

Nussbaum, Martha. "Equity and Mercy." *Philosophy and Public Affairs* 22 (1993): 83–125.

Origen. *Contra Celsum.* Trans. Henry Chadwick. Cambridge: Cambridge University Press, 1953.

Pachomius, St. "Precepts and Judgments." In *Pachomian Koinonia, Vol. 2: Pachomian Chronicles and Rules.* Trans. Armand Veilleux. Kalamazoo, MI: Cistercian Publications, 1981.

Palmer, Paul F., S. J. "Sacraments and Forgiveness." In *Sources of Christian Theology,* vol. II. Westminster, MD: The Newman Press, 1959.

Parker, Theodore. *Speeches, Addresses, and Occasional Sermons.* Boston: Horace B. Fuller, 1876 [originally published 1847].

Pattavina, April, ed. *Information Technology and the Criminal Justice System.* Thousand Oaks, CA: Sage, 1996.

Pavlich, George. "Towards an Ethics of Restorative Justice." In Lode Walgrave, ed. *Restorative Justice and the Law.* Cullompton, UK: Willan, 2002, 1–18.

Percival, Henry R. "The Seven Ecumenical Councils of the Undivided Church." In Philip Schaff and Henry Wace, eds. *A Select Library of Nicene and Post-Nicene Fathers of the Christian Church.* Second series, vol. XIV. New York: Charles Scribner's Sons, 1900.

Peters, Edward. "Destruction of the Flesh—Salvation of the Spirit: The Paradoxes of Torture in Medieval Christian Society." In Alberto Ferreiro, ed. *The Devil, Heresy and Witchcraft in the Middle Ages.* Leiden: Brill, 1998.

———. *Inquisition.* New York: The Free Press, 1988.

———. "Prison Before the Prison." In Norval Morris and David Rothman, eds. *The Oxford History of the Prison.* New York: Oxford University Press, 1995, 347.

———. *Torture.* Philadelphia: University of Pennsylvania Press, 1996.

Pius XII, Pope. "Crime and Punishment." *The Catholic Mind* 53 (1955): 364–84.

———. "The Criminologist and His Important Service to Society." *The Pope Speaks* 1 (1954): 361–67.

———. "International Penal Law." *The Catholic Mind* 52 (Feb. 1954): 107–18.

———. "Prisoners, Punishment, and Pardon." *The Pope Speaks* 4 (1957): 167–76.

Plato. "The Apology." In *Plato: Complete Works*. Ed. John M. Cooper. Trans. G. M. A. Grube. Indianapolis, IN: Hackett, 1997.

———. *Laws*. 2 vols. Trans. R. G. Bury. Cambridge, MA: Harvard University Press, 1926.

Pollock, Frederick. *The History of English Law Before the Time of Edward I*. Cambridge: Cambridge University Press, 1899.

Polycarp, St. "Letter to the Philippians." In *Early Christian Writings*. Trans. Maxwell Stanforth. London: Penguin, 1968.

Pontifical Council for Justice and Peace. *Compendium of the Social Doctrine of the Church*. Washington, DC: United States Conference of Catholic Bishops, 2005.

Poschmann, Bernhard. *Penance and the Anointing of the Sick*. Trans. Francis Courtney, S. J. New York: Herder & Herder, 1964.

Poupko, Chana Kasachkoff. "The Religious Basis of the Retributive Approach to Punishment." *The Thomist* 39 (1975): 528–41.

Pugh, Ralph. *Imprisonment in Medieval England*. Cambridge: Cambridge University Press, 1970.

Quinney, Richard. *The Social Reality of Crime*. Boston: Little, Brown, 1970.

Rahner, Karl. "Penance in the Early Church." In *Theological Investigations*, vol. XV. Trans. Lionel Swain. New York: Crossroad, 1982.

———. *Theological Investigations*, vol. II. Trans. Karl H. Kruger. London: Darton, Longman & Todd, 1963.

———. *Theological Investigations*, vol. VII. Trans. David Bourke. London: Darton, Longman & Todd, 1971.

Ranulf, Svend. *Moral Indignation and Middle Class Psychology*. New York: Schocken Books, 1964.

Ricoeur, Paul. *The Symbolism of Evil*. Trans. Emerson Buchanan. Boston: Beacon Press, 1967.

Roberts, Rev. Alexander, and John Donaldson, eds. *The Ante-Nicene Fathers*, vol. VII. New York: Charles Scribner's Sons, 1925.

Rothman, David. *Conscience and Convenience*. Boston: Little, Brown, 1980.

———. *The Discovery of the Asylum*. Boston: Little, Brown, 1971.

Ruiz, Federico, O.C.D., et al. *God Speaks in the Night: The Life, Times, and Teaching of St. John of the Cross*. Washington, DC: ICS Publications, 1991.

Rusche, Georg, and Otto Kirchheimer. *Punishment and Social Structure*. New York: Russell & Russell, 1968.

Ryan, John, S. J. *Irish Monasticism: Origins and Early Development*. Dublin & Cork: The Talbot Press, 1931.

"S. Quintino Martyre." In *Acta Sanctorum*. 31 Octobris, Tomus XIII. Paris: 1883: 725–820.

Sampson, Robert J., and John H. Laub. *Crime in the Making*. Cambridge, MA: Harvard University Press, 1993.

Sellin, Thorsten. "Dom Jean Mabillon: A Prison Reformer of the Seventeenth Century." *Journal of the American Institute of Criminal Law and Criminology* 17 (1927): 581–602.

———. "Filippo Franci—A Precursor of Modern Penology." *Journal of the American Institute of Criminal Law and Criminology* 17 (1926): 104–12.

——. *Pioneering in Penology*. Philadelphia: University of Pennsylvania Press, 1944.

Sheingorn, Pamela, ed. and trans. *The Book of Sainte Foy*. Philadelphia: University of Pennsylvania Press, 1995.

Shoham, Shlomo. *The Mark of Cain*. Jerusalem: Israel Universities Press, 1970.

Simon, Jonathan. "The Emergence of a Risk Society." *Socialist Review* 95 (1987): 61–89.

——. "Governing Through Crime." In Lawrence M. Friedman and George Fisher, eds. *The Crime Conundrum*. Boulder, CO: Westview Press, 1997, 171–89.

Siricius, Pope. "Epistola ad Himerium Episcopum Tarraconensem." In J. P. Migne, ed. *Patrologia Latina*. Paris, 1845, 13.

Skotnicki, Andrew. "God's Prisoners: Penal Confinement and the Creation of Purgatory." *Modern Theology* 22 (2006): 85–110.

——. "How Is Justice Restored?" *Studies in Christian Ethics* 19 (2006): 187–204.

——. *Religion and the Development of the American Penal System*. Lanham, MD: University Press of America, 2000.

Snyder, T. Richard. *The Protestant Ethic and the Spirit of Punishment*. Grand Rapids, MI: Eerdmans, 2001.

Southern, R. W. *Saint Anselm and His Biographer*. Cambridge: Cambridge University Press, 1963.

Spierenburg, Pieter. "The Body and the State." In Norval Morris and David Rothman, eds. *The Oxford History of the Prison*. New York: Oxford University Press, 1995, 49–77.

——. *The Prison Experience*. New Brunswick, NJ: Rutgers University Press, 1991.

——. *The Spectacle of Suffering*. Cambridge: Cambridge University Press, 1984.

Stern, Laura Ikins. *The Criminal Law System of Medieval and Renaissance Florence*. Baltimore, MD: Johns Hopkins University Press, 1994.

Sumption, Jonathan. *Pilgrimage: An Image of Medieval Religion*. London: Faber & Faber, 1975.

Taylor, Mark Lewis. *The Executed God*. Minneapolis, MN: Fortress, 2001.

Teeters, Negley K., and John D. Shearer. *The Prison at Philadelphia Cherry Hill*. New York: Columbia University Press, 1957.

Tertullian. *Apology*. Trans. T. R. Glover. Cambridge, MA: Harvard University Press, 1960.

——. "De Spectaculis." In Rev. Alexander Roberts and John Donaldson, eds. *Anti-Nicene Christian Library*, vol. XI. Edinburgh: T&T Clark, 1869.

——. "On Penitence." In *Treatises on Penance*. Trans. William P. Le Saint, S.J. Westminster, MD: The Newman Press, 1959.

Teresa of Avila, St. "The Constitutions." In *The Collected Works of St. Teresa of Avila*. Trans. Kieran Kavanaugh, O.C.D., and Otilio Rodriguez, O.C.D. Washington, DC: ICS Publications, 1985.

——. *The Letters of St. Teresa of Jesus*. 2 vols. Trans. E. Allison Peers. London: Burns, Oates, and Washbourne, 1966.

Tonry, Michael. *Sentencing Matters*. New York: Oxford University Press, 1996.

Tracy, David. *The Analogical Imagination*. New York: Crossroad, 1981.

Ullmann, Walter. *The Growth of Papal Government in the Middle Ages.* London: Methuen & Co., 1955.

———. *Law and Politics in the Middle Ages.* Ithaca, NY: Cornell University Press, 1975.

United States Catholic Conference. "A Community Response to Crime." *Origins* 7 (1978): 593–604.

Vaux, Roland de, O.P. *Ancient Israel: Its Life and Institutions.* Trans. John McHugh. New York: McGraw-Hill, 1961.

Vogel, Cyril. "Sin and Penance." In Philippe Delhaye, et al. *Pastoral Treatment of Sin.* New York: Desclee Company, 1968, 177–282.

Wakefield, Walter. "Friar Ferrier, Inquisition at Cannes, and Escapes from the Prison at Carcassone." *The Catholic Historical Review* 58 (1972): 220–37.

———. *Heresy, Crusade and Inquisition in Southern France.* Berkeley: University of California Press, 1974.

Weber, Max. *Economy and Society.* Guenther Roth and Claus Wittich, eds. Berkeley: University of California Press, 1978.

Wilson, James Q. *Thinking About Crime.* Rev. ed. New York: Vintage, 1985 [originally published 1975].

Wolfgang, Marvin E. "A Florentine Prison: Le Carceri delle Stinche." *Studies in the Renaissance* 7 (1960): 148–66.

Zehr, Howard. *Changing Lenses.* Scottdale, PA: Herald Press, 1990.

Index

About the Author

Andrew Skotnicki is professor in the religious studies department at Manhattan College in New York City. He is the author of *Religion and the Development of the American Penal System,* as well as numerous scholarly articles on the theological and moral implications of criminal justice.